Tiakina te Pā Harakeke

Tiakina te Pā Harakeke

ANCESTRAL KNOWLEDGE and TAMARIKI WELLBEING

Edited by
LEONIE PIHAMA
JENNY LEE-MORGAN

HUIA

First published in 2022 by Huia Publishers
39 Pipitea Street, PO Box 12280
Wellington, Aotearoa New Zealand
www.huia.co.nz

ISBN 978-1-77550-724-6

Copyright © the authors 2022
Front cover image © Erica Sinclair 2022

This book is copyright. Apart from fair dealing for the purpose of private study, research, criticism or review, as permitted under the Copyright Act, no part may be reproduced by any process without the prior permission of the publisher.

A catalogue record for this book is available from the National Library of New Zealand.

Published with the assistance of

He Mihi — 1

Acknowledgements — 3

CHAPTER 1 — 5
Introduction
Leonie Pihama and Jenny Lee-Morgan

CHAPTER 2 — 17
Taku Kuru Pounamu:
Cherishing Our Children
Leonie Pihama

CHAPTER 3 — 31
He Raranga Mātauranga:
Weaving Ancestral Knowledge
Donna Campbell

CHAPTER 4 — 41
Te Taonga o Taku Ngākau:
The Wellbeing of Tamariki
within Whānau
Leonie Pihama, Naomi Simmonds
and Waikaremoana Waitoki

CHAPTER 5 — 59
He Mokopuna He Tupuna
Ngaropi Cameron-Raumati

CHAPTER 6 — 75
Whakataukī: Sharing Ancestral
Knowledge through Generations
Hineitimoana Greensill,
Leonie Pihama and Hōri Manuirirangi

CHAPTER 7 — 85
Oriori: He Akoranga Tahito –
Oriori as Knowledge Transmission
Glenis Philip-Barbara and Hiria Barbara

CHAPTER 8 — 101
Tūī, Tūī, Tuituia: Pūrākau to
Keep Us Connected
Jenny Lee-Morgan

CHAPTER 9 — 111
Mātauranga-ā-Whānau: Intergenerational
Knowledge Transmission through
Whānau Pūrākau
Marjorie Beverland

CHAPTER 10 — 125
Te Kura Mai i Tawhiti:
Ancestral Knowledge and Practice in
Kaupapa Māori Early Years Provision
Erana Hond-Flavell, Aroaro Tamati,
Will Edwards, Ruakere Hond,
Gareth J. Treharne, Reremoana Theodore,
Richie Poulton and Mihi Ratima

CHAPTER 11 — 143
Aro ki te Wairua o te Hā:
The Spirituality of Birth
Naomi Simmonds and Teah Carlson

CHAPTER 12 — 159
Raranga Wahakura: Weaving Wellbeing
for Mokopuna and Whānau
Tanya White

CHAPTER 13 — 177
Wahakura and Te Whare Pora
o Hine-te-iwaiwa: Delving Deeply
into Te Pā Harakeke
David Tipene-Leach and Sally Abel

CHAPTER 14 — 189
Oranga Mokopuna –
Ngā Mōtika Tangata Whenua
Paula Toko King, Donna Cormack
and Mark Kōpua

CHAPTER 15 — 215
Whiti-te-Rā: A Māori-centred
Therapeutic Approach to Wellbeing
Andre McLachlan and Waikaremoana Waitoki

Glossary — 237

Index — 245

He Mihi

Kei ngā pārekereke huri noa i ngā motu e tupu whakaritorito ai ngā pā harakeke ā muri nei, he whakamiha noa ake tēnei i a koutou. E tangi wiwini ana, e te tangi wawana ana te ngākau kōhukihuki i ngā tini aituā o te wā e hingahinga mai nā. E noho mōwai rokiroki ana te punga nehenehe i te korenga o ngā kākā tarahae o te pae kua riro ki tua o Paerau ki te huinga o te kahurangi ka oti atu koutou. Tēnā hoki koutou e whakatupuria ana ā tātou tamariki me ā tātou mokopuna ki te hua o te rengarenga, ā, e whakapakari ana i ā tātou whakareanga ki te hua o te kawariki e matomato ai te tupu o ngā māhuri i roto i ngā tini whakawai kei mua i a rātou. Ā, ka whakatairangatia te kōrero, mā te ngakingaki ā mua e tupu, e rea, e puāwai ai ngā hua āpōpō, ā, pihipihi ake nei, pihipihi ake nei.

Acknowledgements

We would like to acknowledge the many people who participated in all of the research projects and programmes that form the basis of many of the chapters published here. In particular, to all of those who attended hui and wānanga; those who were interviewed; those who have worked to bring wellbeing to our tamariki, mokopuna and their whānau, hapū and iwi. All too often, we hear that it takes a pā (village) to raise a child, and as we see in the writings here, it is a particular kind of pā that provides the collective support and responsibility that we need to ensure the wellbeing of current and future generations.

We wish to acknowledge all who have provided support, guidance and advice for the projects 'Tiakina te Pā Harakeke' and 'Te Taonga o Taku Ngākau'. The research projects that provided the inspiration for this publication have been funded by Ngā Pae o te Māramatanga, the Health Research Council, A Better Start National Science Challenge and Cure Kids. We acknowledge that a number of authors and research teams involved with contributing chapters have also received support for their work. Cure Kids again supported the publication of this book and has actively encouraged work, such as that included in this book, to be distributed widely. We acknowledge the support of the University of Waikato, in particular Professor Linda Tuhiwai Smith, who has been an advisor to all of our work, and the operations and business team who supported us during our time at Te Kotahi Research Institute: Herearoha Skipper, Papahuia Dickson and Tammy Tauroa. Many thanks to the kaimahi, especially Catherine Page and Ngahuia Eruera of Ngā Wai a te Tūī Māori and Indigenous Research Centre, and Tuapapa Rangahau – Research and Postgraduate Office, Te Whare Wānanga o Wairaka, Unitec – who have assisted in the final stages to ensure the publication of this book.

Our appreciation to all of our whānau who have provided ongoing support and encouragement throughout the work that has been done to not only bring this publication together but all of the many projects and studies that are documented here. We also acknowledge the contributing authors for their agreement to publish chapters on their work in the area of Kaupapa Māori research, tamariki and whānau ora to enable a wider inclusion of work that can inform, support and affirm our people.

Our acknowledgement to Eboni Waitere and the team at Huia Publishers who were supportive of this book from its conception and who have made the publication process a stress-free experience in what is a stressful time in the world as we all work to keep our tamariki, mokopuna and whānau safe throughout the COVID-19 pandemic.

Ngā manaakitanga.

Introduction

Leonie Pihama
Jenny Lee-Morgan

CHAPTER 1

This book is concerned with the role of healthy whānau (extended family structure) relationships in the raising of tamariki (children). It is about how our tūpuna (ancestors) have passed to us mātauranga Māori (traditional knowledge), in its many forms, which provide us with guidance as Indigenous Peoples in this contemporary world. Di Grennell (2006), a longterm worker in the area of Family Violence prevention has highlighted this in her work:

> Drawing on the wisdom of our tūpuna and traditions is not to return us to a mythic past or golden age – our people have always adapted to new circumstances and experimented with new technology. Rather it is to understand and be guided by the symbols, values and principles that can enhance our capacity to live together peacefully as whānau and communities. Our capacity for resilience as an indigenous people is fed and nourished by our language, traditional practices and oral traditions (p. 1).

Tiakina te Pā Harakeke: Ancestral Knowledge and Tamariki Wellbeing brings to the fore discussions of successful values and practices of Māori childrearing that have been maintained within many whānau, hapū and iwi for generations. It is a sharing of knowledge that supports the belief held by our tūpuna that our tamariki and mokopuna (grandchildren) are treasured parts of whānau, hapū and iwi, as is expressed in the saying 'He taonga te mokopuna'. This knowledge comes in the form of a wide range of Māori research projects and discussions that are grounded upon and which reveal the significant privileging of ancestral knowledge to inform our contemporary understandings of wellbeing for tamariki and mokopuna.

Over the past thirty years there has been a return to a focus on the role of whānau as a site of wellbeing for Māori. This has focused upon providing access to the wisdom, knowledge and approaches, grounded within mātauranga Māori, that support whānau, and those organisations working alongside whānau, to shape positive outcomes and experiences for Māori. *Tiakina te Pā Harakeke* explores a range of contexts that include examples of how our tūpuna believed, lived and acted within Māori cultural frameworks of traditional childrearing. Historical documentation about early contact indicates Māori children were indulged by all generations of a whānau and hapū (Hohepa, 1994). It is clear that physical punishment was unacceptable in the raising of Māori children and therefore there were particular approaches that ensured such discipline was not required. Whānau relations were traditionally embedded within wider hapū and iwi structures and therefore whānau resiliency was also embedded in wider collective and collaborative responsibilities and support.

There is clear evidence that the impact of colonisation has been devastating to whānau wellbeing. The fragmentation of whānau, hapū and iwi through colonisation has meant a denial of the cultural knowledge and practices that can facilitate wellbeing. Over the past thirty years the defining of whānau Māori and parenting has been predominantly through a deficit paradigm (Pihama, 1993). This has been a significant impetus in the denial of tikanga Māori and the transmission of tikanga (cultural practices), including traditional approaches to childrearing. For many Māori, the fragmentation of whānau, limited access to support and a shift in values in regard to the place of tamariki has had serious consequences. The over-representation of Māori in child abuse and whānau violence statistics is a serious indicator of those consequences (Kruger et al., 2004). Issues of denial of te reo, tikanga and mātauranga Māori have been raised as sources of profound disconnection for many whānau that must be actively addressed.

It is against this background that we have seen an increase in the assertion for Kaupapa Māori approaches to whānau health and wellbeing (Jenkins & Harte, 2011), including a growth in whānau-based research approaches that privilege whānau knowing. *Tiakina te Pā Harakeke* engages directly with the importance of whānau, hapū, iwi and Māori knowledge and Māori childrearing practices to draw upon both traditional and contemporary Māori expertise and knowledge that supports a wider aspiration of whānau wellbeing.

Tiakina te Pā Harakeke provides an opportunity to share Kaupapa Māori approaches that draw upon tikanga and mātauranga Māori in relation to whānau ora, which we consider is the fundamental essence of wellbeing for whānau. This book shares with whānau, and others, knowledge about raising children in ways that are grounded within tikanga Māori through providing access to the wisdom and approaches of a diverse range of people who have a depth of knowledge in tikanga and childrearing practices. It is our intention that in doing so we can share important knowledge that helps to identify, learn and practise positive, cultural approaches to childrearing as practised by our tūpuna.

Throughout the book there are consistent themes and concepts referred to that are embedded within the understandings associated with Te Pā Harakeke. Te Pā Harakeke is both a way of understanding and a way of practising whānau ora. At its very core is the wellbeing, nurturing, care and protection of tamariki. This is discussed in a range of ways within each of the chapters. Within the project 'Tiakina te Pā Harakeke', the centrality of the relationship between te pā harakeke and whānau relationships is highlighted by those interviewed:

> I do remember my Nanny on Dad's side because she used to weave as well. She talked about the harakeke being our relationship with the harakeke as a whānau. She would talk about it in a very holistic way whereas opposed to my mum and my grandmother they used it for function and my grandmother, Dad's Nana ... used to talk about it as a very spiritual plant. She used to talk about all the healing properties in it and not only what you use it to make things with and so the connection between pā harakeke and us was just on-going all the time. (Kairaranga interview)

> As you said you know if you've got your pā harakeke, you've got your rito, you've got your mātua on either side. It's really important to nurture both the children and

parents, and grandparents, and then you have your wider whānau unit. And at some stage some of the harakeke will die, the rau will die, so you allow for them to be safely removed, carefully removed, tended to and then others to grow. So I see that as a fundamental, the essence really of how we are in a perfect Māori world that we nurture from the time you're starting with your parents, grandparents, whatever, and then you think about their te ira, e tipu haere ana i roto i te kōpū o te whaea, kōkā. And that nurturing right from the time, even pre-seed, actually. Because if you're not eating well, kāore koe [i] te āta whāngai i te whaea, ka kore kaha tipu tōna ora, te ora rānei o te punua me te kōpū. So it's about nurturing, manaakitanga, aroha. All of those things are essential throughout the whānau in looking after that pā harakeke. (Kairaranga interview)

The knowledge expressed by the kairaranga above are indicated in the image below:

Figure 1:
Te Pā Harakeke.

Pivotal to the sustenance of te pā harakeke is 'te rito', the centre shoot, which also symbolises the importance of the child, sitting at the centre of a protective mechanism of whānau. The rau (leaves) that grow around the rito provide the first layer of sustenance and represent the mātua. The term mātua refers to parents and those of the parent generation. This is aligned to the concepts of whaea, which refers to mother and aunties, and matua, which refers to father and uncles. What we see in these relationships is that, even at the first level of relationships, the tamaiti is surrounded by those who are responsible and obligated to provide for their wellbeing. The rau that extend further from the rito are representative of tūpuna, the grandparent generations that reach out to beyond the physical living grandparents to our ancestors, who provide spiritual sustenance, guidance and protection to all generations. In the image of the harakeke, we also see that there are multiple whānau within te pā harakeke. That is the essence of the term pā, which is a clump or group of things and also refers to a village.

It is a total environment in which, Māori assert, the past stands as a resource to sustain the current and future generations. According to Rokx, Woodham and Joe (1999), concepts or sayings that highlight the growth of Te Pā Harakeke are an indication that whānau is secure and protected and therefore able to grow. Te Pā Harakeke exemplifies the need for the interconnectedness of whakapapa (cultural genealogical layers) that both sustain and nourish human relationships. It highlights the relation of new growth from old, and signifies clearly how each generation is linked to both its ancestral and future lines.

This publication was initiated through the work conducted in two Kaupapa Māori research projects, 'Tiakina te Pā Harakeke' and 'Te Taonga o Taku Ngākau'. Both projects focused on the investigation and identification of Māori approaches to Māori childrearing and parenting. The key aim across the projects was to investigate how we can draw upon such traditional Māori understandings and practices to support healthy relationships within our whānau. It was also emphasised that in doing so we could provide further insights into how we can draw on traditional knowledge as both prevention and intervention in the area of child abuse and child neglect. Where these projects gave the impetus to develop this publication we have ensured there is a wider range of ideas and research shared that goes beyond those particular research projects. *Tiakina te Pā Harakeke* includes chapters that have been developed through research and practice across a range of sectors. In doing so we seek to share insights and information that support whānau and organisations to delve more deeply into tikanga and mātauranga Māori to inform our approaches in helping shape positive outcomes for whānau. Through drawing upon these knowledges and ancestral knowledge, we continue to enhance and strengthen our childrearing approaches within a contemporary context.

Tiakina te Pā Harakeke provides access to the views and understandings of a range of Māori people who have a depth of knowledge in tikanga, te reo and mātauranga Māori, and who can identify and define those success elements that ensured whānau wellbeing within traditional Māori society. There is a strong view among these authors that within tikanga and te reo Māori is a vast amount of knowledge about childrearing and enhancing our ways of doing things in relation to the care of our children. Some articles speak

He Pā Harakeke.

to the place of tūpuna (ancestral) knowledge in the development of approaches that explore whānau wellbeing, while others highlight key tikanga (practices and protocols) that are central to our current efforts to regenerate mātauranga Māori, and others highlight the ways in which we can implement tikanga across a range of sites to enhance wellbeing for tamariki, mokopuna and whānau. As such, this publication seeks to provide some insights into the place of mātauranga Māori in our lives and the ways in which whānau and Māori organisations are working to revitalise mātauranga Māori for the benefit and wellbeing of our people.

Chapter Overview

Chapter 2 opens with key themes that emerged from the 'Tiakina te Pā Harakeke' research project. Where the literature within this article was published previously, the author Leonie Pihama has included interview material from the project itself. Other literature and interview material also appear in the chapters by Donna Campbell, and Hineiti Greensill and Hōri Manuirirangi. This chapter provides an opening by sharing traditional knowledge that highlights the whakataukī 'Taku Kuru Pounamu', which emphasises the sacred place of tamariki Māori.

In Chapter 3, 'He Raranga Mātauranga: Weaving Ancestral Knowledge', Donna Campbell discusses the relationship the kairaranga/whatu weaver has with Te Pā Harakeke. Drawing upon conversations with kairaranga as a part of the 'Tiakina te Pā Harakeke' research project, it is highlighted that the practice of nurturing our harakeke takes us back to whakapapa, to the reality of caring for something other than ourselves. It not only requires that we have knowledge of the environment we live in, but also that we take responsibility for that environment. First, we are reconnecting with the whenua by nurturing and conserving the plants. Then, second, we are learning about ourselves and our tūpuna through practising the tikanga associated with the art forms.

Chapter 4, by Leonie Pihama, Naomi Simmonds and Waikaremoana Waitoki, is titled 'Te Taonga o Taku Ngākau: The Wellbeing of Tamariki within Whānau'. This piece explores the ways in which whānau themselves generate, through purposeful action, wellbeing from within mātauranga and tikanga Māori. This chapter shares findings from 'Te Taonga o Taku Ngākau,' a Kaupapa Māori research project that situates the wellbeing of tamariki within the context of well and thriving whānau. This chapter brings together discussions with whānau on the wellbeing of tamariki within whānau as expressed through the understanding of tamariki as taonga.

Chapter 5, 'He Mokopuna He Tupuna', by Ngaropi Cameron-Raumati, explores the guiding whakataukī, "He tupuna, he mokopuna. Mā wai i whakakī i ngā whāwhārua o ngā mātua tūpuna? Mā ō tātou mokopuna!" It is noted that within Taranaki the economic, political and social trauma not only dispossessed hapū of land, but severely impacted the way mātauranga was conveyed across the generations, disrupting safety mechanisms that placed the wellbeing of tamariki mokopuna at the centre of community life. 'He Mokopuna He Tupuna' is embedded as a guiding reference for whānau, hapū and iwi to improve healing outcomes that return tamariki mokopuna to the centre of community.

Chapter 6, 'Whakataukī: Sharing Ancestral Knowledge through Generations', by Hineitimoana Greensil, Leonie Pihama and Hōri Manuirirangi, examines a number of whakataukī for messages relating to the positioning of Māori children within whānau and the relationship of that to traditional childrearing practices. Many of the whakataukī presented here have been shared with us by kaumātua during interviews conducted for the 'Tiakina te Pā Harakeke' project and have contributed to the development of other publications. Drawing on the examples in this chapter, the writers explore whakataukī as a means by which to bring forward knowledge gifted to us by our ancestors that can inform our contemporary experiences as Māori.

Chapter 7 is 'Oriori: He Akoranga Tahito – Oriori as Knowledge Transmission', by Glenis Philip-Barbara and Hiria Barbara. This chapter explores oriori from the Ngā Mōteatea series. Oriori, it is noted, provide not only a language of love worthy of reflection but also a point of reference around the position of children within whānau in pre-contact Aotearoa. Each line is a blessing, a bestowing of gifts of knowledge and whakapapa upon children and their future. Today, the word we use to describe children, tamariki, is an obvious clue as to the centrality of children in whānau; however, closer examination of oriori provides a series of observable practices and values that bring our ancestral knowledge to life.

Chapter 8 is entitled 'Tūī, Tūī, Tuituia: Pūrākau to Keep Us Connected' by Jenny Lee-Morgan. Based on a section of Jenny's inaugural professorial address delivered at Te Noho Kotahitanga marae in 2019, she argues that pūrākau are critical to keeping us culturally connected and unified. Drawing on a pūrākau about a local landmark, Te Tokaroa – otherwise known as Te Ara Whakapekapeka o Ruarangi – her chapter demonstrates the ways in which ancient pūrākau continue to be used in her whānau. Making story-space not only ensures the memory of the story itself, but provides a tool for a special engagement, discussion and analysis of relevant contemporary issues. The possibilities pūrākau create for generating story-talk that strengthens relationships, and provides insights into each others' worlds for tamariki, rangatahi, pakeke and mātua are plentiful. This chapter encourages valuing pūrākau of the past and present, and continuing to develop them for the future as a source of mātauranga – central for growing a strong, resilient pā harakeke.

Chapter 9 is 'Mātauranga-ā-Whānau: Intergenerational Knowledge Transmission through Whānau Pūrākau', by Marjorie Beverland. This chapter draws upon whānau knowledge, experiences and practices, through pūrākau, that frame mātauranga-ā-whānau as a distinctively Māori approach that centres knowledge and practices that are embedded within whānau, bringing a focus on ways of knowing and being that are transmitted intergenerationally. This chapter explains mātauranga-ā-whānau, and briefly discusses the nature of mātauranga Māori, whānau and Kaupapa Māori in relation to relationships and the transmission of knowledge within whānau. A number of whānau pūrākau are shared and the mātauranga that stems from each of the pūrākau is discussed. It is highlighted that the mātauranga shared through the tūpuna–mokopuna relationship has guided the identification of key principles that form a mātauranga-ā-whānau approach to whānau wellbeing.

Chapter 10, 'Te Kura Mai i Tawhiti: Ancestral Knowledge and Practice in Kaupapa Māori Early Years Provision', is a contribution as a part of the 'Te Kura Mai i Tawhiti' research programme of Te Kōpae Piripono, who are working in partnership with the National Centre for Lifecourse Research (NCLR) at the University of Otago. The focus of the programme is to examine the effects of Kaupapa Māori early life and whānau development programming on Māori educational success and whānau wellbeing over the life course. This chapter is authored by the research team of Erana Hond-Flavell, Aroaro Tamati, Will Edwards, Ruakere Hond, Gareth J. Treharne, Reremoana Theodore, Richie Poulton and Mihi Ratima. Te Kōpae Piripono is a Kaupapa Māori early childhood centre established in 1994 as part of a community development initiative that centred on the reclamation of te reo me ngā tikanga Māori in Taranaki. The founders of Te Kōpae Piripono believe that Māori Taranaki children should have access to high-quality early education within a Māori environment and community, speaking the language of their forebears and living Indigenous concepts and practices.

In Chapter 11, 'Aro ki te Wairua o te Hā: The Spirituality of Birth', Naomi Simmonds and Teah Carlson examine Indigenous spirituality (wairua) and birth for Māori women and whānau in Aotearoa. They note that Māori have a unique and enduring spiritual tradition that values the sanctity of the maternal body and the collective approach to raising children, and in turn children 'raising' whānau, which this chapter will discuss. In this chapter, they weave together the cosmological and historical narratives of Māori with the contemporary experiences of women today to examine the wairua of birth and of the maternal body in a uniquely Māori way. In doing so, they reveal the transformations that are inherent to a Kaupapa Māori approach to maternity care that ensures the wellbeing of tamariki, whaea and whānau.

'Raranga Wahakura', by Tanya White, continues the discussion of wellbeing of pēpē (baby) in Chapter 12. Wahakura are vessels of wellbeing, providing safe sleeping spaces that give tangible form to all applications and processes of Tikanga Pā Harakeke. As such, they are an embodiment of mana, tapu and aroha, and a woven manifestation of whakapapa. This chapter presents a case study of raranga wahakura from a weaver's perspective. Tikanga Pā Harakeke provides a tangible model of practice and serves as a point of access for whānau to connect with te ao Māori and its fundamental nature as a 'woven universe'.

Chapter 13, by David Tipene-Leach and Sally Abel, is titled 'Wahakura and Te Whare Pora o Hine-te-iwaiwa: Delving Deeply into Te Pā Harakeke', and it follows on the discussion of the traditional practices associated with wahakura and tamariki wellbeing. Drawing on the deity Hine-te-iwaiwa, and her role in birthing and overseeing wellbeing through Te Pā Harakeke, this chapter discusses the contemporary development of Te Whare Pora o Hine-te-iwaiwa as a health intervention. The conception of a 'safe shared-sleeping environment' to prevent sudden infant deaths led to the development of the wahakura, the Pēpi-Pod, and the Safe Sleep programme, credited with a 29 percent drop in infant mortality across the years 2009 to 2015. Te Whare Pora o Hine-te-iwaiwa is an antenatal clinic that has no health professionals – just weavers and the stories and traditions of Te Whare Pora of old.

Chapter 14, 'Oranga Mokopuna – Ngā Mōtika Tangata Whenua', by Paula Toko King, Donna Cormack and Mark Kōpua, continues with the place of traditional knowledge and tamariki health. This chapter presents 'Oranga Mokopuna' as an alternative that disrupts Western notions of rights that are assumed to have universal application. Based in te ao Māori, Oranga Mokopuna provides a conceptual frame of reference for the realisation of tangata whenua rights to health and wellbeing. Inherent tangata whenua rights are grounded in tikanga Māori and affirmed by He Whakaputanga o te Rangatiratanga o Nu Tīreni and Te Tiriti o Waitangi, alongside other international human rights instruments. The vision expressed in this chapter is for mokopuna to thrive and flourish as our rangatira of today, through the full realisation of their tangata whenua rights to health and wellbeing.

Chapter 15, 'Whiti-te-Rā: A Māori-centred Therapeutic Approach to Wellbeing', by Andre McLachlan and Waikaremoana Waitoki, discusses the place of Māori cultural beliefs, values and practices in mental-health therapies, and the growth of Māori assertions for Māori health models that recognise the importance of strengthening language, identity and cultural practices; kin relationships; engagement with the environment; and connection to the world of wairuatanga (spirituality). This chapter is presented as a response to the need to update and contribute to Māori health models of wellbeing, and outlines a range of Māori cultural concepts and processes within Māori mental health provision. It is noted that while there is recognition that working with Māori requires knowledge of cultural concepts and practices, there has been a lack of clarity on how to apply these practically to clinical assessments and/or treatment. This chapter provides a discussion of key models and uses a case-study approach to describe how to integrate the models to develop a comprehensive, culturally informed psychological formulation, an interactive treatment/healing plan and processes to evaluate that plan.

References

GRENNELL, D. (2006). *Amokura – Indigenous innovation*. Paper presented at the 10th Australasian Conference on Child Abuse and Neglect (ACCAN), 14–16 February 2006, Wellington.

HOHEPA, M. (1994). Whakatipu Tamariki. *Te Pua, The Journal of Te Puawaitanga*, 3(2).

JENKINS, K., & HARTE, H. (2011). Traditional Māori parenting: An historical review of literature of traditional Māori child rearing practices in pre-European times. Auckland, New Zealand: Te Kāhui Mana Ririki. Retrieved from http://www.ririki.org.nz/wp-content/uploads/2015/04/TradMaoriParenting.pdf

KRUGER, T., PITMAN, M., GRENNEL, D., MCDONALD, T., MARIU, D., POMARE, A., MITA, T., MATAHAERE, M., & LAWSON-TE AHO, K. (2004). *Transforming whānau violence: A conceptual framework: An updated version of the report from the former Second Māori taskforce on Whānau Violence*. Retrieved from https://nzfvc.org.nz/sites/nzfvc.org.nz/files/transforming_whānau_violence.pdf

PIHAMA, L. (1993). *Tungia te ururua, kia tupu whakaritorito te tupu o te harakeke: A critical analysis of parents as first teachers* (Master's thesis). University of Auckland, Auckland, New Zealand.

ROKX, H., WOODHAM, B., & JOE, M. (1999). *Māori programme development: He taonga te mokopuna – The child is precious*. Unpublished Paper. Children & Family Violence: Effective Interventions Now Conference, 4–5 July 1999, Wellington, New Zealand.

Taku Kuru Pounamu: Cherishing Our Children

Leonie Pihama

CHAPTER 2

Introduction

For many years, Māori have advocated that whānau is a site of wellbeing (Durie, 2001; Kingi et al., 2018; Pihama et al., 2019c). A key part of the discussion from Māori has focused on providing access to the wisdom, knowledge and approaches, grounded within mātauranga Māori, that support whānau and organisations working alongside whānau. This chapter provides insights into Te Pā Harakeke, as shared within the research project 'Tiakina te Pā Harakeke', and associated traditional knowledge and practices that can support whānau living and enhance wider whānau wellbeing, in particular for our tamariki (children) and mokopuna (grandchildren). It also explores some key concepts that were raised within the research project 'Tiakina te Pā Harakeke', in particular the place of whānau as a site that has traditionally provided for the wellbeing of tamariki; the significance of connectedness through whakapapa; and intergenerational transmission as a means by which to inform the raising of tamariki in positive and nurturing ways.

Whānau

Whānau is the fundamental building block within Māori society. Whānau is generally translated as 'extended family' consisting of up to three or four generations and was the basic social unit under the direction of elders (Henare, 1988). Whānau structures provide for a system of accountability and responsibility. Whānau has provided a support base from which individuals are located in the wider dimensions of whakapapa and Māori society (Durie, 2001; Lawson-TeAho, 2010; Pihama & Cameron, 2012). It is a structure through which Māori societal and cultural norms may be reinforced and acts as a resource through which to obtain support and knowledge of the world, and to receive necessary values and belief systems essential to both the individual and the society. In a comprehensive discussion of Māori concepts titled *Te Hīnātore ki te Ao Māori: A glimpse into the Māori world* (Ministry of Justice, 2001), whānau is described as:

> The basic unit of Māori society into which an individual was born and socialised ... a unit for ordinary social and economic affairs, and making basic day to day decisions. Its members had close personal, familial and reciprocal contacts and decision-making relationships with each other (p. 30).

Whānau provides the basis for Māori society, upon which other forms of organisation such as hapū and iwi are dependent. It has also been a key target for colonialism, and colonising forces have actively sought to undermine the fundamental values and relationships that are the basis for whānau wellbeing (Ministry of Justice, 2001). Whānau is a crucial cultural structure in Māori society. Meaning both extended family and birth, the word 'whānau' encompasses both creation and support mechanisms for all in the whānau. Whānau brings to the fore collective obligations and responsibilities for each other in the wider sense of wellbeing. Rangimarie Rose Pere (1991) identifies whanaungatanga (relationships) as a critical practice that provides the bond and "an input support system" (p. 26) for whānau members. Whanaungatanga, the maintenance of whānau relationships, is central to Māori society. This was highlighted clearly in the project as follows:

> Ehara i te mea, ka riro koe mā ō mātua anake e tohutohu. Kei reira ō tuākana, ō matua kēkē, ō whaea kēkē e tohutohu ana i a koe, 'Kaua e mahi i tēnā mahi, kaua e whai i tēnā mahi.' (Interview)

Margie Hohepa (1999) describes the various ways in which whānau can be regarded. Whānau, she states, has both traditional and more 'evolved' meanings. Traditional in that the construct of whānau through whakapapa connections remains as a key definition, and evolved through the more recent co-option of the term whānau in the linking of groups of common interest, or common kaupapa (philosophy). She describes these groupings as "Whānau based on unity of purpose rather than whakapapa lines, sometimes termed 'kaupapa whānau' or 'metaphorical whānau', develop around a particular aim or goal" (Hohepa, 1999, p. 18).

Durie (2001) stresses the increased diversity of whānau in contemporary Māori society has come in line with changes that have occurred in Māori society more generally, noting that there now exists a spectrum of whānau types that range from whakapapa whānau to kaupapa whānau. Durie (2001) identifies the following whānau types: whānau as kin, who descend from a common ancestor; whānau as shareholders-in-common, who are shareholders in land; whānau as friends, who share a common purpose; whānau as a model of interaction, for example in a school environment; whānau as neighbours, with shared location of residence; whānau as households, urban dwellers; and virtual whānau, which meets in cyberspace due to geographical separation. As highlighted by Hohepa (1999) and Durie (2001), these forms of kaupapa whānau align to the contemporary needs of many Māori and provide systems of support that are not necessarily grounded in whakapapa. Whakapapa, however, provides a connection between whānau members that is grounded in ancestral relationships.

Whakapapa

Whakapapa is fundamental to Māori society. It is through whakapapa that individuals link to whānau, hapū and iwi (Mikaere, 2005), thus providing a platform for identity and connectedness. Understanding one's whakapapa and the obligations associated with this, however, is also a crucial component of being Māori. In traditional times, all adults would have knowledge of whakapapa associated with their direct line of descent, with some also holding knowledge of the connection between iwi (Pere, 1982). Walker (2013) states:

> Fundamental to the lived experience of whānau is the continuity provided by whakapapa. Not only does it reach back in time and forward into the future to the mokopuna and those yet to be born, it also expands outward on the horizontal plane.

> Within this expansive, dynamic, evolving, layered reality is a typology beginning with the individual and expanding to whānau's widest possible definition, which includes hapū and iwi (p. 115).

Tamariki would have many contexts through which they would learn of their whakapapa connections, including through pūrākau (traditional storytelling) and kōrero whakapapa (histories associated with cultural genealogies). The holistic wellbeing of tamariki is closely aligned to the sense of belonging to a whānau group with strong collective connections within and between whānau (Joseph, 2007; Pere, 1982). Pitama et al. (2002) point out:

> ... just as children had the right to know their whakapapa, to be secure in their identity and to expect support from the adults within their whānau, the prinicple of reciprocity operated to ensure that they also carried responsibilities to the whole whānau (p. 33).

This principle of reciprocity was learned by tamariki through their engagement with other whānau members, in particular with kaumātua. The significance that whakapapa has in ensuring identity and connectedness continues to be acknowledged today, as noted by whānau within the project, who state:

> I think the main thing is whakapapa. It's all, all of it is there and I feel like if we can give them the skills to be able to journey 'ā whakapapa' then that's what we're after. (Interview)

Socially and educationally, whakapapa, connectedness and identity are important factors for the wellbeing of Māori children (Webber, 2012). This is further extended by the nurturing received during childhood. Morehu (2005) stresses the link between whakapapa and nurturing children and states, "children are our whakapapa, and whakapapa is our past, present and future. As whānau and wider community we have a responsibility to nurture our children so that they are provided with opportunities and are encouraged to reach their potential" (p. 46). This way of being supports the nurturing of healthy relationships within whānau.

Traditional Māori childrearing practices developed within a context where whakapapa, whānau and collectivity were central to the way in which society functioned (Joseph, 2007). A woman's role as a child bearer was highly valued and revered (Gabel, 2013; Pere, 1982). The respect and prestige accorded to women was reflective of the belief that they were fundamental to the ongoing survival of future generations and continuation of whakapapa (Pihama, Smith, Simmonds, Seed-Pihama, & Gabel, 2019a, 2019b). This was demonstrated through such acts as pampering an expectant mother during pregnancy, to nurture and provide for her wellbeing and the growth and development of the child (Gabel, 2013). What this highlights is that whakapapa and the nurturing of present and future generations is central to a Māori view of tamariki and our role in raising tamariki in a context of whānau wellbeing. The significance of this was not lost on early Pākehā colonists, who also documented the valued place of tamariki within Māori society and the practice of collective responsibility within whānau: "I saw no quarrelling while I was there. They are kind to their women and children. I never observed either with a mark of violence upon them, nor did I see a child struck" (Marsden and Elder, 1932, p. 128). Colenso (2001) also noted:

> They certainly took every physical care of them; and as they rarely chastised (for many reasons) of course, petted and spoiled them. The father, or uncle, often carried or nursed his infant on his back for hours at a time, and might often be seen quietly at work with the little one there snugly ensconced (p. 30).

Whānau and the Wellbeing of Tamariki

There are multiple accounts within the literature of the level of respect accorded to Māori children in traditional times (Gabel, 2013; Jenkins & Harte, 2011; Pere, 1982; Smith, 1997). Māori children were observed as having been treated with much adoration and indulgence. Traditional pūrākau and oriori also provide accounts of children as having been highly regarded and nurtured as such (Jenkins & Harte, 2011; Nepe, 1991; Pere, 1982). Seen as representations of generations past, and connectors to the future, children were held in high regard and positioned as such within their whānau and hapū communities. Rangimarie Rose Pere (1991) positions tamariki as being of particular importance within Māori society; such importance is embedded within te reo Māori:

> Tamariki: Tama is derived from Tamanuiterā the central sun, the divine spark; ariki refers to senior most status, and riki on its own can mean smaller version. Tamariki is the Māori word used for children. Children are the greatest legacy the world community has (p. 4).

The importance of understanding te reo Māori was noted by a number of whānau within the research project. For example, one person stated:

> ... the language provides the signposts that tell us – embedded in every word for every aspect of whānau is this reinscribing of the importance [of] mokopuna. Beautiful word 'mokopuna', 'tamaiti', 'tamariki', 'whānau', 'iwi', 'hapū'. All of these words tell their own story even in the word, and in of [itself] they talk about interconnection. Back in time and forward, between each other, amongst one another. (Interview)

From the time of birth, the connection between the land and the child is made. The whenua (placenta) of the newborn baby is taken and placed into the whenua (earth), a tikanga that links the child to the land and establishes their tūrangawaewae. Pākehā practices surrounding the disposal of the placenta have caused some dismay to Māori people from as far back as the late 19th century, as expressed by Teone Taare Tikao (1990):

> When a child is born to the Pākehā, the doctor or nurse usually burns the placenta or afterbirth. The Māori did not do this, it would be against the mana of that child and would destroy its mauri (life principle) ... the whenua (placenta) was never burnt, but was carefully buried in the whenua (earth) and I think this is how it got its name, and by this burial the child's mauri and mana is preserved (p. 97).

The return of the whenua to the land also signifies a cyclical view of the world that espouses an ongoing link of the past to the present. As Māori we come from Papatūānuku and return to Papatūānuku, life and death are a continuum; thereby the preservation of the mauri and the mana of the child is crucial to the preservation of future generations (Norman, 1992). This view of the world is the basis of the beliefs and practices employed by Māori people in the care and education of their tamariki and, according to Arapera Royal-Tangaere (1991), expresses the importance of nurturing the child within a holistic philosophy. This was couched within the structure of whanaungatanga (Buck, 1950; Hohepa, 1990; Ka'ai, 1990; Pere, 1991; Royal-Tangaere, 1991).

The care and education of Māori babies and young children traditionally took place within the whānau. This positioning of Māori children within the whānau is also outlined in a number of programmes related to enabling wellbeing for tamariki Māori. The Early Childhood Development Programme 'He Taonga, Te Mokopuna' takes the following line:

> Our approach to tiaki tamariki is based on the traditional viewpoint that children are the lifeblood of generations gone and those to come, and whakapapa links are maintained through and by them. Children were viewed as part of an ongoing whakapapa, their contributions simultaneously fed into the past, present and future and ensured the survival of themselves and their communities. Defining their positions and status integrated them into communities, while informing those communities of their particular obligations to their children. In other words, as the physical embodiment of tīpuna, bringing together the mana, wairua, ihi, wehi, tapu of generations long-gone, and linking with generations to come, children were assured of safety and nurturing within whānau and hapū structures (Rokx, Woodham, & Joe, 1999, p. 2).

Raising children within Māori cultural understandings is a collective effort shared among whānau. This form of childrearing alleviated stress on parents while providing children with an environment conducive to their development and wellbeing (Pere, 1982). Within a collective whānau environment the responsibility of raising children was shared among female and male whānau members alike, each of whom held unique skills from which a child would learn and grow (Gabel, 2013; Pere, 1982). Raising children in a collective environment also enabled younger women who were of a childbearing age to further develop skills and strengths to undertake other roles within their whānau and hapū communities (Mikaere, 2011). As Gabel (2013) purports, "essentially, the traditional Māori approach to the mothering of a child was a robust system that ensured the wellbeing of both mother and child and ultimately the wider whānau and community" (p. 86). Such a system was central to Māori and the continuation of future generations (Ruru, 2005). This also highlights the critical nature of whānau as multi-generational.

Grandparents played a particularly active role in nurturing the children and took on much of the responsibility of ensuring that these tamariki were provided with continued support and guidance throughout their lifetimes (Brown-Sadlier, 2008). Makareti Papakura (1938) describes how children were taught all aspects of life through living with their parents, grandparents and granduncles, through whom they would learn of folklore, traditions, legends, whakapapa and karakia, and of their relationship to the land, sea, rivers, mountains, forests, birds and all aspects of nature. Te Rangi Hīroa (Buck, 1950) notes that for Māori children the earliest instruction was from tīpuna (grandparent relations). This was made possible due to collective whānau living arrangements that embraced at least three generations and which provided a space for children to be raised within a context that allowed for their nurturing and education from their elders (Buck, 1950). He provides the following example:

> A friend of mine, little older than myself was brought up by a Grand-uncle who still thought that young chiefs should be trained to become successful military leaders. They slept in the same room in separate beds. In the early mornings, the old man went outside to satisfy certain needs. On his return, he slapped the sleeping child and went back to his bed muttering his disappointment. This went on for some time, until one memorable morning the now apprehensive child heard the old man leave the room. When he returned to slap the sleeper, the child gazed up at him with wide open eyes. A pleased look came to the old man's eyes and he returned to his bed saying "Now I have a grandchild who will be a bulwark of defence to his tribe". After that they played a game. Some mornings the man got up earlier, others later, but always the child gazed up at him wide awake. The training had had its effect, and the child roused at the slightest sound (Buck, 1950, p. 359).

Those interviewed in the project also emphasised that grandparents shared a special and unique relationship with their grandchildren, especially those who held the role of primary caregiver. The following provides two examples given in the research:

> In terms of tikanga the most important influence in my life was my nan, my kuia, my mother's mother … We were a very transient whānau, so my nan's pragmatic approach to that was to make sure that as kids we went back to Gisborne and the coast every holidays … That relationship, that connectedness, was developed very strongly through the insight and foresight of my kuia. (Interview)

> Kaha ana au ki te kōrero ki aku mokopuna, ngā mea e kite ai au, koirā tētahi mea ko te noho pātata mai o te mokopuna ki te tīpuna te mea nui. (Interview)

Pere (1982) explains the significance of the grandchild–grandparent connection:

> … tīpuna can mean ancestors or grandparents, mokopuna can mean grandchild(ren) or descendent(s), so that the two terms are linked together as one unit and are a part of each other. The tīpuna link up the mokopuna with the past, and the mokopuna link up the tīpuna with the present and the future (p. 49).

This relationship was seen as an unbreakable bond. Grandparents, through love, support and guidance provided educational, mental, emotional and spiritual nourishment to their grandchildren. Their contribution to the rearing of children was pivotal to the wellbeing of the whānau and hapū (Ka'ai, 2005; Smith, 2008).

Traditionally, fathers and grandfathers also provided infants and children with care and affection, and, as Pere (1982) recalls, were likely to have "spent as much time with their young offspring as mothers and grandmothers" (p. 65). It was pivotal to a child's growth and development that fathers and grandfathers had a role in their upbringing. For some whānau this practice continues; however, the reality for many others is that fathers are less active or absent from a child's life. Edwards, McCreanor, and Moewaka-Barnes (2007) found that, while present, fathers did not feature as central figures in many of the participants' lives; they were more distant. Mothers, however, held significant roles as nurturers, providing support and protection. As found in the research by Edwards et al. (2007), "the strong relationships with mothers and inconsistent bonds to fathers reflect the stresses and impacts of living in conditions of scarcity and marginalisation arising from the ongoing effects of colonisation on Māori whānau" (p. 12). The role of fathers was noted by a number of participants in the research project 'Tiakina te Pā Harakeke', including the following:

> I think my father was a loving man I think one of the nicest of their family. I think he was a giving man and so we loved our father because he treated us like we wanted to be treated. Love. Although we didn't have much, the love, I've always felt it, and I think all my sisters … my sisters have said that we talk about our parents a lot. And because of that love we're close even now and I think that stems from how our parents raised us. (Interview)

What this comment highlights is the importance of healthy relationships within whānau. There is no doubt that traditional Māori practices emphasise whānau support as crucial to the wellbeing of children. This means working against the limited, colonial, gendered beliefs that serve against the interests of whānau through the reduction of relationships to the construct of the nuclear domestic family (Pihama, 2001; Pihama, Simmonds, & Waitoki, 2019c). Edwards et al.'s 2007 study of adolescents within the South Auckland area showed all participants had active relationships with extended family members, and many lived with grandparents. Within the study they also found "another significant family member was an aunty and for a number of participants, the aunty was the surrogate parent who provided a sanctuary (sometimes long term) at times of conflict with their parents" (Edwards et al., 2007, p. 10). This practice is similar to traditional Māori childrearing practices in which whānau provided an alternative care environment to that of birth parents, to ease stress and tension (Pere, 1982). Morehu (2005) believes that without the practical support of the extended whānau and traditional pedagogies, many Māori children and whānau are vulnerable within a Western, individualised, consumerist society. The traditional intergenerational support within whānau provided enormous support in maintaining wellbeing. Te Rarawa elder Ruta Wakefield (cited in Metge, 1995) underlines this by stating that "where whānau were strong and well-integrated, the involvement of older relatives in child-raising provided an effective safeguard against abuse" (p. 266).

Traditional childrearing practices, such as collective care, are described as supportive for parents and children alike. According to Pere (1982), "the kinship parenting system included an open display of strong affection and caring for children" (p. 65). In a contemporary context, grandparents and other extended whānau members continue to play a critical role in supporting whānau and protecting children, particularly in situations where parents are experiencing hardship and dealing with a range of issues that impact on their ability to safely care for their child (Smith, 2008). One interview in our project highlighted the centrality of the wellbeing of tamariki, in which the experience of poverty was overcome through feeling central in the lives of their whānau, and also the skill of knowing how to catch eels, as learned from a grandparent:

> My mother was like that. She really was adorable, she was really, really special … she would let anybody come to our house, we were pōhara, but we were never hungry, never hungry, kei reira te awa. Something we learned from our nanny. One of the jobs she used to make us do was threading the toki … making those … worms for them to go down the creek for the eels. (Interview)

Māori grandparents have always played a significant role in the lives of whānau. Such roles include overseeing and leading whānau, holding and disseminating whakapapa and whānau knowledge (Families Commission, 2012). Support provided by grandparents is demonstrated in a variety of ways, from assisting parents with childrearing duties and providing primary care, to passing on cultural knowledge and traditions. The importance of whānau was not solely that of nurturing, but was the key social formation through which cultural norms were transmitted, reproduced and maintained.

Ako ā-Whānau: Learning within Whānau

The whānau has been recognised within traditional understandings as the key site for the education of Māori children. Edwards et al. (2007) note, "whānau are key sites for the intergenerational transfer of knowledge, wealth and power in Māori society and every opportunity to strengthen and build these structures will benefit Māori and the wider community" (p. 13). Te Rangi Hīroa (Buck, 1950) states that for the Māori child the earliest personal instruction was received from their grandparents. This was made possible due to the whānau living arrangements. Tamariki lived within an environment that embraced at least three generations and were exposed to a lifestyle that allowed for their nurturing and education from their elders. Kaumātua provided the initial introduction to a wealth of knowledge and the skills that pertained to their development, and it was they who took responsibility for the education of their mokopuna (Pihama, 1993).

Tamariki received knowledge at a pace suited to their needs and as required to maintain their positioning within the whānau (Pere, 1988). Tamariki were collectively nurtured, raised and educated within whānau, hapū and iwi relationships. This ensured the child had access to a range of adults and siblings who all contributed to their accumulation of knowledge, language, values and belief systems essential to the maintenance and continuance of Māori societal structures (Pere, 1988). This is also asserted within our research project by those interviewed:

> Our kaumātua and adults taught freely and openly in front of children. They didn't exclude them from kōrero. They spoke freely and openly, and tamariki were around and they either absorbed it, in which case they were ready to hear that kōrero, to learn from those kōrero or they didn't because it went off the top of their head because they weren't ready for those kinds of kōrero, those kinds of teachings. (Interview)

> Kei te hoki aku mahara, e pēpi tonu ana au, kua āhei au te tū. Ko tētahi mahi i tīmata atu au ko te mahi rō māra. Kāore koe i tohutohungia, "Ei, me haere koe ki roto i te māra." Kua purua koe, nā wai rā nā ka ako koe. Ērā tūāhuatanga, ā, pakeke noa ka mōhio koe i ngā āhuatanga i roto i te māra. Nō te mea nei nā, i roto i te māra mahi ai tōku māmā mā te maramataka. (Interview)

Learning processes for tamariki took many forms and included practical exercises as well as stories, games, waiata, karakia, whakapapa and much more. All these provided the child with explanations as to their place in the scheme of things, their positioning in society, descriptions of places, events and people of historical significance, as well as aspects of tribal lore necessary for the child to be knowledgeable of the day-to-day expectations of them within the whānau.

The process of intergenerational learning and teaching started prior to birth, with babies being sung and spoken to while in the womb (Pere, 1982). Hemara also highlights that Māori began teaching children before they were born. Learning was located within whānau and whakapapa relationships and often grounded upon the familiar, as Hemara (2000) states:

> While the content of the lessons may have been complex and difficult, the learning was incremental and familiar. New knowledge, skills and activities were related to preceding and following lessons. The basis for lessons was what children had already become familiar with. Those lessons included genealogical and geographic locations, social behaviours and cultural imperatives as well as ways and means of generating mana and political and economic power (pp. 9–10).

It was understood that children learn through experience and observation, and by being in a supportive, nurturing environment (Rickard, 1998). Traditionally, Māori children were provided with this type of setting in which they were encouraged to be inquisitive, attentive and to interact with a range of people of all ages (Pere, 1982) in order to flourish and make sense of the world.

The education of tamariki within the whānau may therefore be expressed in a philosophy that seeks to prepare the child for all aspects of living, in order to ensure that each child will ultimately have the opportunity to take an active, participatory role within Māori society. Teaching and learning was an integrated philosophy that sought at all times to acknowledge and validate the absolute uniqueness of the child and their position in their whānau, hapū and iwi (Pere, 1988). Tamariki were taught through tikanga the significance of protocols and laws, and through such means came to understand that there was a correct or incorrect way of doing things (Pitama et al., 2002). The collective obligations we all hold within whānau are noted in the following interview comment:

> … it's about all us pulling together to serve the people and serve the kaupapa and so trying to imbue that in her and in our children, it's my whole life has been, that's what my mother imbued in us, that's what those nannies imbued in me, you know you serve the people and you take care, everybody takes care of everybody. (Interview)

According to Tuakana Mate Nepe (1991), the traditional notions that were a part of whānau educating tamariki have been articulated in contemporary times through the doctrine of 'Te Aho Matua', which provides a clearly articulated Māori philosophical foundation for the education of the Māori child:

> Te Aho Matua is a philosophical doctrine that incorporates the knowledge, skills, attitudes and values of Māori society that have emanated from a purely Kaupapa Māori metaphysical base. As a product of the combination of Kaupapa Māori metaphysics and Māori societal relationships, Te Aho Matua sets standards and pedagogical procedures for the significance of Kaupapa Māori education as a system of intervention that is highly applicable today (p. 41).

As a philosophy that is based on tikanga Māori, Te Aho Matua establishes as imperative the positive educating of tamariki. The Māori child is a "descendant of Māori ancestry that link[s] back to Io Matua Kore" (Nepe, 1991, p. 41) and hence the nurturing and rearing of the child relates not solely to the child but to their entire ancestral lineage.

Conclusion

Over the past forty years whānau Māori have been defined predominantly within deficit and deprivation models in social policy, in which whānau has been regarded as maintaining 'undesirable' characteristics. Historical literature, however, indicates that whānau provides a cultural structure that is enabling of Māori. It provides a process of nurturing, education and sustenance on all levels, within all domains. Research has highlighted the importance of whānau in providing a context of wellbeing for tamariki. It has also consistently noted the place of tamariki as 'taonga', or treasures.

Identity and cultural connectedness are essential components of wellbeing for tamariki Māori. Understanding whakapapa and its many intricacies and responsibilities provides a foundation for this to occur. Those who understand their whakapapa connections and have an active role within their whānau, hapū and iwi groups develop a strong sense of identity; this then leads to the likelihood of more positive life outcomes (Webber, 2012). Grandparents and whānau continue to play a vital role in supporting children. Edwards et al.'s 2007 study of adolescents showed a large proportion of participants had active relationships with extended whānau. The role of grandparents and extended whānau was seen as key in ensuring healthy outcomes.

Raising tamariki in an environment where colonial beliefs of individuality and independence are promoted as ideal values can be an exceptionally challenging experience for many whānau Māori. Despite the destructive process of colonisation, however, Māori continue to draw from traditional knowledge as a guide to contemporary childrearing. This is evident in the developments within Māori education in which whānau have worked together within their communities in the establishment of Māori educational initiatives that nurture tamariki and provide support for whānau. It is critical that we look to traditional practices to inform our ways of being today. Traditional support systems for Māori consisted of a collective environment, with whānau and hapū members contributing to childrearing. Collective care was not only a positive support mechanism for parents and primary caregivers, but also provided tamariki with an enhanced and nurturing learning environment. Childrearing within a whānau environment that supports and nurtures tamariki growth and potential is vital for the wellbeing of the child and the whānau as a whole.

References

BROWN-SADLIER, M. (2008). *Motherloss*. Paper presented at the Te Tatau Pounamu: The Greenstone Door. Traditional Knowledge and Gateways to Balanced Relationships 2008, Auckland, New Zealand.

BUCK, P. (TE RANGI HĪROA). (1950). *The coming of the Māori*. Second Edition. Wellington, New Zealand: Māori Purposes Fund Board.

COLENSO, W., & NEW ZEALAND EXHIBITION. (2001). *On the Māori races of New Zealand* (new ed.). Christchurch, New Zealand: Kiwi.

DURIE, M. (2001). *Mauri Ora: The dynamics of Māori health*. Auckland, New Zealand: Oxford University Press.

EDWARDS, S., MCCREANOR, T., & MOEWAKA-BARNES, H. (2007). Māori family culture: A context of youth development in Counties/Manukau. *Kōtuitui: New Zealand Journal of Social Sciences Online*, 2(1), 1–15. doi: 10.1080/1177083X.2007.9522420

FAMILIES COMMISSION. (2012). *Tūpuna – Ngā Kaitiaki Mokopuna: A resource for Māori grandparents*. A Families Commission research report. Wellington, New Zealand: Families Commission.

GABEL, K. (2013). *Poipoia te tamaiti ki te ūkaipō* (Doctor of Philosophy thesis). University of Waikato, Hamilton, New Zealand. Retrieved from http://researchcommons.waikato.ac.nz/handle/10289/7986

HEMARA, W. (2000). *Māori pedagogies: A view from the literature*. Wellington, New Zealand: New Zealand Council for Educational Research.

HENARE, M. (1988). Ngā tikanga me ngā ritenga o te ao Māori: Standards and foundations of Māori society in *The Royal Commission on Social Policy*. Wellington, New Zealand: Governement Printer.

HOHEPA, M. K. (1990). *Te Kōhanga Reo hei Tikanga Ako i te Reo Māori* (Unpublished Master of Arts thesis) University of Auckland, Auckland, New Zealand.

HOHEPA, M. K. (1999). *'Hei Tautoko i te Reo': Māori language regeneration and whānau bookreading practices* (Unpublished Doctor of Philosophy thesis). University of Auckland, Auckland, New Zealand.

JENKINS, K., & HARTE, H. (2011). *Traditional Māori parenting: An historical review of literature of traditional Māori child rearing practices in pre-European time*. Retrieved from http://www.ririki.org.nz/images/pdfs/TradMāoriParenting.pdf

JOSEPH, R. (2007). Whānau mentoring, Māori youth and crime: Possible ways forward. *Childrenz Issues*, 11(1), 26–35.

KA'AI, T. (1990). *Te Hiringa Taketake: Mai i te Kōhanga Reo: Māori pedagogy, Te Kōhanga Reo and the transition to school* (Unpublished Master of Arts thesis). University of Auckland, Auckland, New Zealand.

KA'AI, T. (2005). Te Kauae Mārō o Muri-ranga-whenua (The jawbone of Muri-ranga-whenua): Globalising local Indigenous culture – Māori leadership, gender and cultural knowledge transmission as represented in the film *Whale Rider*. *PORTAL Journal of Multidisciplinary International Studies*, 2(2). Retrieved from http://epress.lib.uts.edu.au/journals/index.php/portal/article/view/92/59

KINGI, T., DURIE, M., ELDER, H., TAPSELL, R., LAWRENCE, M., & BENNETT, S. (2018). *Maea te Toi Ora: Māori health transformations.* Wellington, New Zealand: Huia Publishers.

LAWSON-TE AHO, K. (2010). *Definitions of Whānau: A review of selected literature.* Wellington, New Zealand: Families Commission

MARSDEN, S., & ELDER, J. S. (ED.) (1932). *The letters and journals of Samuel Marsden, 1765–1838, senior chaplain in the colony of New South Wales and superintendent of the Mission of the Church Missionary Society in New Zealand.* Dunedin, New Zealand: Coulls, Somerville Wilkie, Ltd. and A. H. Reed for the Otago University Council.

METGE, J. (1995). *New growth from old: The Whānau in the modern world.* Wellington, New Zealand: Victoria University Press.

MIKAERE, A. (2005). Cultural invasion continued: The ongoing colonisation of tikanga Māori. *Yearbook of New Zealand Jurisprudence Spcial Issue – Te Purenga*, 8(2), 134–172. http://www.waikato.ac.nz/_data/assets/pdf_file/0003/32799/Yearbook-of-NZ-Jurisprudence-vol-8-issue-2-2005.pdf

MIKAERE, A. (2011). *Colonising myths Māori realities: He rukuruku whakaaro.* Wellington, New Zealand: Huia Publishers.

MINISTRY OF JUSTICE. (2001). He Hīnātore ki te Ao Māori: A glimpse into the Māori world. Wellington, New Zealand: Government Print.

MOREHU, C. (2005). *A Māori perspective of whānau and childrearing in the 21st century case study* (Master of Education thesis). University of Waikato, Hamilton, New Zealand. Retrieved from http://researchcommons.waikato.ac.nz/handle/10289/2321

NEPE, T. M. (1991). E Hao Nei e Tenei Reanga: Te Toi Huarewa Tipuna: Kaupapa Māori, an educational intervention system (Master's thesis). University of Auckland, Auckland, New Zealand.

NORMAN, W. (1992). He aha te mea nui. *Te Pua, The Journal of Te Puawaitanga*, 1(1), 1–9.

PAPAKURA, M. (1938). *The old-time Māori.* London, England: V. Gollancz.

PERE, R. R. (1982). *Ako: Concepts and learning in the Māori tradition.* Wellington, New Zealand: Te Kōhanga Reo National Trust Board.

PERE, R. (1988). Te Wheke: Whaia te Māramatanga me te Aroha. In S. Middleton (Ed.), *Women and education in Aotearoa* (pp. 6–19). Wellington, New Zealand: Allen & Unwin New Zealand Ltd.

PERE, R. (1991). *Te Wheke: A celebration of infinite wisdom.* Gisborne, New Zealand: Ao Ako Global Learning.

PIHAMA, L. (1993). Tungia te Ururua, kia Tupu Whakaritorito te Tupu o te Harakeke: A critical analysis of parents as first teachers. RUME Masters Theses Series Number 3. Auckland, New Zealand: University of Auckland.

PIHAMA L. (2001). *Tīhei Mauri Ora: Honouring our voices. Mana Wāhine as a Kaupapa Māori theoretical framework* (Unpublished Doctor of Philosophy thesis). University of Auckland, Auckland, New Zealand.

PIHAMA, L., & CAMERON, N. (2012). Kua Tupu Te Pā Harakeke: Developing healthy whānau relationships. In W. Win & M. Yellowbird (Eds.), *For Indigenous minds only: A decolonization handbook* (pp. 225–244). Sante Fe, NM: SAR Press.

PIHAMA, L., & MARA, D. (1994). Gender relations in education. In E. Coxon, K. Jenkins, J. Marshall, & L. Massey (Eds.), *The politics of learning and teaching in Aotearoa New Zealand* (pp. 215–250). Palmerston North, New Zealand: Dunmore Press.

PIHAMA, L., SMITH, L. T., SIMMONDS, N., SEED-PIHAMA, J., & GABEL, K. (EDS) (2019A). *Mana Wahine reader: A collection of writings 1987–1998. Volume 1,* Hamilton, New Zealand: Te Kotahi Research Institute.

PIHAMA, L., SMITH, L. T., SIMMONDS, N., SEED-PIHAMA, J., & GABEL, K. (EDS) (2019B). *Mana Wahine reader: A collection of writings 1999–2019. Volume 2,* Hamilton, New Zealand: Te Kotahi Research Institute.

PIHAMA, L., SIMMONDS, N., & WAITOKI, W. (2019C). *Te Taonga o Taku Ngākau: Ancestral knowledge as a framework for wellbeing for Tamariki Māori.* Report to Better Start National Science Challenge & Cure Kids. Hamilton, New Zealand: Te Kotahi Research Institute.

PITAMA, D., RIRINUI, G., & MIKAERE, A. (2002). *Guardianship, Custody and Access: Māori Perspectives and Experiences.* Wellington, New Zealand: Ministry of Justice.

RICKARD, S. (1998). Koi patu koi mamae: Disciplining Māori children. *Social Work Now, 11,* 4–9.

ROKX, H., WOODHAM, B., & JOE, M. (1999). *Māori programme development: He Taonga, Te Mokopuna – The child is precious.* Children & Family Violence: Effective Interventions Now Conference 4–5 July 1999, Wellington, New Zealand.

ROYAL-TANGAERE, A. (1991). *Kei hea te Komako e kō? Early childhood education: A Māori perspective.* Fifth Early Childhood Education Convention, Dunedin, New Zealand.

RURU, J. (2005). Indigenous peoples and family law: Issues in Aotearoa/New Zealand. *International Journal of Law, Policy and the Family, 19*(3), 327–345.

SMITH, C. (2008). *Māori grandparents: Raising Mokopuna fulltime.* Paper presented at the Te Tatau Pounamu: The Greenstone Door. Traditional Knowledge and Gateways to Balanced Relationships 2008. Auckland, New Zealand.

SMITH, G. H. (1997). *The development of Kaupapa Māori theory and praxis* (Unpublished PhD thesis). School of Education, University of Auckland, Auckland, New Zealand.

TIKAO, T. T., & BEATTIE, H. (1990). *Tikao talks: Ka taoka tapu o te ao kohatu: Treasures from the ancient world of the Maori.* Auckland, New Zealand: Penguin.

WALKER, T. W. (2013). *Ngā Pā Harakeke O Ngāti Porou: A Lived Experience of Whānau* (Unpublished Doctor of Philosophy thesis). Victoria University, Wellington, New Zealand.

WEBBER, M. (2012). Identity matters: Racial-ethnic identity and Māori students. *set 2012. Te Māori i ngā ara rapu mātauranga – Māori Education, 2,* 20–27.

He Raranga Mātauranga: Weaving Ancestral Knowledge

Donna Campbell

CHAPTER 3

The practices of raranga and raranga whatu not only transform the materials the kairaranga is using, but also the kairaranga themselves. These practices are self-affirming, culturally affirming and ultimately decolonising (Campbell, 2019, p. 2).

This chapter is founded on the relationship the kairaranga/whatu weaver has with Te Pā Harakeke – the transformative relationship that envelops not only the weaver but also the wider whānau in the reclamation of mātauranga Māori and the wellbeing this accords. It privileges the voices of weavers who have contributed to my own raranga journey and to the overall research project of 'Tiakina te Pā Harakeke: Māori Traditional Understandings of Caring for our Children'. The plant harakeke has developed into a living metaphor for human and family wellbeing, with many kairaranga/whatu seeing themselves as repositories, linking the knowledge of the past with that of the future. The practice of nurturing our harakeke takes us back to whakapapa; this requires of us not only knowledge of the environment we live in, but also that we take responsibility for that environment. First, we are reconnecting with the whenua by nurturing and conserving the plants. Then, second, we are learning about ourselves and our tūpuna through practising the tikanga associated with the art forms. The expressions of raranga and whatu originate from te ao Māori, our unique worldview. Through working with native materials, the consciousness of the Māori world as embodied in the art form arises.

I have experienced raranga as cultural regeneration in my own artistic practice, and through the teaching of these artforms I have witnessed the transformative power of raranga in myself and others. Embodied within the practices of raranga and whatu are te reo and tikanga that affirm the centrality of the Māori worldview. Through the senses – the smell, the feel, the sound of raranga – when weaving, I have felt a timelessness, a weightlessness that I believe is the experience of 'being in' mātauranga Māori. For me, the act of practising tikanga associated with raranga and whatu enlivens a cultural wellness through enacting spiritual awareness as well as self-awareness. The connection with the whenua in the harvesting and the preparation of materials takes us back to the land and the knowledge of conserving our materials for future generations. Then, creating taonga from the knowledge that can be discovered in the physical exemplars of raranga and whatu that our tūpuna have left for us provides access to mātauranga Māori and to the creative spirit.

The relationship between the material and the weaver is explained in Erenora Puketapu-Hetet's 1989 book *Māori Weaving*, the first publication to provide insights into weaving from the perspective of a female weaver: "There is a phrase – I ngā rā o mua – which refers to the past. But the word 'mua' also means 'in front of you'. In our concept of time we cannot separate ourselves from our ancestors or the generation in front of us. Our past is our future, and also our present. Like the eternal circle" (cited in Jahnke & Ihimaera, 1996, p. 123).

Hetet affirms that this concept is very important to the kairaranga/whatu because they see themselves as repositories, the links to the practices of the past, the present and the future. My position is that in engaging with our native plants, while enacting our tikanga pertaining to the arts, we connect through all the senses to that cultural imprint otherwise articulated as whakapapa. Engaging the senses of the body with the tactile nature of weaving stimulates a rhythm of thinking, and the mind eases and allows the body to take over. Memories embedded in the body arise as a gathering of thought into the present-day experience of art making and knowledge formulation. In other words, the creative practices of raranga and whatu ignite the connections to our tūpuna.

Raranga and whatu are often carried out through wānanga collective practice that creates an environment of support, of sharing and learning and a sense of solidarity. I have had many teachers, and the work created is not only mine but also belongs to those who have contributed to my learning through the passing on of tūpuna knowledges. Our tūpuna are always acknowledged as those who have passed this gift on to us, and constant revisiting of taonga tuku iho informs new directions in contemporary practice. Taonga tuku iho inform the practices of raranga and raranga whatu, including the tikanga that guide the practice. Through their practice, kairaranga enact taonga tuku iho; through the practice we experience dignity and self-esteem, asserting our identity in an ultimate decolonising of the mind. In considering Indigenous People's realities in a colonised world, Reverend Māori Marsden (2003), the Tai Tokerau scholar, minister and philosopher, explains that through the process of assimilation and cultural genocide, tangata whenua have suffered the loss of dignity, self-esteem and identity, resulting in spiritual and psychological insecurities. I claim that practising our arts, especially raranga and raranga whatu, addresses cultural erosion and assimilationist polices by validating Māori knowledges, while at the same time acknowledging and encompassing the future generations or the "succeeding generations that add their quota of knowledge and fresh discoveries to the corpus of [our] cultural heritage" (Marsden, 2003, p. 39). Raranga and whatu are our cultural heritage practices, articulated through textiles that are functional artistic expressions of narratives pertaining to the Māori worldview. Our visual arts, raranga and whatu in the context of this chapter provide a lens, a portal, an access point to the unique expression of our Māori world. The practice of making engages all the senses; working with our native plants I engage not just the physical senses, but the spiritual senses as well.

This relationship is expressed by the tikanga that surrounds the practice of weaving. First and foremost, weavers acknowledge the life force of weaving, recognising the deity and histories associated with these artforms. Hine-te-iwaiwa, the deity of all womanly things, is but one of the cultural entities that inform weavers today. She is responsible for childbirth, nurturing and caring for others. These values are reflected in the tikanga of collecting harakeke for weaving. On harvesting, only the outer leaves are taken. The three central leaves are left to grow. The central leaf is the shoot, referred to as te rito and sometimes te pēpi. The outer leaves that protect te rito are referred to as ngā mātua because of their role in protecting the young shoot of the plant, hence the term whānau o te harakeke.

Cathy Schuster reflects on how te pā harakeke represents whānau in this way:

> [W]hen I'm harvesting and taking off those outer leaves and leaving the centre three, I always think about the māmā, the pāpā and the pēpi. And on those occasions when you do have to take that third one off, always feel really bad, always talk to them, its ok you'll be alright and when you can relate that to all the tamariki out there who are in one parent families, and they can thrive and they can be OK, you know, with support. So you go back and you check on that next time and I think there is that relationship there and it is, it's in my mind when I'm cutting. (Interview)

This harvesting practice is central to the survival of the plant; in addition, any dried leaves not suitable for weaving are cleaned away. Keeping the plant clear of dried and decaying leaves allows the plant to breathe and lets in the sunlight. It was once common practice to leave the pūkaha (leaf trimmings) of harvesting with the plant, but studies have shown that this practice encourages pests and has since been in decline. Plants need regular harvesting and cleaning; a harakeke plant that is not used will overgrow and the leaves will become tough and dry, and the dry leaves will overtake the healthy ones. It is said that the health of the pā harakeke on a marae reflects the state of ahi kā.

Wikitōria Tāne emphasises the importance of caring for te pā harakeke and Kahutoi te Kanawa reflects on growing up with te pā harakeke:

> Manaakitia te pā harakeke is the epitome of whānau ora. It is the ultimate example from Papatūānuku of nurturing of the infant/child (te rito) by its parents, whānau (awhi rito), and community in order for the community, whānau and child to thrive. Hine-te-iwaiwa is the female essence that exemplifies that nurturing. (Interview)

> Growing up, as a child, when you go to harvest harakeke or take care of it with your parents you get the jobs of taking the pūkaha away – you know, the rotten leaves and things like that – and put [them] in a separate pile. My grandmother and mum used to do this all the time; they used to actually take all those discarded ones away and put [them] in a totally different pile, so that it frees the harakeke plant to rejuvenate quicker, and simply also because they were using it all the time. Now that is the relationship that we've had with it because they were using it all the time and we'd always make sure when you look at the pā harakeke from a distance and it's starting to become a mass you realise that … it's just like your hair, when your hair grows, oh it's time for a haircut, well it's the same with the harakeke. So, we would always have to trim it back and in the end offer to go and get the harakeke for mum and nana. (Interview)

The phrase "the harakeke won't wait for you" was said to me by Matekino Lawless many years ago. By this short statement she meant that you have to make time for raranga and whatu, make the time to create the taonga you are working on. It is not good enough to go and harvest, then run out of time and let the harakeke dry out and be of no use. This maxim means that you need to make sure that you complete your taonga; it is a wisdom that teaches us to plan ahead, to focus, to commit, to complete. Another of our teachings from Tikanga o te Pā Harakeke is tā koha. The practice of tā koha relies on the completion of taonga before they are gifted. It is said that you must koha the first taonga you create on your raranga journey. Why? One of the main reasons is that you enact reciprocity by passing on a taonga in which you have invested time and aroha, and another is that you keep on creating taonga to develop skills as a kairaranga. Woven taonga are often passed down through the generations, and acknowledged for their mauri, and these taonga are often given back to Papatūānuku when they have completed their life journeys.

Hinekura Smith and Joy Wikitera remind us of the lessons to be learned from te pā harakeke:

> There are some great lessons in the process of raranga, particularly for our children and teenagers in this sort of day and age where everything's instant, short and sharp kind of stuff; there's a real skill in being able to sit down for an hour, two or three hours sometimes, to complete something. It's about being still. The perseverance to finish something and the patience to do it. And I see that with our oldest girl, she's still at that stage where … oh just gotta hurry up and do it cos gotta go and do something else, but just that patience to sit there and to be still and to find the mistake rather than just moving on … One of the things I love about raranga is that if you've got a mistake, you can't keep going; it's quicker to go back and fix it. I think there's some good lessons in life about that. (Interview)

> My moko always play with the harakeke. They could be up-and-coming weavers. It's good to get them used to it and instruct them how to use it. My moko doesn't cut harakeke; I will always cut it, but she likes making putiputi and weaving with it – tries to do as much as she can without my interference and I just let her go. What she makes is what she makes. (Interview)

Through the engagement of all the senses, an internal understanding of self, otherwise unarticulated, can be brought forth. Through the feel, the sound and the smell of the harakeke, with the opportunities and sometimes challenges of creating taonga that your tūpuna have made before you, being involved in this expression of being Māori has transformative power. Raranga and whatu are active processes on an essential level. These practices unite mind and body, "embracing the totality of our sensual perception and experience rather than intellectual activity alone" (Schneider & Wright, 2006, p. 16). Accordingly, experience can become knowledge; you know because you have been in it. These practices are taonga, which are defined by Rose Pere and Te Kōhanga Reo Trust (1994) as "the highly prized practices and beliefs of our forebears, our ancestors" (p. 69). Putting these beliefs into practice is to manifest mātauranga Māori drawing on every experience of life. As the practices of raranga and whatu are passed on to us from our ancestors, they are imbued with mātauranga Māori. As Pere and Te Kōhanga Reo Trust (1994) illustrate, the knowledge of ancestors is valued in the present, and through creative practice in the fibre arts we can maintain and pass on these treasures. Aroha Mitchell credits raranga with her development as a wahine Māori and an artist:

> Raranga affects every part of my life. This art form has connected me to my culture, my tūpuna and to the whenua. It has changed my life in a positive way; it grounds me, [has] taught me patience and provided many amazing opportunities. (Interview)

Discussing culture and identity, Marsden (2003) writes that Māori culture is Māoritanga, a term affirmed by tangata whenua (Māori) to specify our unique view of the world. Māori culture, he states, "is a complex whole of beliefs/attitudes/values/mores/customs/knowledge acquired" (Marsden, 2003, p. 34) dictated by responses to the environment, evolving and transmitted by the people as guiding principles. The guiding principles Marsden is suggesting here are a corpus of knowledge providing the cultural endurance that weaves together the societal fabric of a culture. He goes on to declare that despite the colonising forces that have disrupted Māori ways of cultural identification, tangata whenua have never totally surrendered the value systems of our culture. Therefore, cultural identity, according to Marsden (2003), is grounded within the prevailing understanding of a society's basic convictions. However, cultural identity also operates and responds within a dynamic flux of changing environments.

Representations of cultural identity underpin Māori creative practice as assertions of a distinctive Māori worldview. The Māori worldview is elucidated by Ngāti Raukawa and Ngāti Porou legal scholar Ani Mikaere (2011) in this way:

> The worldview bequeathed to us by our ancestors is at the very heart of what makes us unique. It provides a lens through which we view the world. It determines the way in which we relate to one another and all other facets of creation. It enables us to explain how we came to be here [and] where we are going. It forms the very core of our identity (p. 308). (Interview)

Mikaere (2011) affirms that through a Māori worldview we express our cultural identity as gifted to us through ancestral connections. Accordingly, at the heart of my own creative practice is a Māori worldview that informs my identity and the expression of that identity. Te Arawa and Tūhoe writer, scholar and feminist activist Ngahuia Te Awekotuku (1991) writes of the Māori worldview as expressed through taonga tuku iho. According to Te Awekotuku (1991), echoes of taha wairua and taha tinana are embodied in the Māori ancestral arts created from natural resources:

> Taha wairua, the way of the spirit in matters Māori, permeates our world so profoundly that to isolate and analyse it is almost like threatening the very fabric itself. Spirituality and art making have formed an integral part of the Māori worldview from ancient times until the present day (p. 135).

As Te Awekotuku (1991) observes, essential to the creation of Māori art is spirituality, while also acknowledging the intellect, and the body, as ornately embodied within the practice of our art forms. The ancestral arts such as raranga and whatu are created from the whenua through designs and forms responding to and inspired by the whenua. Cultural identity is reflected through these designs, forms and materiality as unique to this place, this whenua.

Matiu Rau reflects on the holistic nature of te pā harakeke:

> Harakeke, like whānau, consist of pēpi which are to be nurtured, mātua which are needed to provide the nurturing, mātua tūpuna who have lived, passed on their knowledge and at some point must leave us in light of another journey. This cycle will continue as long as we continue to uphold its value and [the] principles of manaakitanga and whanaungatanga. (Interview)

The kairaranga knows that through the practices of raranga and whatu all the senses are ignited through the hands. There are no tools between the kairaranga and the harakeke when practising raranga and whatu; the hands and the materials transmit energy. The senses are activated by experiencing the material, then through the senses we are enacting our value systems, exploring our intellectual worlds, and engaging in mātauranga Māori. Māori scholar Charles Royal (2009) explains that "Mātauranga Māori is a modern term for a body of knowledge that was brought to these islands by Polynesian ancestors of present-day Māori. Here this body of knowledge grew according to life in Aotearoa" (p. 87).

These bodies of knowledge were impacted in many and significant ways by the arrival of European settlers, endangering the veracity of Māori knowledge systems, but "Important fragments and portions – notably the Māori language – remain today" (Royal, 2009, p. 87). I would add to Royal's discussion that the visual arts of raranga, raranga whatu and whakairo rākau are also important "fragments and portions" that remain to inform and inspire us today.

Hinekura Smith reflects here on the holistic nature of mātauranga Māori:

> Whilst I am harvesting, preparing, and weaving the wahakura, I am thinking about pēpi, weaving my aroha for pēpi into each whenu. If I consider that my DNA is literally worked into the weaving through handling and processing the kōrari then I have a responsibility to ensure that my intentions and thoughts about pēpi are pure, as this is where he will sleep. (Interview)

Conclusion

> Take the single line, such as the aho tapu of the weaver, the genealogical line. Follow it to its logical conclusion. It doubles, triples, quadruples. Eventually there is a mosaic of interwoven lines, a fabric of history, an infinite number of references surface. That single line reflects the mana of the people and a history that can go beyond the present to another time long, long ago (Ford, cited in Smith & Smith, 2001, p. 12).

Te aho tapu is the first and sacred line of weaving. This is the first weft thread that is strung across two sticks or turuturu anchored in the ground. It is the beginning thread that the warp threads are suspended from. Without this first thread a korowai cannot be made. Te aho tapu is integral to the construction of kākahu and korowai, and is also integral to the fabric of Māori society. The notion of the eternal thread can be applied to the way that a whiri in a kete is integral to the beginning of a kete, and no kete is complete without the whiri on the top edges. Without the whiri the kete would not hold together; it contains the whakapapa of pattern and binds all together to create one fabric. Raranga, akin to the revered korowai of old, holds a visual language of its own, a record of history and provenance embodying genealogy. Te aho tapu is used in Māori society as a metaphor for our connection to the past. This ancestral thread not only connects us in the present to the past; it is also our connection to the future.

The wonderful qualities of te pā harakeke manifest in the taonga created by kairaranga/whatu. The physical and spiritual layers fuse to embody connections to the whenua, to our tūpuna and to ourselves. I believe I am a much healthier and more aware mother, partner, daughter, sister and friend because of the legacy of raranga and whatu passed down to us from our tūpuna.

Acknowledgements

Many thanks to the kairaranga/whatu who have contributed your thoughts and wisdom to this chapter: Wikitoria Tāne (Ngāti Maniapoto), Kahutoi te Kanawa (Ngāti Kinohaku, Uekaha, Maniapoto, Waikato, Tūwharetoa), Hinekura Smith (Te Rarawa), Joy Wikitera (Ngāpuhi), Aroha Mitchell (Te Arawa, Ngāti Porou), Matiu Rau (Ngāti Korokī-Kahukura, Ngāti Haua, Ngāti Maniapoto), Cathy Schuster (Ngāti Pākehā).

References

CAMPBELL, D. (2019). *Ngā kura a Hine-te-iwaiwa: The embodiment of Mana wahine in Māori fibre arts* (Doctoral dissertation). University of Waikato, Hamilton, New Zealand. https://hdl.handle.net/10289/12583

HETET, E. (1989). *Māori weaving.* Auckland, New Zealand: Pitman.

JAHNKE, R., & IHIMAERA, W. (1996). Te rito o te harakeke: The tender shoot of life. In S. Adsett, C. Whiting & W. Ihimaera (Eds.), *Mataora the living face* (pp. 122–125). Auckland, New Zealand: Bateman.

MARSDEN, M. (2003). *The woven universe: Selected writings of Rev. Māori Marsden* (Ed. T. C. Royal). Otaki, New Zealand: The Estate of Rev. Māori Marsden.

MIKAERE, A. (2011). *Colonising myths – Māori realities: He rukuruku whakaaro.* Wellington, New Zealand: Huia Publishers.

PERE, R., & TE KŌHANGA REO TRUST. (1994). *Ako: Concepts and learning in the Maori tradition.* Wellington, New Zealand: Te Kōhanga Reo National Trust Board.

ROYAL, T. C. (2009). *Let the world speak: Towards Indigenous epistemology.* Porirua, New Zealand: Mauriora-ki-te-ao/Living Universe.

SCHNEIDER, A., & WRIGHT, C. (2006). *Contemporary art and anthropology*, Oxford, England: Berg.

SMITH, J., & SMITH, P. (2001). *Making connections: John Bevan Ford, Māori Artist.* Lower Hutt, New Zealand: Gilt Edge Publishing.

TE AWEKOTUKU, N. (1991). *Mana wahine Māori: Selected writings on Māori women's art, culture and politics.* Auckland, New Zealand: New Women's Press.

Te Taonga o Taku Ngākau: The Wellbeing of Tamariki within Whānau

Leonie Pihama
Naomi Simmonds
Waikaremoana Waitoki

CHAPTER 4

Introduction

The whakataukī 'Te Taonga o Taku Ngākau' translates as the 'treasure of my soul/heart'. Pihama, Tiakiwai, and Southey (2015) note that in a contemporary context this relates to the wider notion that children are a gift of life. It is argued that by reclaiming our knowledge of Māori childrearing traditions, a deeper understanding of the importance of collective practices and responsibility emerges. From that understanding, Māori values that inspire connectivity and relationality strengthen Māori language and cultural practices, and provide transformative action that will enable our children and communities to grow and flourish.

'Te Taonga o Taku Ngākau' is a Kaupapa Māori research project that situates the wellbeing of tamariki (Māori children) within the context of well and thriving whānau. The purpose of the research is to consider the frameworks, values and actions for whānau transformation that exist within mātauranga Māori. Importantly, the research seeks to demonstrate the ways in which whānau themselves generate, through purposeful action, wellbeing from within mātauranga and tikanga Māori. This chapter seeks to synthesise the key findings of this research project.

Using a Kaupapa Māori methodology, the project involved interviewing traditional knowledge holders, Māori mental-health providers and whānau Māori to better understand how whānau define and practise wellbeing; the role of mātauranga and tikanga in creating well and thriving whānau; and the collective responsibility to the wellbeing of tamariki within a whānau context. By effectively using the knowledge held by those at the front line working with tamariki and their whānau, and by whānau themselves, this research seeks to demonstrate the collective community, hapū and iwi involvement in the care and wellbeing of our children.

In this chapter we reassert the fundamental principles of Kaupapa Māori and their value in transformation for whānau. In doing so, this research contributes to growing a much-needed body of evidence that reaffirms the centrality of whānau to the mental wellbeing of tamariki. In what follows, an overview of the research questions, background to the research, and research context is provided. The chapter then focuses specifically on conceptualisations and understandings of whānau wellbeing, and the wellbeing of tamariki within whānau, by unpacking the Kaupapa Māori principle of whānau.

Mātauranga Approaches for Raising Tamariki

This project investigates how mātauranga Māori related to the raising of Māori children can be used to develop prevention and intervention tools that support tamariki and whānau who are experiencing mental-health issues in Aotearoa. The overarching research question is: How can mātauranga Māori provide an evidence-based cultural intervention that will improve the mental health and wellbeing of tamariki Māori and their whānau?

Broadly speaking, the research sought to carry out an interdisciplinary Kaupapa Māori research project that explored mātauranga Māori with key knowledge holders, and to think through culturally responsive tools and frameworks to improve the mental health and wellbeing of tamariki within the context of whānau. The project team worked with key knowledge holders, practitioners and whānau to consider the collective mechanisms for change and transformation within whānau. In doing so, we sought to generate a Kaupapa Māori framework for whānau that means collective responsibility is of foremost importance.

'Te Taonga o Taku Ngākau' is grounded in mātauranga Māori and informed by a Kaupapa Māori research methodology. Framing this research with the whakataukī 'Te taonga o taku ngākau' locates both the theoretical and methodological approaches within a Kaupapa Māori research approach. All components of this project were designed to align with Kaupapa Māori through the delivery of research processes that meaningfully engaged with and responded to Māori communities; prioritised Māori approaches and mātauranga Māori throughout all phases of the project; engaged with a research area that is important to Māori and has wellbeing as a central focus; and had a strong Kaupapa Māori approach, led by experienced Māori researchers and providers.

Kaupapa Māori recognises that the tradition of 'research' extends back to our ancestors. Not simply the subjects of colonial research agendas, our tūpuna had ways of 'researching' and 'investigating' the world around them (and beyond) that were ancient in their origins. As their descendants, we, as Māori, inherit a tradition of 'research' that enables us to be unique and creative in the ways we share, teach and learn new and old knowledges. Importantly, our tūpuna have taught us how to be flexible and adaptable in our knowledges and practices, while at the same time upholding their power and tapu. Kaupapa Māori theory and methodology are not singular; rather, they have multiple expressions that ensure whānau, hapū, iwi and Māori communities are able to create approaches that prioritise the tikanga, kawa, te mita o te reo and mātauranga that are unique to their regions or focus of work (Pihama, 2001).

Today, many whānau have been separated from this cultural support network, causing disruption to traditional and collective childrearing values and practices, with devastating effects for whānau, and specifically for tamariki. There are numerous studies that highlight the range of negative indices experienced by whānau Māori, including economic inequality, child abuse, partner violence, suicidality, high smoking rates and mental-health issues (Fergusson, Horwood, & Gibb, 2011; Lawson-Te Aho, 2016; Marriott & Sim, 2014; Seymour, Cooper, & Stanton, 2016). Within dominant research, however, it is not always made clear that these negative indices have their roots in a long colonial history burdened with land theft, urbanisation, destruction of collectivity and the marginalisation of traditional knowledges. Instead whānau are pathologised, made the problem and not the solution, or, in the case of mental wellbeing and children, whānau are often left out of the discussion and decision making all together.

The social and economic positioning of whānau Māori as a result of historical and ongoing colonialism further affects the capacity of whānau Māori to thrive and impacts on the mental health and wellbeing of tamariki.

Kaupapa Māori Principles – Active Frameworks for Change

The key principles of Kaupapa Māori theory, which underpin this project, are outlined below. This is provided to give an understanding of where the 'whānau' principle that is discussed in this chapter is situated. Drawing on the work of Smith (1997) and Pihama (2001), Kaupapa Māori principles may be summarised as follows:

TINO RANGATIRATANGA (The self-determination principle)

This principle is defined through the framing of tino rangatiratanga within Te Tiriti o Waitangi (Treaty of Waitangi, 1840). Tino rangatiratanga has a multitude of translations, including independence, sovereignty, iwi autonomy, chiefly authority and self-determination. In summary, Smith (1997) states, "The principle of 'tino rangatiranga' reinforces the goal of seeking more meaningful 'control over one's own life and cultural wellbeing'" (p. 466).

TAONGA TUKU IHO (The cultural aspirations principle)

This principle refers directly to all 'taonga' or treasures, valued ways of being and practices, both tangible and intangible, that have been handed down through the generations by our ancestors and which we will hand to our descendants. It relates to te reo, tikanga, mātauranga and all cultural ways of being that are encompassed within te ao Māori.

AKO MĀORI (The culturally preferred pedagogy)

Ako refers to all forms of Māori cultural processes of learning and teaching. As Māori pedagogical practices, we affirm the interconnectedness of all learners and teachers, and the reciprocal relationship that is central to the learning and transmission of Māori knowledge and associated practices.

KIA PIKI AKE I NGĀ RARURARU O TE KĀINGA
(The socioeconomic mediation principle)

This principle focuses on providing the ways in which we draw upon cultural understandings and practices to provide support for those who are experiencing difficulties. It is referred to as mediating the ill effects of the impacts of colonisation and the means by which we create forms of intervention that Smith (1997) states, "[speak] to the need to alleviate the negative pressures of the marginal socio-economic positioning of any Māori families which impacts on learning" (p. 468).

WHĀNAU (The extended family structure principle)

Whānau is the foundation collective within te ao Māori. Whānau provides for the collective wellbeing of all its members and is central to Kaupapa Māori approaches. This principle centralises cultural relationships and is the basis for the larger cultural groupings of whānau and hapū. Collective relationships and responsibility are a key focus of this project in relation to the wellbeing of tamariki and whānau.

K A U P A P A (The collective philosophy principle)

Kaupapa refers to the central philosophy that informs our approaches to particular events, issues and contexts. It is both a foundation and platform on which our understandings are shaped and is the basis upon which our approaches are grounded. Collectively, these elements provide principles and practices within which all aspects of te reo, tikanga and mātauranga Māori can be drawn upon. Pihama (2001) has indicated there are some elements that require further emphasis or need to be named more explicitly, such as discussions of decolonisation, whakapapa, te reo and tikanga. It is clear these are embedded within the principles of tino rangatiratanga and taonga tuku iho.

What follows are excerpts and analysis of kaikōrero in the research that are specifically focused on the principle of whānau.

Whānau: Collective Networks for Wellbeing

Māori communities have always had measures of health and wellbeing that were collectively defined. These measures were holistic, intimately connected to the wellbeing of the environment, spiritually mediated and collectively supported. In other words, the wellbeing of an individual in Māori communities was the responsibility of many. Smith (1999) highlights that we need to think about the measures and frameworks we must understand, and know when we have achieved good health and wellbeing as individuals and as whānau.

Following colonisation, Māori health and wellbeing has consistently declined (Kukutai & Pool, 2014). The impact of diseases, the confiscation of lands and the denial of Māori healing processes have had a significant impact and unfortunately this is still the case today (Robson & Harris, 2007). The evidence is clear that the disparities experienced by Māori in the health sector and across all domains of life continue to impact significantly on the lives of whānau, hapū and iwi, both individually and collectively. There are many statistics that indicate this is the case, and statistics on the inequities for tamariki Māori are stark. It has been highlighted that state-defined interventions in mental wellness have often been found lacking, and have even reproduced violence and trauma for Indigenous Peoples (see de Leeuw et al., 2010). In more contemporary times, several models have have been developed that describe a Māori view of health, including 'Te Whare Tapa Whā', 'Te Wheke' and 'He Waka Eke Noa', among many others (Kingi et al., 2018). All these models emphasise the importance of the wellbeing of the whānau. The implication is that unless the whānau is strong and healthy, the individual will not be.

The institution of whānau is posited as a cornerstone of Māori society (Jenkins & Harte, 2011; Pihama, 2001; Smith, 1999). The meaning of whānau as it is used here is not simply meant to denote the nuclear family – whānau is much more. It can include extended family and – wider still – hapū and iwi. Indigenous families have endured a lot of trauma through colonisation and part of decolonisation requires that we rework understandings of family. It has been argued that colonisation and the impact of colonising systems affect Māori on a daily basis (Simmonds, 2014). The systemic nature of colonisation has been identified as reproducing inequalities and disparities that underpin economic poverty and the marginalisation of te reo and tikanga Māori, thus creating contexts in which experiences of cultural, political, economic and social disconnection negatively affect the wellbeing of many whānau. The consequences of colonisation have been widely felt by Māori.

In the health sector, Harris et al. (2006) have noted that the significant health disparities experienced by Māori can be sourced directly to colonisation and the processes of the ongoing personal and structural marginalisation of Māori in the health sector. In education, it is well documented that the denial of te reo and tikanga Māori was an intentional strategy in the establishment of dominant educational systems grounded upon practices of assimilation (Pihama, 2001). It is clear that from the outset of colonial permeation, Māori collectivism was philosophically at odds with the settler ethic of individualisation. Urbanisation and land confiscations, as well as Christian ideologies about the status of men and women, have had devastating effects for whānau Māori and specifically for Māori women.

As the whānau unit became progressively smaller, the responsibilities of individuals grew. Whānau became dislocated from traditional means of support and cultural knowledge, including mātauranga and tikanga, which would have been learned in a communal setting (Mikaere, 2003). This is a direct reflection of the nuclear family structure that has significantly permeated our society and has had a huge impact on our day-to-day living. The individualised nature of Western family units provided the right conditions to undermine the collectivity of whānau and the power and strength that came from living, learning and thriving as whānau in the very broadest sense of the word (Gabel, 2013). Colonisation sought to undermine our collectivity in every way: by physically separating our ability to connect to our lands through confiscations; by denying the practice of returning the whenua ki te whenua; by denying te reo Māori; by outlawing our spiritual experts and healers; and through urbanisation and assimilatory policies.

The marginalisation of whānau collectives continues today, as does the marginalisation of mātauranga and tikanga Māori. Across Aotearoa, Australia and the Pacific, Western systems and structures of health, including mental health and wellbeing, continue to foster, maintain and reproduce 21st-century colonialism (Pihama et al., 2014). Programmes implemented here continue to deny the history of violence that underpins the extremely high rates of family violence and sexual violence, poverty and ill health in this country. The denial of this history can be described as selective amnesia. It is an act of erasure. It serves to deny the role of both colonisation and successive colonial governments in the reproduction of violence, and as such reinforces the deficit, colonial views of Māori people.

There is no doubt that Māori are over represented in negative health statistics (Mental Health Commission, 2012); however, the deficit approaches taken have worked to reproduce existing inequities. Within this way of thinking, Māori ethnicity itself is posited as an unfavourable 'deficit' variable, in line with dominant deficit discourse, and there is no consideration of the ways in which Māori are systematically and historically positioned regarding colonisation. The focus on our people as 'deficit' continues to be privileged across the health sector. However, our people have stated for many years that we are not the problem; we are the solution. The risk factors are in fact colonisation and systemic racism, and the ways in which they continue to impose oppressive structures upon our people. As Green (2011) states, the representation of Māori as 'problem' is more than an imagining. Instead, it has a materiality in the form of how knowledge and power are produced and how these are implemented in the health policy sector. Smith (1999) describes problematising Indigenous Peoples as a Western obsession.

The representation of Māori as 'problem' justifies the growth of the institutions and instruments involved in the surveillance, the management and the control of Māori sexual and reproductive health (Green, 2011). Nash (2001) states that this contributes to the construction of key barriers regarding Māori, including: (i) the privilege given to forms of statistical explanation that favour a positivist over a hermeneutic account, embedded in the practical, theoretical 'at risk' concept; (ii) the preference for behaviourist and reductionist models that isolate behaviour from its social context; and (iii) the support given to an authoritative concept of culture that inhibits recognition of actual and lived cultural practices. It is not surprising to Māori and Indigenous communities around the world that we shoulder a disproportionate burden of mental and physical illness (Nelson & Wilson, 2017). There is a dominance of research within the mental health and wellbeing literature that pathologises tamariki Māori and whānau and continues to theorise the inequities in a range of indices from a deficit model. This research challenges such approaches and argues that collective approaches to raising children within mātauranga Māori uplift and empower whānau in their experiences and transform the wellbeing of tamariki and whānau in Aotearoa.

Māori health and wellbeing research makes the point that Māori mental illness is a contemporary issue and that, traditionally, whānau were a protective mechanism for individuals. Te Kani Kingi (2005) points out that mental health problems were mediated by cultural practices and structures, particularly the whānau, and as such Māori culture offered a protective mechanism, a basic structure through which mental-health problems were unable to develop or, at the very least, unable to take hold in the way that they have since colonisation. The point that whānau wellbeing is vital as a protective mechanism for individuals has been reiterated across multiple research programmes and Māori health initiatives. In the report *Te Oranga Hinengaro* (Russell, 2018) about Māori mental wellbeing, this was reiterated – highlighting that it is not simply about the numbers of people surrounding an individual but about the connectivity, support and manaakitanga an individual can rely on. The report points out that alongside strong familial relationships and good social support, being able to manaaki others is another indicator of wellness for Māori that may protect against social isolation (or loneliness). Those who find it easy to provide help to others in need are significantly less likely to report feeling socially isolated. Mounting Māori evidence supports the notion that a secure cultural identity derived from cultural and social connection is vital for better Māori mental wellbeing.

Reclaiming Whānau

Whānau is central to the wellbeing of tamariki and mokopuna. Whānau voices, whānau wānanga, whānau understandings and whānau aspirations provide us with understandings of the necessity to ensure the wellbeing of whānau both as a structure and as a focus of wellbeing. One of the key points made by all whānau kaikōrero (those whānau interviewed) is that whānau means much more than simply the English word 'family'. It is multifaceted, complex and broadly defined. Within te ao Māori it is understood that children are born into whānau – not just to a mother and father. This was expressed, in various ways, by several whānau kaikōrero as highlighted below:

> My concept of whānau I probably draw upon from my own, which is quite intergenerational, but also not just whakapapa by blood, but whakapapa by upbringing and support. So, I have a whāngai sister who is no less my sister, for example, than my birth sister, and her children are no less my irāmutu than my own biological sibling's children. So, within my own whānau context there are my parents; all their parents have passed on now but, like myself and my siblings and their partners and all our children, are very much a part of each other's lives. So, when I talk about whānau I immediately think about the context of my own, which is not just me, husband or children. My whānau is me, my biological siblings, my siblings – who, by the way, are divorced and have married again and have divorced again, but they are still a cohesive subsystem as parents with a narrowing whānau context. Then of course we have cousins, some of which are third cousin[s] twice removed, but have grown up entrenched within our whānau system, so they are cousins and they are probably not even as close as some other ones, but they are a part of the whānau unit. (Whānau kaikōrero)

> I guess what came to mind is some of the reading I had done a while ago around how our tūpuna raised their children and it wasn't a nuclear type of [family]. If you want to use that term, that we tend to have from a Western perspective, that yes there were parents, mum and dad acknowledged as important but the wider whānau were responsible and involved in raising and supporting those children. That would include aunties and your grandparents and siblings of your grandparents and older cousins and so on. From some of the things I read from Rose Pere, I think it was, there wasn't a word for parenting, that it was tiaki tamariki, or tiakitanga might be the closest term to think of, but that wasn't specific to mother and father. (Whānau kaikōrero)

> I guess I think of whānau in lots of different ways. Like there is whakapapa whānau that we have, which includes parents, grandparents, siblings, children, mokos, aunties and uncles, but wider and broader whānau as well. I guess most of the time I'm thinking about whānau it's the whānau that I grew up with that I'm more immediately engaged with day to day. Like which for me, is siblings, would be parents if they were around, and my own child and grandchildren. But I also think about the broader whakapapa of our whānau. That's important to me, still working on strengthening those connections. (Whānau kaikōrero)

What these narratives highlight is that the limited definition of family and Western appropriations of whānau can be particularly damaging. Pihama (1998) argues that whānau should not be defined or constrained to a Western Pākehā notion of the colonial heterosexual nuclear family. She makes the point that:

> The limited definition of the 'family' as nuclear, heterosexual and constructed within limited gender roles is not 'natural', but is constructed by certain groups to benefit their own interests ... Such a definition is not only limited but it also imposes restrictions on how different groups wish to construct their families. With the nuclear heterosexual family being centred as the 'norm', the standardised version of family, everything else is measured against it and labelled and judged accordingly (Pihama, 1998, pp. 179–207)

Connections through whakapapa sit at the centre of our understanding of traditional structures of whānau. Within our whakapapa, relationships, concepts, values and practices that enable us to project ourselves with confidence into the future are shared and transmitted. Moreover, whakapapa tells us that we have a heritage of hardship and richness, struggle and joy, that we are descendants of creative, courageous and sometimes outrageous people. Whakapapa also enables us to feel supported in being well. More than simply genealogy, whakapapa is very much a relational and multiple-layered term. Whakapapa is about connections and growth and it is within our whakapapa that we can find a wealth of resources that enable us to make sense of and transform our lived realities. Ani Mikaere (2011) talks about whakapapa, writing:

> Whakapapa embodies a comprehensive conceptual framework that enables us to make sense of our world. It allows us to explain where we have come from and to envisage where we are going. It provides us with guidance on how we should behave towards one another and it helps us to understand how we fit into the world around us. It shapes the way we think about ourselves and about the issues that confront us from one day to the next (pp. 285–286).

This point was made in thinking about the ways in which mokopuna are reflections of their ancestors and that connecting to those gifts of our ancestors enables and facilitates wellbeing:

> Just a quick example, it's like to say mokopuna, being like the imprint of our ancestors, so as soon as I know and understand that, changes it from being just this is a grandchild, the offspring of my own child to, wow, this a connection that is from the spirit world because this child has come through from my ancestors who dwell in another place. Knowing all those stories, as well, about where we come from, our connection to the stars originally and coming through from te kore ki te ao mārama, so just that one word, mokopuna, can help me feel spiritually connected. And know that I am a mokopuna too, and my mokopuna, all our mokopuna are connected spiritually and our reo and knowledge about cosmology and all sorts of information from our tūpuna is incredible for spiritual support and wellbeing, definitely. Karakia of course, absolutely, and recently ... using romiromi healing and karakia within that too, but again understanding how we are influenced by those unseen forces and sometimes how that can impact our wellbeing in ways that aren't good, but there is something we can do about that. (Whānau kaikōrero)

Whakapapa, then, is much more than 'genealogy'. It is an intricate web of connections, intersections and relationships that serve to connect whānau to enduring lifeways that are ancient in origin but that will carry them into the future and enable them to navigate the complex systems of power that are part of our colonised realities.

Many of the people involved in this research also discussed the wide reaches that their understandings of whānau had, beyond those with whakapapa ties to those who had shared values, shared kaupapa and who were part of a larger network of support. This point was reiterated by another whānau kaikōrero:

> Whānau, I've experienced whānau in different shapes and forms and so have my kids. Back home in the pā, whānau is whānau. So that term really applies to all my cousins and aunties and uncles and stuff like that so even though we belong to different hapū groups within our tribe, whānau is whānau. I can go anywhere in the world and ring up someone and say hey cuzie, and to me that's whānau. That line of whakapapa connection I suppose, there is no term for it, it's just we are whanaunga, we are part of the same collective. But in terms of being away from the centre back home, I've had to create what I call whānau up here with people who aren't even whakapapa, don't [whakapapa] ā-toto, they are not linked to me by blood. But in terms of a collective kind of thought and, for example, our kids all went to kōhanga, so for us whānau was the kōhanga whānau. Then you move from the kōhanga into a kura and then you have another whānau, and then you move from the kura into, one of my kids went to a mainstream kura so we had a whānau there and my other youngest daughter went to kura, so we had a whānau there. (Whānau kaikōrero)

The different kind of work required to establish and maintain these relationships was discussed by some whānau kaikōrero as examples of establishing connections and the ethics of care that they saw as important to maintain the relationships. In this way, a multiplicity of collectives is required and finding lateral connections as opposed to just generational ones is important. Whatever way whānau is defined – and this is an important point – whānau is multiply defined and should be to fit the needs of each collective – there is little doubt that the whānau unit is pivotal to wellbeing and to mental wellbeing. One whānau kaikōrero points out the changes that have occurred to collective ways of defining whānau over time:

> I guess when thinking about our tūpuna we think of things as a large collective, so I think the concept of whānau was probably based on our hapū approaches. Everyone played a part in the development of the pā I guess, and I think in the modern day there are still some of us who lived that same lifestyle, and I think particularly in the urban environment that's probably a little bit different, but when you do have different things like [kura] and the movement of kapa haka you can also get that hapū or pā lifestyle in those urban settings now. I think those that are disconnected from it for many different reasons ... are missing out on quite an important part of their identity ... so when I think about how our tūpuna did things, when I think about the concept of wellbeing, I guess that was just a secondary outcome for them. All of their kaupapa was just based on, I guess, survival, and so being out and about was part of them being able to feed themselves and create housing, create waka, being

able to transport themselves from places. And the outcome was they were getting stronger, they were getting faster, they were getting fitter, but that wasn't quite the primary goal of each of those things – in my opinion, anyway. (Whānau kaikōrero)

The broad and inclusive nature of whānau was also reflected in the discussion by one participant:

I wonder how the word whānau was used and how it came up in conversations – your whānau, my whānau, we were all whānau. I have on a number of occasions thought about how the term and the idea of whānau has been appropriated and used in so many different ways and misappropriated, mispronounced – 'far-now' – and how it's become almost one of those words that's part of our New Zealand English, and how when a word is used over and over and over and over again in different contexts how it starts to shift and change its meaning. For our tūpuna, I am not sure how our tūpuna might have understood it. I guess I can only go from what some of our other words tell or indicate that whānau might have been understood, the idea that a whaea can be a mother and an aunt, it's not just one role, or a matua. There weren't words for step-sister or half-sister, I imagine that you would have just been part of the whānau without those terms that somehow seem to exclude in different ways or put on another label or something like that ... in my experience those labels are often used to put you in your place, you know, you are the half-sister, or you are the so and so. I would imagine that our tūpuna would have used whānau as a really all-encompassing kind of term, and in that way if I think about these things here, tamariki, wellbeing and mental health, that by having an encompassing term like that there isn't an exclusion, or if there was there was probably a really good ... I don't know how people might of been excluded from that, but you know without question that you are part of this thing, this collective, this concept. (Whānau kaikōrero)

This is an important point with regard to the wellbeing of individuals, that perhaps this wasn't the primary goal, but instead the necessary work to live, learn and love collectively was a much healthier (physically, spiritually and emotionally) way to live than current lifestyles.

Definitions of whānau extend beyond the realm of people and when discussing wellbeing many whānau kaikōrero talked about the environment as part of their whakapapa network and thus part of the equation when it comes to wellbeing. There is a growing body of Indigenous work that considers the dialogic relationship between land, the environment and ancestral places, and the health and wellbeing of individuals and collectives (Kimmerer, 2013; Schultz et al., 2016). Indigenous knowledge frameworks that sit within the land were undermined and cast as 'inferior' to Western biomedical and biophysical approaches to health. The dominant ideology that people and land can be treated as separate is challenged through Indigenous knowledge frameworks that demonstrate the inextricability of human wellbeing from the health of our lands, waters and environment (Kingi et al., 2018; Moewaka Barnes & McCreanor, 2019).

Indigenous health researchers continuously affirm the relationship to 'all of our relations' as a critical indicator of health and wellbeing. Embedded within significant places is a multitude of interventions that can serve to transform physical, emotional and mental wellbeing for our whānau (Moewaka Barnes, Eich, & Yessilth, 2018; Pihama et al., 2014; Simmonds, 2014). Māori models of health emphasise holistic understandings and multiple dimensions that cannot be separated. In 2018, for Mental Health Awareness Week, the Mental Health Foundation and Hāpai Te Hauora selected the theme "Let nature in, strengthen your wellbeing – Mā te taiao, ka whakapakari tōu oranga!" (Hāpai Te Hauora, 2018). This was a resounding theme across whānau kaikōrero. The relationship between the environment and the wellbeing of whānau was highlighted by the following comments:

> So, an example for us on the awa is when the awa is sick like it is now, our tuna are dying in the tributaries because the water is too warm, we are still unwell. So, there's that reciprocity of not just looking after ourselves, but looking after ourselves and our tūpuna for the sake of being able to have that collective wellness. It's not just about tuna dying. (Whānau kaikōrero)

> I think, being connected, that would tie into being connected to our land, our waters. Definitely like our view of wellbeing, generally, as Māori is like our health and the health of our land are completely connected, our environment, not just the whenua but our rivers, our awa, our moana and our kai, all of those things, cultivating gardens. If our environment was healthy then we could be healthy and vice-versa, so I guess you could look to the environment as a sign of whānau wellbeing too. (Whānau kaikōrero)

Conclusion

When asked what Te Taonga o Taku Ngākau meant, the importance of whakapapa and the empowering collective approach to raising tamariki resounded among the whānau kaikōrero. Each kaikōrero had their own understanding of the concept; however, there was a general consensus that tamariki were 'te rito o te harakeke' (the centre shoot of the harakeke plant) and therefore the wellbeing of the whole was paramount to protect the child in physical, spiritual and mental terms. As one kaikōrero explained:

> When I first heard that, the first thing I thought of was the waiata for the kōhanga reo tamariki. I guess for me it would probably be essentially it's (that) our whakapapa line is our taonga. Our whakapapa line is the ultimate taonga because we come from somewhere and we are about to pass down our mātauranga to the next generation, who is going to pursue something eventually. That whakapapa then means that it could be our kuia, our koroua, it could be mum, could be dad, could be your whanaunga, could be your pēpi, they are essentially going to hold a part of your ngākau. But the thing that binds us all together is our whakapapa, so when I think about that phrase in particular it's something bigger and larger than all of us to be honest, and not necessarily a particular thing or person or item … Yeah, whakapapa is the thing I think of when I think of Te Taonga o Taku Ngākau. (Whānau kaikōrero)

> When I think of Te Taonga o Taku Ngākau I just think of my family cause that's what makes me happy and that is where I feel most safe. (Whānau kaikōrero)

> For me, Te Taonga o Taku Ngākau means that every little characteristic that they have each been gifted by their tūpuna, by their whakapapa and that have come through into te ao mārama is unique and special to them and that loving them for who they are and everything that they are is so important to me, and uplifting their unique differences; and understanding that those tūpuna markers that have come through with them are there for a reason … (Whānau kaikōrero)

To conclude, for Māori there is a need to provide clear understandings about the advantages of returning to traditional practices of 'matua rautia' in which children are parented and cared for by communities as well as their direct whānau. This is a move away from individualised approaches that focus on the deficits within communities and toward one that brings positive change by drawing upon our collective strengths within whānau, hapū, iwi and community. What we are advocating is that Kaupapa Māori provides an opportunity for both knowledge generation and the development of clear principles and practices, based upon mātauranga Māori, to be affirmed within broader approaches for the wellbeing of our children, and the necessity to decolonise wellbeing discourses and mental wellbeing within the context of whānau. Specifically, the research has signalled that tamariki cannot move alone in considerations of health and wellbeing, and that to decolonise approaches to mental health and tamariki we must enable whānau to take control of their own transformations (in the plural).

As Taina Pohatu (2011) has stated, we have both the definitions and the answers; we are all mokopuna and tūpuna and we are all kaitiaki of each other. A critical part of research related to the wellbeing of tamariki Māori is the expectation that the research will be transformative. This requires strong connections to whānau, hapū, iwi and broader Māori communities. Research shows that cultural connectedness makes a significant impact on Māori wellbeing (Durie, 2001; Smith, 1997). There is an urgent need to use mātauranga Māori in the development of approaches to the mental and physical wellbeing of our children and whānau (Grennell, 2006; Kruger et al., 2004). Hinemoa Elder (2018) points out that developing mechanisms to help whānau with practical supports is most relevant and that we "need to consider how cultural factors or philosophies can be used for therapeutic benefit and lead to more innovative interventions" (p. 148).

Linda Tuhiwai Smith (2006) asks, "How do we know as a people when we are well?" (n.p.). Māori communities have always had measures of health and wellbeing that were collectively defined. These measures were holistic, intimately connected to the wellbeing of the environment, spiritually mediated and collectively supported. In other words, the wellbeing of an individual in Māori communities was the responsibility of many. As Linda Tuhiwai Smith highlights, we need to think about the measures and frameworks that we must understand and know when we have achieved good health and wellbeing as individuals and as whānau.

A whakataukī, in the context of childrearing, is "Ehara taku toa i te toa takitahi, engari he toa takitini – My strength is not mine alone but the strength of many". Once again, this whakataukī emphasises that it is not one person's sole responsibility to raise a child, but rather it is a collective responsibility. What this also means is that the collective strength that comes from the sharing of childrearing responsibilities with others ensures not only the wellbeing of the children, but also the wellbeing of parents by supporting them through any difficult experiences. Importantly, reclaiming a whānau collective approach to raising well tamariki situates our tamariki at the centre and also connects them to an ancestry that is theirs and that provides them with strength, resilience, wisdom and vibrancy. As stated by one kaikōrero:

> Te Taonga o Taku Ngākau? Isn't that beautiful. That is what I call my pōtiki [youngest] … Her wairua [spirit], her āhua and my āhua and I guess more so our mauri that easily intertwines with each other's, and so that's what I call her. But I guess when I reflect upon it, I think about our mokopuna and that is exactly what they are, taonga. Ngā taonga o taku ngākau … I love them. I can see the moemoeā [dreams] of our tūpuna in the faces of our mokopuna … I look at them and that is what I see. I see the moemoeā. (Whānau kaikōrero)

References

DE LEEUW, S., GREENWOOD, M., & CAMERON, E. (2010). Deviant constructions: How governments preserve colonial narratives of addictions and poor mental health to intervene into the lives of indigenous children and families in Canada. *International Journal of Mental Health and Addiction*, 8(2), 282–295. doi:10.1007/s11469-009-9225-1

DURIE, M. (2001). *Mauri Ora: The dynamics of Māori health*. Auckland, New Zealand: Oxford University Press.

ELDER, H. (2018). He tamariki wāwāhi tahā: It is in the nature of children to break things. In T. Kingi, M. Durie, H. Elder, R. Tapsell, M. Lawrence & S. Bennett (Eds.), *Maea te toi ora: Māori health transformations* (pp. 79–91). Wellington, New Zealand: Huia Publishers.

FERGUSSON, D. M., HORWOOD, L. J., & GIBB, S. J. (2011). Childhood family income and later outcomes: Results of a 30 year longitudinal study. *Children*, 79, 24–28. Retrieved from http://www.occ.org.nz/assets/Uploads/Journals/Children-79.pdf

GABEL, K. A. (2013). *Poipoia te tamaiti ki te ūkaipō* (Doctoral dissertation). University of Waikato, Hamilton, New Zealand. Retrieved from http://hdl.handle.net/10289/7986

GREEN, J. A. (2011). *A discursive analysis of Māori in sexual and reproductive health policy* (Master's thesis). University of Waikato, Hamilton, New Zealand. Retrieved from https://researchcommons.waikato.ac.nz/handle/10289/5711

GRENNELL, D. (2006). *Amokura – Indigenous innovation*. Paper presented at the 10th Australasian Conference on Child Abuse and Neglect (ACCAN), 14–16 February 2006, Wellington, New Zealand.

HĀPAI TE HAUORA. (2018). *Communities connect with Mātauranga Māori this Mental Health Awareness Week to strengthen wellbeing*, Media release. Retrieved from https://mentalhealth.org.nz/news/post/communities-connect-with-matauranga-maori-this-mental-health-awareness-week-to-strengthen-wellbeing

HARRIS, R., TOBIAS, M., JEFFREYS, M., WALDEGRAVE, K., KARLSEN, S., & NAZROO, J. (2006). Racism and health: The relationship between experience of racial discrimination and health in New Zealand. *Social Science & Medicine*, 63(6), 1428–1441.

JENKINS, K., & HARTE, H. M. (2011). *Traditional Māori parenting: An historical review of literature of traditional Māori child rearing practices in pre-European times*. Auckland, New Zealand: Te Kahui Mana Ririki. Retrieved from http://www.ririki.org.nz/wp-content/uploads/2015/04/TradMaoriParenting.pdf

KIMMERER, R. (2013). *Braiding sweetgrass: Indigenous wisdom, scientific knowledge and the teachings of plants*. Minneapolis, MN: Milkweed Editions

KINGI, T. (2005). *Māori mental health: Past trends, current issues, and Māori responsiveness*. Wellington, New Zealand: Massey University. Retrieved from https://www.massey.ac.nz/massey/fms/Te%20Mata%20O%20Te%20Tau/Publications%20-%20Te%20Kani/T%20Kingi%20Maori%20mental%20health%20past%20trends,%20current%20issues%20and%20maori%20responsiveness.pdf?E50260ED98B353D7CF7782575952A73A

KINGI, T., DURIE, M., ELDER, H., TAPSELL, R., LAWRENCE, M., & BENNETT, S. (2018). *Maea te Toi Ora: Māori health transformations*. Wellington, New Zealand: Huia Publishers.

KRUGER, T., PITMAN, M., GRENNELL, D., MCDONALD, T., MARIU, D., POMARE, A., MITA, T., MAIHI, M., & LAWSON-TE-AHO, K. (2004). *Transforming whānau violence – A conceptual framework* (2nd Edition). Wellington, New Zealand: Te Puni Kōkiri.

KUKUTAI, T. H., & POOL, I. (2014). From common colonization to internal segmentation: Rethinking indigenous demography in New Zealand. In F. Trovato & A. Romaniuk (Eds.), *Aboriginal populations: Social, demographic, and epidemiological perspectives* (pp. 441–468). Edmonton, Canada: University of Alberta Press.

LAWSON-TE AHO, K. (2016). He waka eke noa – Māori and indigenous suicide prevention: Models of practice, lessons and challenges. In W. Waitoki, J. S. Feather, N. Robertson, & J. J. Rucklidge (Eds.), *Professional practice of psychology in Aotearoa New Zealand* (3rd ed) (pp. 229–246). Wellington, New Zealand: The New Zealand Psychological Society.

MARRIOTT, L., & SIM, D. (2014). *Indicators of inequality for Māori and Pacific people*. Working Paper 09/2014. Wellington, New Zealand: Victoria University. Retrieved from https://www.victoria.ac.nz/sacl/centres-and-chairs/cpf/publications/working-papers/WP09_2014_Indicators-of-Inequality.pdf

MENTAL HEALTH COMMISSION. (2012). *Blueprint II: How things need to be*. Wellington, New Zealand: Mental Health Commission. Retrieved from https://www.hdc.org.nz/media/1075/blueprint-ii-how-things-need-to-be.pdf

MIKAERE, A. (2003). *The balance destroyed: Consequences for Māori women of the colonisation of Tikanga Māori*. Auckland, New Zealand: The International Research Institute for Māori and Indigenous Education.

MIKAERE, A. (2011). *Colonising Myths Māori Realities: He Rukuruku Whakaaro*. Wellington, New Zealand: Huia Publishers and Te Wānanga o Raukawa.

MOEWAKA BARNES, H., EICH, E., & YESSILTH, S. (2018). Colonization, Whenua and capitalism: Experiences from Aotearoa New Zealand. *Continuum: Cultures of Capitalism*, 32(6), 685–97.

MOEWAKA BARNES, H., & MCCREANOR, T. (2019). Colonisation, hauora and whenua in Aotearoa. *Journal of the Royal Society of New Zealand*, 49(1), 19–33, DOI: 10.1080/03036758.2019.1668439

NASH, R. (2001). Teenage pregnancy: Barriers to an integrated model for policy research. *Social Policy Journal of New Zealand*, 17, 200–213.

NELSON, S., & WILSON. K. (2017). The mental health of Indigenous peoples in Canada: A critical review of research. *Social Science & Medicine*, 176, 93–112.

PIHAMA, L. (1998). Reconstructing Meanings of Family: Lesbian/Gay Whānau and Families in Aotearoa. In V. Adair & R. Dixon (Eds.), *The family in Aotearoa New Zealand* (pp. 179–207). Auckland, New Zealand: Addison Wesley Longman.

PIHAMA, L. (2001). *Tīhei Mauri Ora: Honouring Our Voices. Mana Wahine as a Kaupapa Māori Theoretical Framework* (Doctoral dissertation). University of Auckland, Auckland, New Zealand.

PIHAMA, L., TE NANA, R., REYNOLDS, P., SMITH, C., REID, J., & SMITH, L. T. (2014). Positioning historical trauma theory within Aotearoa New Zealand. *AlterNative: An International Journal of Indigenous Peoples*, 10(3), 248–262.

PIHAMA, L., TIAKIWAI, S., & SOUTHEY, K. (EDS.) (2015). *Kaupapa Rangahau: A reader – A collection of readings from the Kaupapa Rangahau workshop series* (2nd Edition). Hamilton, New Zealand: Te Kotahi Research Institute.

POHATU, T. (2011). Mauri – Rethinking human wellbeing. *MAI Review*, 3, 1–12.

ROBSON, B., & HARRIS, R. (EDS.). (2007). *Hauora: Māori standards of health IV. A study of the years 2000–2005*. Wellington, New Zealand: Te Rōpū Rangahau Hauora a Eru Pōmare.

RUSSELL, L. (2018). *Te Oranga Hinengaro: Report on Māori mental wellbeing results from the New Zealand Mental Health Monitor & Health and Lifestyles Survey*. Wellington, New Zealand: Health Promotion Agency/Te Hiringa Hauora.

SCHULTZ, K., WALTERS, K., BELTRAN, R., STROUD, S., & JOHNSON-JENNINGS, M. (2016). "I'm stronger than I thought": Native women reconnecting to body, health, and place. *Health and Place*, 40, 21–28.

SEYMOUR, F., COOPER, E., & STANTON, S. (2016). Child abuse and neglect. In W. Waitoki, J. S. Feather, N. Robertson & J. J. Rucklidge (Eds.), *Professional practice of psychology in Aotearoa New Zealand* (3rd edition) (pp. 131–143). Wellington, New Zealand: The New Zealand Psychological Society.

SIMMONDS, N. B. (2014). *Tū te turuturu nō Hine-te-iwaiwa: Mana wahine geographies of birth in Aotearoa New Zealand* (Doctoral dissertation). University of Waikato, Hamilton, New Zealand. Retrieved from https://researchcommons.waikato.ac.nz/handle/10289/8821

SMITH, G. H. (1997). *The development of Kaupapa Māori theory and praxis* (Doctoral dissertation). University of Auckland, Auckland, New Zealand. Retrieved from https://researchspace.auckland.ac.nz/handle/2292/623

SMITH, L. (1999). *Decolonizing methodologies*. New York, NY: Zed Books.

SMITH, L. T. (2006). Facilitator 1: Opening address. In J. S. Te Rito (Ed.), *Proceedings of the Mātauranga Taketake: Traditional Knowledge Conference 2006* (pp. 213–220). Auckland, New Zealand: Ngā Pae o te Māramatanga.

He Mokopuna He Tupuna

Ngaropi Cameron-Raumati

CHAPTER 5

Introduction

In 2013 Tu Tama Wahine o Taranaki (TTW) undertook a research project, 'He Mokopuna He Tupuna: Investigating Māori Views of Childrearing Amongst Iwi in Taranaki', as part of a process of reclaiming and revitalising traditional knowledge that communicates the position and status of tamariki mokopuna within our whānau as defined within tikanga ā Taranaki.

For the last thirty years TTW has been organising, planning and implementing different approaches to address whānau violence within the Taranaki region; this work is based upon Kaupapa Māori philosophies and values. TTW was established in 1989 and incorporated in 1994; the name Tu Tama Wahine o Taranaki was given to the organisation by Matarena Rau-Kupa (OBE) and Dr Huirangi Waikerepuru in recognition of the work being undertaken by its members to support Taranaki whānau and to encourage TTW kaimahi to continue to challenge ongoing colonial behaviour and practices. The name of the organisation is significant and unique; it dates to the 1881 plunder of Parihaka. At that time, specific instructions were given by Te Whiti o Rongomai to the women remaining on the papakāinga to continue upholding the work and words of their tūpuna, and to take on the roles and responsibilities of their exiled men, by upholding tikanga and maintaining the care and wellbeing of whānau.

Currently, TTW provides a number of community-based development and social justice services designed to enhance whānau wellbeing; these have their base in education, counselling, learned social behaviours, whānau therapies and tangata whenua community development projects. Projects are designed to reclaim community intelligence, lift Māori thinking and expectations towards developing tikanga-based solutions that have more relevance to a values base upon which to realise a Māori reality for living. These programmes have been developed by TTW in conjunction with whānau and other relevant stakeholder groups. TTW maintains a deep commitment and profound desire to help transform the lives of whānau. This commitment is held in the vision that "Taranaki whānau have a secured sense of identity and connection to each other where all are able to contribute and participate in the maintenance of a peaceful, prosperous community" (Tu Tama Wahine o Taranaki, n.d., para. 3).

The release of the UNICEF report 'Kids Missing Out' (2013) and a range of reports over five years from the Child Poverty Action Group highlight that there are substantial and growing numbers of tamariki in Aotearoa who are living in poverty. This situation is unacceptable. What is also unacceptable are the large numbers of tamariki mokopuna who experience neglect, abuse and/or live in a context of family violence. Both those reports, interrelated to poverty and to abuse and violence within whānau, highlight a wider societal issue about how tamariki mokopuna are positioned. That was also a focus of the TTW research project.

The project was inspirational because participants brought to the forefront the exceptional insight of tūpuna who toiled for generations to ensure that the tikanga and reo of Taranaki would remain on our whenua for those present and those yet to come. The affection and deep love felt by tūpuna for their future generations, and the commitment to Taranaki tikanga as a means to ensure mokopuna wellbeing, were revealed in participants' kōrero.

Whakataukī

The expression 'He Mokopuna He Tupuna' provides Tu Tama Wahine o Taranaki with a cultural framework for understanding the positioning of tamariki mokopuna within te ao Māori, and it is derived from the following whakataukī:

> He tupuna, he mokopuna. Mā wai i whakakī i ngā whāwhārua o ngā mātua tūpuna? Mā ā tātou mokopuna! He mokopuna, he tupuna.

This whakataukī draws us to the essence of intergenerational whakapapa relationships. It asserts that we are all mokopuna and we are all tūpuna. Put simply, it is stating that the mokopuna in future generations will fill the spaces vacated by tūpuna. All grandchildren in time become grandparents and each generation links through whakapapa to each other, which means that we are a magnificent reflection and continuance of our ancestral lines, and thus the sacredness of those connections is preserved.

What is also implicit in the conceptualisation of 'He Mokopuna He Tupuna' is the understanding that tamariki and mokopuna, like tūpuna, must be treated with respect and, many would say, reverence. Clearly the research was located in te ao Māori; however, it has implications for non-Māori, for the simple reason that it requires more in-depth examination and dismantling of the misogynist and child abusive practices imported into Aotearoa with the structured racist system of colonialisation, from which non-Māori have benefitted. It is essential that the lives of our future generations are accorded more status within Aotearoa New Zealand society, because only then will we see authentic, informed prevention and intervention happening at multiple levels of whānau, hapū, iwi, communities and government agencies. At the end of the day, we may find that possibly the only thing that both cultures have in common is that we are all born mokopuna of someone and, when we die, we die as mokopuna of someone.

Methodology

This research project was developed to provide insights into tikanga ā Taranaki and traditional childrearing beliefs and practices. The project was visioned, developed and undertaken by iwi researchers and providers in Taranaki. It was informed by Kaupapa Māori research methodology and this was expressed more fully through whakapapa and whanaungatanga approaches to each aspect of the research. Key cultural concepts and practices within a Kaupapa Māori methodology provided us with strategies for our research practices. We are honoured that whānau provided their knowledge and understandings for this project. The overarching intention is that the knowledge, the tikanga, the stories are to be shared with whānau, hapū, iwi and organisations in Taranaki as part of a collective desire for wellbeing for our tamariki and mokopuna. The original project proposal for 'He Mokopuna He Tupuna' included a literature and archival review to be located alongside a series of qualitative interviews and workshops. The literature review was not funded and therefore the project focused on the facilitation of three workshops and the gathering of knowledge and data through qualitative interviews.

Methods

The process for identifying participants and participant focus groups involved whanaungatanga. Information relating to the research topic processes and objectives was provided at various Taranaki community and iwi forums. Specific research workshops and information sharing sessions were held across Taranaki (North, Central and South Taranaki) to engage and inform Taranaki-wide whānau, hapū and iwi. These included the Tū Tama Wahine o Taranaki Community Kōrero session (North Taranaki), joining with a pre-existing marae-based rongoā wānanga (Central Taranaki) and joining the whānau/hapū/iwi political and spiritual gatherings held at Parihaka on the 18th and 19th of every month (South Taranaki).

The majority of research participants self-identified as a result of information provided in these community forums. The Kaupapa Māori qualitative methods used were kanohi ki te kanohi (face-to-face) interviews with Taranaki whānau, kaumātua and individuals with a knowledge of the tikanga (philosophy and practices) associated with the notion 'He Mokopuna He Tupuna' and Māori childrearing practices. The qualitative interviews were undertaken by staff members from Tu Tama Wahine and included a combination of individual and focus group interviews. These were considered to be whakawhiti kōrero, or engaged discussions, with the researcher and the whānau involved. Tikanga provided the framework for these discussions and the focus groups were arranged by kaupapa, the topic being discussed, and whakapapa, the relationships between whānau involved.

Interviews

The qualitative interviews involved asking whānau to comment in three key areas that included a range of questions. Those broad areas were Muru me te Raupatu: events that interrupted or disrupted the intergenerational transmission of knowledge; Te Whanaketanga: knowledge and experiences growing up of tikanga and mātauranga Māori approaches; and Kōrero Whakatepe: concluding thoughts – drawing on traditional knowledge on childrearing in contemporary times. A focus of the research was enabling conversations about traditional knowledge and how we can, in current and future generations, draw upon that knowledge to enhance whānau relationships; our approaches to childrearing; prevention and intervention in negative situations; and informing tikanga healing practices for whānau.

Muru Raupatu

With no difficulty, participants identified what they considered to be beliefs, values and practices that disrupted or interrupted the transmission of tikanga tūpuna, ancestral knowledge that is grounded within the concepts of tiaki tamariki, tikanga and te reo o Taranaki, and why that knowledge is not readily available or accessible to many whānau. The term "muru me te raupatu" refers to acts of colonisation – historically traumatic events that have impacted on the overall wellbeing of whānau, hapū and iwi around the maunga. The multiple ways in which the theft and plunder of hapū lands have impacted upon connectedness both to whenua and tikanga were still felt deeply when spoken about.

> If they want the work, they will take the work. But if they want land, they'll take the land ... So, these have gone, and so are the ways of living in the old times, that have slowly gone into the history books. (Interview)

The process of disconnection and how it was achieved was highlighted in many differing ways, including disconnection from marae and access to knowledge of tikanga, and transmission of knowledge disrupted between generations. Further concerns about the loss of kaumātua and the knowledge held in that generation were also seen as a critical issue, with some urgency noted in terms of listening to and receiving that knowledge for future generations. It also means having fewer exemplars and models. For some whānau this meant there was an interruption to the process and continuity of tikanga and doing things in a Māori way.

> The line of communication has been lost so I don't know how to pick that back up. (Interview)

Some participants spoke of smacking becoming a means by which whānau sought to 'teach' children. It was also deemed to be a means of delivering a 'short, sharp lesson'. The introduction of smacking in the past three generations within whānau, hapū and iwi aligns with the significant changes that occurred in the transmission of te reo and tikanga Māori. Some whānau reflected on the fact that their grandparents' experiences of being hit at school influenced their decision not to teach their mokopuna to speak te reo Māori. It was their way of preventing their mokopuna from being physically assaulted at school. The increase in child abuse was seen as a significant interruption of traditional views and approaches to our tamariki, and the depth of pain associated with that was summed up clearly in the statement from one whānau member who said:

> It is a sore point for me; when I hear that our babies are dying, I cry. I don't even know who the whānau is but I cry because it is our babies. (Interview)

As has been noted previously there is ample historical evidence to indicate that, traditionally, tamariki were treated with respect and their mana was acknowledged in their own right. Tamariki were adored and treasured. Tamariki were indulged and supported as independent people and participant whānau explored views about how those understandings and practices have changed for many of our people. The implications of such disruptions and interruptions in the transfer of tikanga and mātauranga Māori have had significant consequences, none more so than the increase of whānau violence and child abuse.

Te Whanaketanga

Te Whanaketanga refers to the process of growing up, and in the discussions about their experiences of traditional knowledge, whānau shared how tikanga influenced them and how tikanga has guided the way they raised their tamariki mokopuna. Whanaungatanga was warmly talked about by participants and included a strong ethic of valuing whānau and looking after each other. Whanaungatanga enhances and affirms collective responsibility and obligations to one another that are reciprocal in nature. Working together as a whānau was a consistent enriching theme. Working and supporting the wider whānau was essential to wellbeing and accountability, and necessitated everyone playing their part, which meant working for the collective good.

> Everything was about the value of our whānau … and how we looked after each other. (Interview)

Whānau is defined as comprising at least three generations and therefore is inclusive of broader relationships than those present in terms of a nuclear family structure. A number of those interviewed spoke of coming from families that included thirteen or fourteen tamariki, and living in ways that enabled both extended relationships and communal living situations, while working collectively for the wellbeing of all. Whānau also provided a structure by which protections and safety of tamariki could be ensured. Whānau support can intervene in issues that arise through isolation that may be caused by a nuclear family construct. Traditional marae life and the experiences of being on the marae meant that tamariki learned the values and importance of whānau. Respect for each other was clearly a part of daily life, and a part of the relationship between tamariki, mātua and tūpuna. That respect also enabled tamariki to understand notions such as whakaiti, humility and to appreciate what whānau had. Tūpuna were also seen as key to showing aroha through actions to tamariki: awhi atu, awhi mai; so tamariki see that through your actions and practices you can show caring.

> The kuia, during the time I had been at that marae that kuia used to give me cuddles … I can remember about times when I was a little kid and that kuia, I would do anything for her. That's where you have aroha; if you have loved her, they give it back to you. (Interview)

The place of grandparents in people's lives is a compelling theme that was raised consistently by whānau. Tūpuna had significant influence in the lives of tamariki and the relationship of the grandparent generation to mokopuna is considered critical in the wellbeing not only of tamariki but of the whānau as a whole. A number of people interviewed talked of being raised by their grandparents in a supportive and caring environment and the significant sense of security they felt. Grandparents' identity as 'first' teachers was acknowledged, and it was recognised that grandparents and other kaumātua were always present and that considerable efforts were made by whānau to ensure tamariki had time with their grandparents if they did not live in close proximity. Many reflected on the importance of values about behaviour and etiquette to their grandparents, and how they sought to model those to their mokopuna. Mokopuna also supported tūpuna and were encouraged to help care for elders and for their teina (younger siblings). There was no difference made between caring for an elder, a young child or a baby.

> It was our job to go and get our kuia and our koro a plate of kai and take it to them rather than expect them to … Making sure the tamariki were fed at the same time. (Interview)

Within te ao Māori, a process of honouring tūpuna is through naming a person, ngā hononga. Naming also strengthens the significance of whānau connections, providing a means by which to pass on the knowledge and respect of that ancestor through their mokopuna. Being named after tūpuna was highlighted with a sense of honour and a feeling of pride associated with that. Maintaining intergenerational links is important, with some participants noting that they have that role within their whānau to ensure links both within and between generations are maintained.

> [I am] named after my kuia … I think I have carried her name well … [I] feel quite proud of who I am. (Interview)

> Taurima is a tikanga that has continued being practised in Taranaki and gives both tamariki and tūpuna ways of sharing. In other iwi the term used is that of whāngai. The sharing from one whānau shows the depth of the relationship and the significance of whāngai and taurima for all. Not having had any children of my own, but living at the pā now, and we've had a number of children living with us. Seven, nine, two children at a time. And so it's been sort of a learning curve for me as well. Imparting what I know with them, and sometimes I get it wrong. But you know, so we don't make that mistake again. It's been helping me as well, to be able to communicate with children on their level. Because I noticed when I first came back, and speaking to your children and after quite a while I thought oh, they probably don't understand a word I'm saying. Cause I'm using words that they never heard of. To me it was just natural. And so I had changed my thinking and my language too, to use more simple words that they would understand. And then teaching, children are full of questions all the time. I had to dig deep for some of them. But when I was sharing with them what I know, and what I thought was right and wrong, and it's been good and I thought, oh, will they ever come to me for advice or anything, or do they think I'm a silly old woman or whatever. But it's quite a privilege you know, when they come to me and ask me for advice or different things. (Interview)

Taurima was referred to as both permanent and temporary care arrangements that provide support and care for tamariki; what was important was the wellbeing of the tamariki.

A range of traditional pedagogical practices were evident, including caring for each other, which was also articulated in terms of tuakana–teina (older–younger sibling) relationships within the whānau. Tuakana and teina were supported in reciprocal relationships because this enabled learning and teaching practices to be reinforced while providing tamariki with processes to support and care for each other as they grow together. This was a practice through which tamariki learned to express manaakitanga within whānau.

> [A]nd brought up by older teenage cousins, they looked after me until mum came from the pā or from the farm. In time I did the same thing for one of my cousins. (Interview)

The need to maintain links between generations was seen as important, as was developing ways to support your own tamariki and mokopuna in a context of work and living, which helped address economic issues as well as maintaining relationships. Supporting their own children by caring for mokopuna enabled whānau members to seek employment opportunities that would otherwise be difficult to achieve.

> She was going to put him into day care so I said no, I'll look after him. (Interview)

As a part of learning tikanga values and what constituted appropriate behaviour, whānau talked of how, when they were directed by elders, they did what was required, without question. It was a process of learning tikanga – manaaki tāngata; a key element of tikanga is that of manaakitanga. Manaaki is the value and practice of showing hospitality and caring for others, and as a part of the process manaaki enhances relationships. Caring for others is an essential part of tikanga Māori and tikanga Taranaki, and it was a part of learning from a very young age. Another aspect of manaakitanga shared in interviews was that of respect towards all, and ensuring people are well cared for and fed. Manaakitanga was expressed in many ways, including a non-violent philosophy, which promoted a need to support, and not impose hurt on others. It also promoted a notion of inclusiveness of all tamariki, ensuring all children were treated with respect and their mana affirmed.

> She never laid a hand on her children, none of us got a smack ... she always said don't hurt one another, don't yell at one another just talk nicely to each other and just support each other. (Interview)

Wairuatanga – spiritual knowledge, influence and connections – and karakia were a natural and normal part of life, as the process of acknowledgement and giving thanks was a part of understanding our deeper connections within te ao Māori. We learned to live in line with the environment in sustainable ways, which required knowing the seasons and what kai and rongoā were available, and remembering that there is a need to ensure that kai and natural resources were available for future generations.

> And before I went to school, I was going down to the beach myself, but it was constant learning from Mum. I said, "Mum, we just passed a reef over there, and there is plenty of kai there, mātaitai tērā." And we'll go to the next one. And the next one. And we'd walk all over there to go and get our kai, and then come back ... we had to carry a food bag for miles. I learned over the years that what she was teaching me was rotational grazing ... She said, "You'll get it sooner or later." (Interview)

Ako

The concept of 'ako' relates to the principles and practices of learning and teaching within te ao Māori. In traditional contexts the role of whānau and the place of intergenerational transmission of tikanga were central to how te reo, tikanga and mātauranga were passed through the generations. The ways in which tamariki developed understandings both of their place and role in the whānau, and their roles and behaviours within the wider hapū and iwi were shared in the discussions. The process of learning and teaching by example and through following elders and siblings was highlighted; tamariki were corrected when things happened or their actions were deemed inappropriate and those corrections were rarely questioned. Corrections to behaviour were made at the time the lapse occurred; things were not left to fester or gather momentum as the days progressed. "Me whakatika te hē," correct the mistake quickly, was a frequent explanation. Tamariki were also provided with clear guidelines by which to make decisions with regard to their own wellbeing.

> We weren't to venture out into the water above our knees. So we knew that as we grew, the knees were the spot. If you went out that far, you were to come back in. So yes, that was so crucial to our existence. So crucial to our survival. So crucial for us to respect. (Interview)

The transmission of tikanga, reo and mātauranga to each generation is fundamental to the survival of cultural understandings and worldviews. Whānau gave a range of reflections on the processes of sharing what they had learned from their whānau, and in particular from their tūpuna. Sharing knowledge with the next generation was also seen as a way of both remembering and honouring what they had been taught and the knowledge passed to them from their kaumātua. It was highlighted that reclaiming tradition and tūpuna knowledge needed to be done for tamariki from a young age so it was embedded in their understandings.

> From the time you were seven, you were quite equipped. You could go hither, and thither, and be safe. (Interview)

A key process of learning and teaching identified was the ability to observe. Tamariki were encouraged to listen, observe and participate in activities that supported the development of particular knowledge and skills. Safe and appropriate practices were modelled under the guidance of whānau.

> They listen, even the young tamariki we would teach them the proper way, the safe way and you know just take your time. So, every time we had a tangi we would take our children down to the river. I would be cooking at the back at Parihaka at night, we used to gather all the mātaitai down ... and go along the bridge. (Interview)

A strong aspect alongside listening, observation and participation was purposeful activity. Purposeful activity was seen as a part of that process of learning and tamariki were encouraged to participate in outcome-oriented, purposeful activities.

> If we went to the park it was for a reason, had to go do some work, help weed the gardens or rake up the rubbish, it was for something, it was never just to play or just to go and see my friend … So all of your waking time was put to work, it was for a purpose; it wasn't just to sit there daydreaming. (Interview)

Pūrākau, traditional forms of storytelling, were identified as a means by which tikanga and mātauranga were transmitted both intergenerationally and within whānau, hapū and iwi (Lee, 2015). They were also a process by which whānau sought to pass on their memories and experiences to their tamariki and mokopuna.

> Often I'm telling them stories about when I was growing up … what I heard when I was growing up. (Interview)

Te reo Māori is a mechanism by which whānau can bring back traditional knowledge to enhance wellbeing. Within te ao Māori words are seen to have their own inherent mana. Sayings such as "he mana tō te kupu" highlight that we must be aware of the words we use, their strength and their sacredness. The power of words to do harm is noted in the following whakataukī: "He tao rākau ka taea te karo, he tao kupu kore rawa. A spear may be parried but a word cannot." Speaking to tamariki in respectful and affirming ways is important to their sense of worth. As such, the way we speak to tamariki and what we say is critical. This is seen as an essential understanding that needs to be reinforced.

> Get our kids back to Māori, te reo Māori. And then they will understand. They will understand. Te mana, te ihi, te wehi o te tangata. They will understand you don't do those things to your sister, your brother, or to your whānau, or to your friends. Te mana. I think it needs to get back to communicating. (Interview)

Ngā Kupu Whakatepe

In line with the research project 'He Mokopuna He Tupuna' and a number of other research projects undertaken, TTW has developed several practise 'tools' for whānau they can use to support behaviour recovery and whānau healing journeys. Whānau wellbeing is the priority and specific attention is paid to self-responsibility in respect to whānau autonomy: rangatiratanga. Encouragement and help is given to maximise opportunities to dispel the illusion that violence within whānau Māori is considered normal by some people, when in fact it is not normal. Backing is also offered to maximise opportunities to remove the opportunity for violence to occur within whānau by addressing poverty, education needs, affordable housing, employment prospects, health and medical needs and other issues whānau are struggling with.

Whānau are supported to secure resources so that collective action can be taken to facilitate opportunities for transformation that whānau can successfully measure. These could be actions identified by the whānau they can implement relatively quickly themselves, or activities they might require assistance to address; the quality of changes or improvements are to be judged by the whānau themselves and the whānau will determine whether or not the changes can be maintained. Most important is the validation of whānau desire for change that is understandable to the whānau and that reconnects them to creative concepts within te ao Māori. Therefore, the endorsement of Māori language, values and models is crucial so whānau become familiar with them and confident that they are legitimate, innovative and valid concepts that can support and maintain behaviour reclamation and transformation.

FIGURE 1

This is one side of a two-sided educative practice tool that illustrates six cultural values with a relatively stress-free application foundation. The flip-side of this practice tool displays six of the Whānau Ora goals and how they can be applied when aligned with the six cultural values.

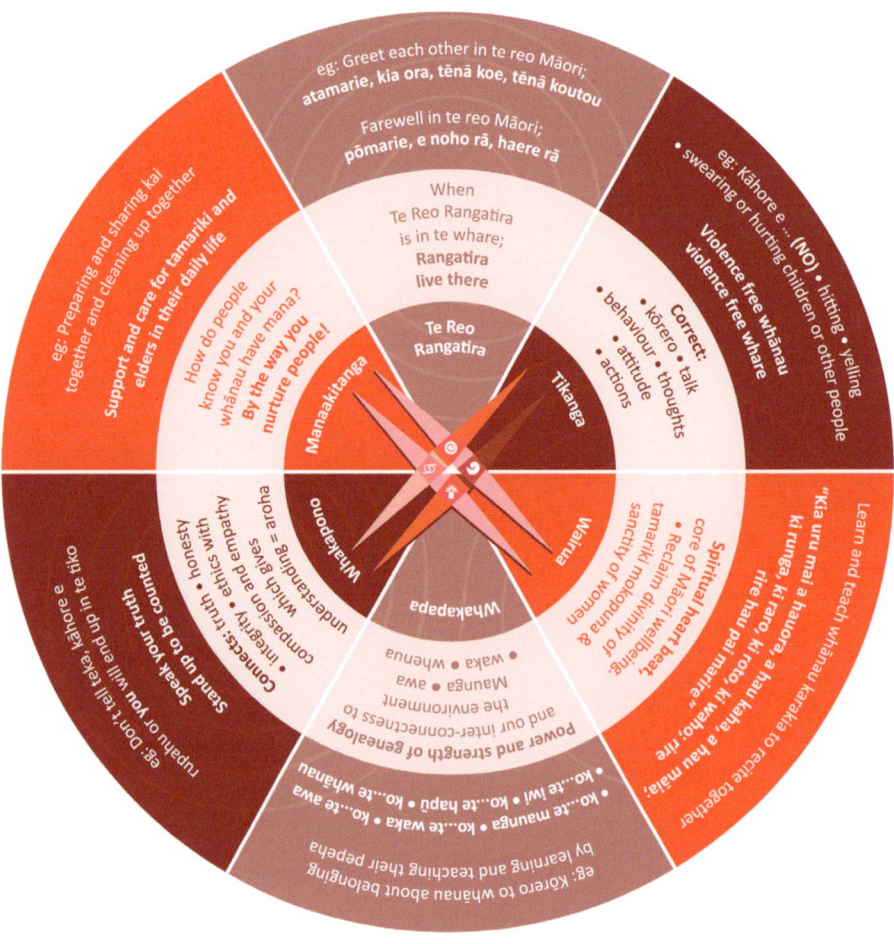

FIGURE 2

This is a wipeable (reuseable) whānau planning tool, designed to be user-friendly so both whānau and practitioners can use it in a variety of situations and contexts. It is an organising, planning, action tool. This tool is a simple visual reminder that our tūpuna existed as independent nations of strategists. They strategised to address all manner of crises: immediate, short-term, long-term, intergenerational and across continents. This tool is intended to once again normalise planning and collective strategic action within whānau by providing a resource they can apply repeatedly themselves. It can include, if desired, but does not require, an intermediary such as a clinician or practitioner to complete it with or for the whānau.

"The most powerful weapon in the hands of the oppressor is the mind of the oppressed"
- Steve Biko

FIGURE 3

This is a practice tool to help whānau identify and reflect on details that matter most to them as individuals and as whānau. This tool requires practitioners to engage in different conversations – those centred on mana-enhancing reflections, thinking and activities, rather than problems identified to be 'fixed' from a needs-based assessment. This is a practical way to progress thinking and actions that are self-identified priorities and can also strengthen positive aspects of whānau functioning.

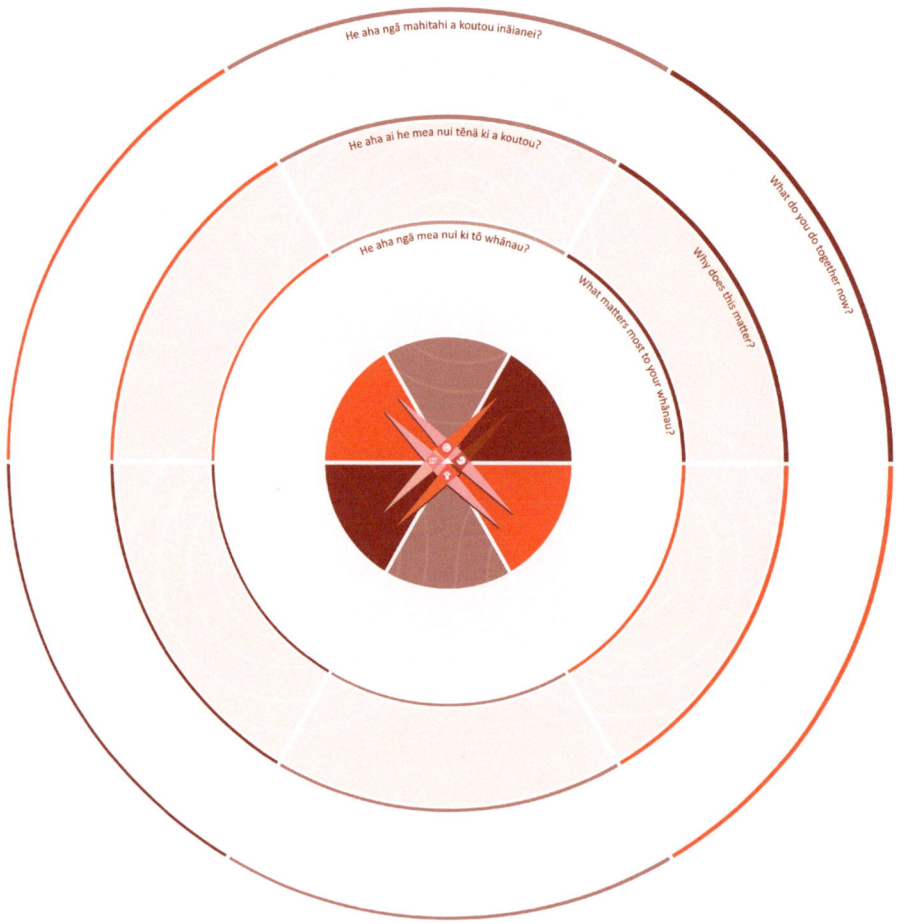

**"Me kore rawa koe e taka!
Don't ever give up!"**
- Ngaropi Cameron

Conclusion

The place of our mokopuna reflects the aspirations of our tūpuna. The mana of our mokopuna reflects the mana of our tūpuna. If we live with these fundamentals as the underpinning ways in which we understand our place in this world, and the centrality of tamariki and mokopuna within whānau, we can and will achieve Taranaki whānau ora for those generations yet to come.

> It is up to us old people to have a good go and talk about it and put it into respect, put it into action. It is the older people ... we talk about the best way we show tikanga for our tamariki. (Interview)

He mokopuna, he tupuna. He tupuna, he mokopuna.

References

LEE, J. B. J. (2015). Decolonising Māori narratives: Pūrākau as method. In L. Pihama & S. Tiakiwai (Eds.), *Kaupapa Rangahau: A reader* (pp. 95–104). Hamilton, New Zealand: Te Kotahi Research.

TU TAMA WAHINE O TARANAKI. (N.D.). *About Tu Tama Wahine o Taranaki.* http://www.tutamawahine.org.nz/about

UNICEF NZ. (2013). *Kids Missing Out. A summary of the first twenty years of the UN Convention on the Rights of the Child in Aotearoa New Zealand.* Wellington, New Zealand: Unicef

Whakatauākī:
Sharing Ancestral Knowledge through Generations

Hineitimoana Greensill
Leonie Pihama
Hōri Manuirirangi

CHAPTER 6

Introduction

In te ao Māori, the values, beliefs and philosophies that underpin our culture are embedded within our language and knowledge systems. Drawing upon a whakatauākī coined by Sir James Henare, "Ko te reo Māori te kākahu o te whakaaro, te huarahi ki te ao tūroa", we recognise that our way of thinking and being can be best understood through our language; a language that can also provide guidance for the way in which we live our lives. This understanding is echoed in the words of Rēweti Kōhere (1994): "Ka ngaro tō tāua Māoritanga ina ngaro tō tāua reo te poutokomanawa o tō tāua Māoritanga" (p. 49). The words of Kōhere – written in the early 20th century, at a time when the number of speakers of te reo Māori was beginning to decline – warn us that if our language is lost, then the very essence of who we are as Māori will also be lost. Kōhere describes the language as the poutokomanawa, the central pillar that holds up our ancestral meeting houses, a powerful and stabilising force that has carried the knowledge of our ancestors from one generation to another for as long as we can remember.

While settler-colonial policies in Aotearoa disrupted the transmission of te reo Māori from generation to generation – a disruption that extends far beyond the transmission of language alone – traditional repositories of Māori knowledge ensure the messages embedded in the language remain with us today. The knowledge, history and ideas of our tūpuna have been preserved in a variety of oral texts, including pūrākau, mōteatea and whakataukī, or ancestral proverbial sayings, many of which can also now be found in written form. As a part of the Māori language regeneration movement in Aotearoa there has been a resurgence of knowledge drawn from our ancestral sayings as expressed through whakataukī and whakatauākī. These knowledge forms teach us about the ways in which our ancestors viewed the world and our multiple relationships with all our relations and everything in the world around us. They provide today's generation with insight and lessons from the past to guide us in all that we do. These expressions describe, urge and at times dissuade certain types of behaviour, and in some cases they serve as warnings or reminders. One particular example of this is the well-known whakatauākī, "E kore e piri te uku ki te rino, ka whitingia e te rā ka ngahoro" (Seed-Pihama, 2004, p. 90). Composed by the revered Taranaki prophet Tohu Kākahi in the late 1800s, its powerful message conveyed through metaphor still resounds within the minds of today's generation. A man of peace, Tohu warned his people of outside influences, reminding them that clay will not adhere to iron, for as soon as it is dried by the sun's rays, it will fall. He, along with Te Whiti o Rongomai, encouraged Māori throughout the nation to take pride in one's true identity and origins. Traditional whakataukī and whakatauākī such as these have enabled the intergenerational transmission of knowledge and ideas through oral and written expression, "He kōpaki i te māramatanga o te tangata ki tētahi rerenga kōrero" (Royal, 2016). To truly appreciate and understand the concepts expressed within these messages, one must understand te reo Māori, as the language itself is the medium that enhances and reflects our cultural perspectives and knowledge. Knowing one's ancestral tongue is vital to achieving a deeper understanding of one's own history and culture, for, as Pere (1982) states, "The Māori language is basic to the retention and maintenance of the Māori heritage for it enshrines the ethos, the life principle of the Māori people" (p. 19).

In transmitting this knowledge, it was understood that tamariki would learn through experience, observation and by being in a supportive nurturing environment (Pere, 1982; Rickard, 1998). Traditionally, Māori children were provided with this type of setting, where they were encouraged to be inquisitive, attentive and to interact with a range of people of all ages (Pere, 1982) in order to flourish and make sense of the world. The acquisition of mātauranga Māori (Māori knowledge and ways of knowing) occurred through multiple processes of storytelling and sharing of ways of being that included pūrākau (Māori storytelling), waiata (chants and song) and whakataukī (ancestral proverbial sayings). All these processes were used to convey educational messages, guidance and learning. Through such cultural media, children were taught about protocols and laws, behaviours and relationships, and that there are ways of doing things that are considered tika (correct) (Pihama, Greensill, Campbell, Te Nana, & Lee, 2015). As a child grows, their needs change, physically, emotionally and spiritually. Within the collective care environment, it was an expectation that those who were primarily responsible for the child would be aware of the child's changing developmental needs (Pere, 1982), to ensure the child's holistic needs were met. It was of great importance that children were raised in this manner to ensure the continuation and survival of each generation.

The aim of this chapter is to examine a number of whakataukī for messages relating to the positioning of Māori children within whānau and the relationship of that to traditional childrearing practices. Many of the whakataukī presented here have been shared with us by kaumātua during interviews conducted for the 'Tiakina te Pā Harakeke' project and have contributed to the development of other publications, including *Taku Kuru Pounamu* (Pihama et al., 2015). Drawing on the examples in this chapter, we explore whakataukī as a means by which to bring forward knowledge gifted to us by our ancestors that can inform our contemporary experiences as Māori.

Mātauranga Māori

Mātauranga Māori is a system of knowledge grounded in the Māori world, but also very much connected to our histories, worldviews and practices as people of Te Moananui-a-Kiwa (Sadler, 2007; Smith, Maxwell, Puke, & Temara, 2016). What we know as mātauranga Māori today is imprinted with this whakapapa, yet it also carries the unique experiences and knowledge of te ao Māori that have evolved in Aotearoa. While mātauranga Māori continued to develop and flourish for hundreds of years before the arrival of foreign settlers on our shores in the 18th century, European colonisation of Aotearoa meant that

Māori "political and social structures were superseded by Western knowledge systems" (Sadler, 2007, p. 34). Assimilationist policies later introduced by the settler–colonial government not only disrupted the transmission of te reo Māori, but also disrupted the transmission of the cultural understandings inherent in the language itself (Walker, 2004). Despite such disruptions, traditional knowledge forms such as whakataukī have remained as pātaka kōrero, storehouses of knowledge that can help us to recover, reclaim and reassert our own ways of knowing and being.

Whakataukī and Whakatauākī

Whakataukī have been referred to variously as Māori proverbial sayings (Metge & Jones, 1995), ancestral sayings (Seed-Pihama & Te Mātāhauariki Institute, 2005) and pēpeha (Mead & Grove, 2001). Whakataukī are mostly short, pithy sayings that are reflective of people and the environment. They are also didactic by nature – that is, they have an instructive or educational purpose – and the origins of the whakataukī are not normally known. In any discussion about whakataukī, is it also important to acknowledge the relationship between whakataukī and whakatauākī.

Like whakataukī, whakatauākī are also instructive by nature. Where they differ is that whakatauākī may vary in length and may also have a known author or source, "ko te nuinga o ngā whakatauākī nā te tangata whai mana i whakatakoto" (Moorfield, 2004, p. 39) – the majority of whakatauākī have been made by people of status. For the purposes of this chapter, both forms will be referred to simply as whakataukī. The function and purpose of whakataukī and whakatauākī is to encapsulate the traditional wisdom of our ancestors. They advise, inform and give directions on customary practices in a concise way that remains relevant to contemporary times. In describing the nature of whakataukī, we often hear the saying "Iti te kupu, nui te kōrero" to express the notion that, while there may be few words, the message is profound. That is the intent and nature of whakataukī.

Whakapapa: Maintaining Identity and Belonging

The importance of maintaining links, knowing one's whakapapa, remaining connected to one's identity and having a sense of belonging are essential elements to the wellbeing of children. A range of whakataukī refer to maintaining whānau, hapū and iwi relationships in order to stand tall as a person.

Hokia ki tō ūkaipō
Return to your place of origin

The whakataukī "Hokia ki tō ūkaipō" speaks to the significance of place for Māori. The ūkaipō is a place where you were fed by the breast of your mother and is symbolic of the intimate relationship Māori have with ancestral lands. This whakataukī advocates returning to one's ūkaipō to maintain that connection. Failure to do so will undoubtedly impact on future generations, who in time may perhaps never return to their roots.

> *Mā ngā pakiaka e tū ai te rākau*
> *With strong roots a tree will stand*

The metaphor of a tree (rākau) and its roots (pakiaka) is also used to elucidate the importance of whanaungatanga. The roots, in this context, are one's links to whānau, hapū and iwi. Knowing who we are and where we come from ensures a strong sense of belonging and a solid foundation on which one can stand as a person.

> *Tamaiti piripoho, he aroha whāereere*
> *A mother's love, a breast clinging child*

A common variation of this whakataukī is 'He aroha whāereere, he pōtiki piripoho'. While the reference here is to the bond between mother and child, it is also possible to interpret this whakataukī in a broader sense. When a child is given love and attention by their parents, and is cherished by their whānau as a whole, the child will grow up feeling secure and be more likely to remain close with their whānau (Ministry of Justice, 2001; Pihama et al., 2015).

Tiakina te Pā Harakeke: Nurturing the Wellbeing of Children and Whānau

In Māori society a child is considered to be like a seed, which must be nurtured and fostered so it may develop and grow well. The time we have to nurture and raise our children is incredibly limited. Nurturing love in our future generations is perhaps the most significant role of a parent. A number of whakataukī stress the importance of caring for our children and are often embedded with cautionary messages. Many of these whakataukī also demonstrate an intimate connection to, and knowledge of, the environment, using plants as symbols for children. The harakeke plant, which symbolises the whānau, is one such example. The rito, or young shoots in the centre of the harakeke, represent the child, while the protective outer leaves represent parents, grandparents and ancestors. The pā harakeke provides us with many teachings about whānau relationships and the interconnectedness of whakapapa – teachings we see embodied in the whakataukī that follow.

> *Kotahi te kākano, he nui ngā hua o te rākau*
> *A tree comes from one seed, but bears many fruit*

The hua or fruit referred to in this whakataukī is children, while the kākano, or seed, refers to the parent/s. This whakataukī is used as praise for producing an abundance of children. While having many children is seen as something positive, the way in which they are treated is just as important. If a child isn't cared for in the early stages of life, the result will be the same as it is for a plant. Neglecting to weed around the base of a young plant may result in the tree, or its fruit, rotting; however, if the plant is properly tended, it is much more likely to flourish. A whakataukī often used in this context is the following:

Parapara waerea a ururua, kia tupu whakaritorito te tupu o te harakeke
Clear away the overgrowth, so that the flax bush will put forth many new shoots

The horticultural advice offered in this whakataukī can also be interpreted in the context of whānau wellbeing, as expressed by Metge and Jones (1995):

> ... we all know that plants grow best when we clear away the weeds that compete for space and nourishment. But when we follow out the analogy between flax bush and whānau, a deeper meaning becomes apparent. If families, large and small, are to fulfil their functions effectively, we must cultivate them carefully, ensuring they have the room and resources they need for continuing growth (p. 4).

Other whakataukī also emphasise the importance of manaakitanga, of nurturing and caring for others, in the context of whānau wellbeing. We explore two specific examples here that urge us to think carefully about our own behaviour as adults and about the kind of impact it may have on our children.

Nā te moa i takahi te rātā
The rātā was trampled by the moa

This whakataukī refers to a young sapling that has just begun to sprout up out of the earth when it is trampled by a moa. The roots remain in the ground, but the sapling itself lies in the way it was trampled, continuing to grow, but growing crooked. What is implied in this whakataukī is that early influences in the life of a child play an important part in their development. Further interpretation indicates that it also relates to the importance of providing appropriate models of conduct early on in life.

Te piko o te rākau, tērā te tipu o te māhuri
As the tree is bent, so shall it grow

The metaphor of a young tree, or māhuri, is also used in this whakataukī to stress the importance of nurturing and guidance in the early stages of one's life. Just as a young tree is malleable and easily moulded, so too is a child. For the full potential of our children to be realised, the appropriate care needs to be provided by parents and whānau. This sentiment is echoed by Patu Hohepa who, in turn, offers a sober warning should we fail to care for our children:

> *Nā, ko ēnei tamariki, āhua rite nei ki te pēpi rākau e tupu ake ana, māu e tiaki, māu e atawhai, māu e poipoi. Mehemea ka whatia e koe, kua ngaro te tamaiti.* Like tender, young saplings, our children need to be nurtured. For if they are broken they will be lost.

Ki te Kāpuia e Kore e Whati: Collective Approaches to Childrearing

Recognising the strength of the collective is a theme that permeates a number of whakataukī and other forms of ancestral sayings. An example of these are the prophetic sayings unique to the Tainui dialect, termed 'tongikura', which are similar in function to whakataukī, "Ko tēnei mea te tongikura, he tūmomo whakataukī, he whakatauākī, he pepeha" (Roa, 2009, p. 8). One tongikura that reinforces this notion of unity was shared by Kīngi Tāwhiao.

Ki te kotahi te kākaho ka whati, ki te kāpuia e kore e whati
When reeds stand alone they are vulnerable, but bundled together they are unbreakable

While this tongikura is often used to talk about kotahitanga, or unity, it also provides a powerful metaphor that speaks to the strength that can be drawn from a collective approach to raising children, a shared view illustrated in the following whakataukī:

Matua rautia
Raise your children collectively

This whakataukī refers to the nature of parenting in the Māori world. Encapsulated in these two words is the philosophy that raising a child is not an individual endeavor, but rather a job for the entire whānau, or community. As a child, aunties, uncles, grandparents and other members of the wider whānau network would be there to guide and instruct you, not just your parents. Such an approach to raising children not only bolsters the confidence of the child, but also provides a great deal of support and relief for the parents.

Ehara taku toa i te toa takitahi, engari he toa takimano
My strength is not mine alone, but the strength of many

This whakataukī, in the context of childrearing, is similar, and emphasises that it's not one person's sole responsibility to raise a child, but rather a collective responsibility. What this also means is that the collective strength that comes from the sharing of childrearing responsibilities with others ensures not only the wellbeing of the children, but also the wellbeing of parents by relieving them of unnecessary burden.

Tū ana ki te Marae, Tau ana: Supporting Appropriate Behaviour

In looking for models of appropriate ways of guiding the behaviour of children, it becomes apparent that there is an absence of sayings that advocate any form of physical punishment. Sayings in English used to promote physical violence against children in the 19th century and beyond, such as "Spare the rod and spoil the child" have no equivalent in Māori. Instead, whakataukī relating to correcting inappropriate behaviour in the Māori world infer thoughtful and compassionate practices aimed at making a child more cognisant of their actions.

Tamaiti akona ki te kāinga, tū ana ki te marae, tau ana
A child who learns at home stands on the marae with dignity

The modelling of appropriate behaviour and values in the home also helps to ensure positive outcomes later in life. Providing appropriate guidance and instruction, while always being compassionate, ensures that a child knows how to conduct themselves in the world around them.

Waiho mā te whakamā e patu
Embarrassment is punishment enough

A number of whakataukī indicate that the behaviour of children was regulated by developing a sense of mindfulness about the consequences of one's actions, as is the case with this whakataukī. Rather than advocating for physical punishment, this whakatukī implies that the embarrassment felt by someone who has done wrong can be more than enough to dissuade them from such action again. This is especially true when one is aware that in the Māori world a wrong committed by an individual is seen as the fault of the collective, thus the saying, "Hē o te kotahi, hē o te katoa" – the wrongdoing of one belongs to everyone. Knowing that your actions reflect badly on your entire whānau and hapū and cause them shame is a much more potent deterrent to negative or inappropriate behaviour than any notion of individual responsibility.

Another form of supporting children to make good decisions are whakataukī that operate as kōrero whakatūpato, or warnings. These appear to be used in a similar way, that is, to encourage children to be mindful of their actions.

Kia mahara ki a Rona
Remember Rona

In the example provided here, attention is drawn to the story of Rona, the woman who lives with the moon. Rona was out fetching water one night when the moon hid behind the clouds, causing her to stumble. Rona cursed at the moon and was taken away for her transgression. This pūrākau is a reminder that we must always be careful of our actions. Jenny Lee (2005) also tells us that the story of Rona "serves to remind people of the power of atua (gods), if we should cause offence" (p. 2).

Conclusion

The lessons we gain from rediscovering and applying ancestral knowledge are both invaluable and necessary. These whakataukī are a small but very much empowering sample of Māori worldview, perspective and lifestyle.

Within the repertoire of whakataukī outlined here, fundamental beliefs, values and practices relating to Te Pā Harakeke have been carefully embedded in the language of our ancestors. In some cases, accessing the cultural understandings inherent within these whakataukī has been fairly straightforward; in others, it has been a bit more challenging. Unpacking the messages within these whakataukī provides us with a rare insight into a way of being and a way of living that has much to offer us in the troubled times in which we live today.

While the whakataukī in this chapter are by no means a complete list, they do, however, give us some useful examples that demonstrate not only the value of children in the Māori world, but also provide a number of guiding principles to ensure the wellbeing of both our tamariki and te pā harakeke in the decades to come. Nō te uranga o te rā ki tōna torengitanga, tērā e manakotia ana ka tiaho mai te māramatanga ō rātou mā kua whetūrangitia. From the rising to the setting of the sun, may the wisdom of our ancestors continue to enlighten us.

References

IHAKA, K. (1957). Nga Whakatauki me nga Pepeha Maori. *Te Ao Hou*, 18, 41–42.

KŌHERE, R. (1994). *Ngā Kōrero a Reweti Kōhere Mā*. Wellington, New Zealand: Victoria University Press.

LEE, J. (2005, JUNE 24). *Māori cultural regeneration: Pūrākau as pedagogy* [Paper presentation]. Centre for Research in Lifelong Learning International Conference, Stirling, Scotland.

MEAD, S. M., & GROVE, N. (2001). *Ngā pēpeha a ngā tīpuna: The sayings of the ancestors*. Wellington, New Zealand: Victoria University Press.

METGE, J., & JONES, S. (1995). 'He taonga tuku iho nō ngā tūpuna: Māori proverbial sayings – a literary treasure'. *New Zealand Studies*, 5(2), 3–7.

MINISTRY OF JUSTICE. (2001). *He hīnātore ki te ao Māori – A glimpse into the Māori world*. Wellington, New Zealand: Ministry of Justice.

MOORFIELD, J. C. (2004). *Te Whanake 4: Te Kōhure*. Auckland, New Zealand: Longman/Pearson Education.

PERE, R. (1982). *Ako: Concepts and learning in Māori Tradition*. University of Waikato Department of Sociology Working Paper No. 17. Hamilton, New Zealand: University of Waikato.

PIHAMA, L., GREENSILL, H., CAMPBELL, D., TE NANA, R., & LEE, J. (2015). *Taku Kuru Pounamu*. Hamilton, New Zealand: Te Kotahi Research Institute.

RICKARD, S. (1998). Koi Patu Koi Mamae: Disciplining Māori children. *Social Work Now*, 11, 4–9.

ROA, R. (2009, DECEMBER). He tongikura. *Te Hookioi*. https://ndhadeliver.natlib.govt.nz/delivery/DeliveryManagerServlet?dps_pid=IE1579415

ROYAL, T. A. (2016). *Whakataukī Series 1, episode 1*. (R. Papa, Interviewer). Retrieved from https://www.maoritelevision.com/shows/whakataukī/S01E001/whakataukī-series-1-episode-1

SADLER, H. (2007). Mātauranga Māori (Māori epistemology). *International Journal of the Humanities*, 4(10), 33–45.

SEED-PIHAMA, J. (2004). *Te waka pakaru ki te moana: A translation and examination of various Taranaki ancestral sayings* (Master's thesis). University of Waikato, Hamilton, New Zealand.

SEED-PIHAMA, J., & TE MĀTĀHAUARIKI INSTITUTE. (2005). *Māori ancestral sayings: A juridical role?* Te Mātāhauariki Institute occasional paper series, No. 10. Hamilton, New Zealand: Te Mātāhauariki Institute, University of Waikato.

SMITH, L. T., MAXWELL, T., PUKE, H., & TEMARA, P. (2016). Indigenous knowledge, methodology and mayhem: What is the role of methodology in producing indigenous insights? A discussion from mātauranga Māori. *Knowledge Cultures*, 4(3), 131–156.

WALKER, R. (2004). *Ka Whawhai Tonu Matou: Struggle Without End* (revised edition). Auckland, New Zealand: Penguin.

Oriori: He Akoranga Tahito – Oriori as Knowledge Transmission

Glenis Philip-Barbara
Hiria Barbara

CHAPTER 7

Introduction

Ngā Mōteatea (2004) is a four-volume collection of hundreds of traditional Māori songs in the Māori language with exquisite English language translations, compiled by Apirana Ngata and Pei te Hurinui Jones (2004a, 2004b, 2004c, 2004d). They were, quite literally, a labour of love for everyone who worked on them. The waiata or songs are helpfully organised in numerical order across all four volumes from song 1 to song 393. They remain one of the most significant windows into our ancestral knowledge, and have remained in the public domain since the first publication of Part 1 in 1928.

These mōteatea feature a collection of twenty-nine oriori or chants composed for children. The four books carry 393 songs in total, and it is noted here that song 1 and song 393 are both oriori; a significant indication of their importance. McRae and Jacob (2011) discuss oriori in depth, noting that Ngata may have positioned an oriori first in the *Ngā Mōteatea* collection because they are so informative, and are especially notable for references to mythology and tribal history, territory and genealogy. Each song also contains an explanatory 'note', providing a rich, whakapapa-informed context, an insight into what inspired the composer, their relationship to the people or children written for or about, and the place that inspired the composition.

Jenkins and Harte, in their 2011 report for Te Mana Ririki, described waiata oriori as lullabies that were sung to babies to reinforce the purpose and the spiritual nature of the child's life. They are beautiful poems, and were composed to build up and mould the child as a useful member of the whānau and hapū; that is, they were a socialising tool. They linked the child to the gods as their spiritual helpers. The child's grandparents or parents usually composed an oriori for the baby. It was sung repeatedly so all listeners learned it and all knew the whakapapa and qualities of the child and, thus, the special treatment they required. Oriori were a poetic and repetitive way to fix personal, whānau and cultural messages in the minds of the listeners.

This collection demonstrates clearly that the practice of oriori was well established among our tīpuna. Children were seen as the link to the future and as such were regarded as worthy receivers of sacred knowledge. This attitude and practice is well evidenced in the many oriori remaining today. Babies and children were immersed in their knowing, so that by the time they grew to maturity, the many reference points required to navigate whakapapa and whenua were firmly established in their hearts and minds.

Wayne Ngata, in his 2009 thesis, describes oriori as the most important waiata composed for children destined to lead within their hapū. According to Ngata (2009), oriori contained important information to support their future leadership and therefore the focus of the composition. The approach to the central kaupapa and each word was approached with the utmost care. Oriori were a fundamental component of ako in terms of intergenerational knowledge transmission. The stories, histories and, importantly, territories a child connected to through their whakapapa were embedded in the oriori and frequently activated, and therefore remembered through singing together as a whānau. Kōkā Rose Pere (1994) wrote about the fluid and dynamic nature of ako in her seminal paper published by Te Kōhanga Reo National Trust, reminding us that to learn and teach is indivisible. In an oriori context, the knowledge transmitted, although intended for a baby, enriched everyone participating, including the composer – yet another example of ako in action. The process of ako was constant; it did not operate in isolation from everyday Māori life. Rather, ako was integral in the creation, transmission, conceptualisation and articulation of Māori knowledge (Lee, 2005).

In Te Wheke, Kōkā Rose's wellbeing framework (Pere, 1991), she reminds us that wellbeing is made up of a dynamic relationship with and between all aspects of our divine and physical experience of living. Reviewing the subject matter of the oriori within *Ngā Mōteatea*, it is immediately apparent that the sharing of knowledge through oriori does not occur in a cerebral vacuum, but rather draws on all aspects of Kōkā Rose's wellbeing framework to create an experience that is felt through all eight ihirangaranga (senses). The practice of oriori draws whānau together, identifies the unique mana of the whānau and the child, draws on and exudes the mauri of the whānau, connects the whānau to their deeper spiritual relationships with others and those who have long passed, expresses reverence for the relationship between pakeke and mokopuna, and expresses total wellbeing while exemplifying a healthy outpouring of emotion. Oriori also share a common tone or approach; that is, reverence for the child. Oriori are easily identifiable by the terms of endearment in every line. There can be no doubt that children lucky enough to have had oriori composed for them were loved and adored by their whānau.

Much-loved pakeke Amster Reedy (2008) observes, "The practice of oriori while the child is in the womb, during birth and as the child grows instils the importance of relationships; with parents, caregivers and kin." His observations highlight the centrality of whakapapa knowledge and the maintenance of whānau connections for children, and the role of oriori in ensuring that this knowledge became intrinsic to a child from their earliest stages of development.

Theorists and practitioners alike have drawn clear conclusions about the importance of children and their role in receiving knowledge from birth onwards to help guide them into roles of leadership, in particular. Oriori, as a means to transmit whakapapa and other knowledge, exemplify how one might engage all eight senses (Pere, 1991) in the transmission of knowledge as a whānau. In this way, the practice of oriori expands our 'modern' ideas of mātauranga Māori through the creation of a unique pedagogical process: waiata. Oriori acts in this context as a thread that draws all aspects of a child's identity together, delivering it through song in a particular vibration containing content rich in information.

For this chapter, we have worked together as whānau, as whaea (mother) and tamāhine (daughter) to explore some of the concepts and practices within oriori that can provide insights into the understandings our tīpuna held in regard to tamariki and the raising of children. Outlined below are the themes drawn from our analysis of the oriori in *Ngā Mōteatea*. They highlight significant learnings and guidance from our tīpuna and their approaches to raising tamariki and mokopuna that we can draw upon in our experiences of raising tamariki and mokopuna in contemporary Aotearoa. It is our view that these oriori provide us all with deep knowledge that can, and must, inform our current-day practices of raising current and future generations of tamariki Māori. To support this, we have included as a key part of this chapter an overview of oriori that are documented within the *Ngā Mōteatea* volumes as a means by which to assist whānau and others to reach into this powerful collection and to explore more fully the mātauranga that comes from each of our own hapū and iwi.

Children are Cherished

In the time of our tīpuna, children were adored from the moment their existence was known of. There are terms of endearment that remind the child how important they are to the whānau and the composer in every oriori. Jenkins and Harte (2011), when considering the status of children in the traditional Māori world, conclude that "The atua imbued children with mana, enfolding them within the embrace of the supreme beings. This mana of the children accruing from the atua tapu underpinned the beliefs our tīpuna had of children, their socialisation."

This is beautifully evidenced by Whakaawe of Ngāti Tūwharetoa, who begins his composition with the line:

E tama i kimihia [Oh child who was sought diligently] (Song 75)

This kind of thinking and composing directly challenges the colonised view of children (and women) as mere 'chattels' of men. For a child to be so wanted conveys a completely different sense of the power dynamic within whānau pre-colonisaton.

In the oriori composed by Taoho of Ngāti Whātua for his son Rairoa, he says:

Me kōhanga tāua [Let us nestle together] (Song 158)

There are two important ideas conveyed in the oriori by Taoho. First, the father is tender toward his son, inviting him to snuggle as war rages around them. This is in stark contrast to the toxic Māori masculinity portrayed in films such as *Deadlands* or *Once Were Warriors*.

In the eight verses of *He oriori mō Tuteremoana*, composed by high priest Tuhotoariki of Ngāi Tara for his mokopuna, the first two lines are exquisite and speak directly to the sacredness of the child in the minds of our tīpuna:

Nau mai e tama, kia mihi atu au, i haramai rā koe i te kunenga mai o te tangata
[Welcome oh child, let me greet you, you have come from the origin of mankind] (Song 201)

This body of ancestral knowledge presents an entirely different view for us to consider about children and their place in society than that of the coloniser. These oriori suggest that children and babies were held in high regard, were cherished and adored, rather than relegated to a lower level of importance within a family structure.

Whakapapa

Whakapapa is critical knowledge in terms of both who we are and where we are from. Whakapapa is literally the source of our identity as Māori people; it is fundamental not only to our knowing who we are, but also to our connections to place and whānau. Whakapapa knowledge also supports our process of working to make sense of the world around us. According to Pihama, Simmonds, and Waitoki (2019), "Whakapapa is about connections and growth and it is within our whakapapa that we can find a wealth of resources that enable us to make sense of and transform our lived realities."

Many oriori convey, for the child, a complex network of geographical and genealogical connections, with the oriori composed as a journey taken from place to place, with relatives often named and in place to provide support as the journey is undertaken.

In the oriori below, composed by Te Maperetahi of Ngāti Porou for Ta-maunga-o-te-Rangi, explicit instructions are given over the course of nine verses, each describing in detail both the terrain and the names of the relatives to be found at each place.

Arahina atu rā hai Te Umukuri,
Te Weka a Umutapu, hai Mairenui, ē;
Ka tāwhi tō ringa, kāti ka hoki mai;
Ka ō koe kai roto kai te tapui, nā.

You are to be escorted to Te Umukuri,
And to Te Weka a Umutapu at Mairenui;
You will wave your hands in salutation before returning;
For you are now with your kinsfolk. (Song 209)

Oriori as Pedagogy

The practice of singing our knowledge to our children strengthens our collective knowing and understanding of who we are. Oriori is an example of knowledge transfer between adults and children. Ako is the process of teaching and learning simultaneously; it is dynamic, contextual and ever-evolving in accordance with the situation. Lee (2005) considers that "Ako was largely determined by the interaction of Māori cultural notions that generated knowledge and understandings of being Māori within our whānau, hapū, iwi and whakapapa relationships" (p. 5).

Oriori as a practice is as multi-layered as the concept of ako itself. It provides a pedagogical practice that uplifts our own processes of learning and teaching (Pere, 1994; Pihama, Smith, Taki, & Lee, 2004). The composer writes for a child, soon to be or just born. While the child may be the intended recipient of the knowledge contained therein, everyone in the whānau who sings the oriori will benefit from the practice of singing it frequently. The markers and stories, whakapapa references and markers of place benefit everyone with a shared whakapapa – and so the shared intent to 'educate' the child becomes an opportunity for the entire whānau system to reinforce their knowledge over many years.

This approach is captured in the oriori written by Hinekitawhiti for her mokopuna Ahuahu-ki-te-rangi. Her oriori begins:

*Kia tapu hoki koe, nā Tuariki, ē! [May you be set apart,
as is fitting for a descendant of Tuariki] (Song 1)*

In the four verses of this oriori, this mokopuna is introduced to various places within the territories of her whakapapa or genealogy, drawing together those two important aspects of life: genealogy and geography.

Collective Knowledge Sharing

Another critical part of oriori as pedagogy is the means by which we prepare our children for the future through the sharing of knowledge. This was noted by McRae and Jacob (2011) in consideration of the work of Ngāti Porou poet Hinekitawhiti and the oriori she composed for her granddaughter Ahuahu-ki-te-rangi when they said, "She speaks of the child as an infant, but anticipates the adult highly informed about her tribe" (p. 95).

This is again in stark contrast to English ideas that children ought to be 'seen and not heard' – with children's knowledge conveyed in oriori including sacred rites and rituals, details of battles fought in the past, including outcomes, and learnings and instructions for taking up one's rangatira functions. The notion that a child should wait until they are 'old enough' to be admitted to the depth of tribal knowledge is not consistent with what we see conveyed in this collection of oriori.

The practice of oriori is dynamic, adaptable and portable, with every situation considered in the range of compositions focused specifically on ensuring that children receive their life's instructions through each line. A great example of this is the oriori composed for children who died in infancy. Their deaths inspired the composition of oriori so their journey beyond the veil would be conducted with the appropriate knowledge of whānau and whakapapa connection to those who would be there to meet and guide them. Ripeka Paiatehau of Ngāti Porou wrote this oriori for Te Ua-o-te-Rangi with words chosen that bring tears to the eyes as one imagines the pain of loss for the composer and the whānau:

Nā Papa koe i te rangi [Alas now, oh child, thou art soaring on high]

Hurihia ki runga rā hei tō tuahine.
Hei a Te Aokaui-Rangi,
Māna koe e karanga mai

[Carried away on high was thy cousin.
She who was called Te Aokaui-Rangi,
and she will call the welcome for thee] (Song 121)

In some instances, the responsibility to hand down critical information was so important that some women also composed oriori for the children they were never able to have, singing them to inanimate objects in the same way they would croon to a loved child (Songs 219, 270, 272, 273). The drive to fulfil one's whānau obligations are powerfully captured in these oriori.

Oriori as Whānau Ora Practice

The core concepts drawn from this collection of oriori speak consistently to the fact that our children are cherished in their own right and treated as an important link to the future and the past for whānau and hapū. In many respects the selection of kupu within these oriori and the way they are conveyed to babies and children within a whānau collective strongly suggest that the very best of what we had was given to them.

The critical nature of whakapapa knowledge, as it pertains to both genealogical and geographical connection, is reinforced in each oriori, with detailed accounts captured in the compositions and conveyed through the singing of the oriori itself to whānau and hapū groups.

It is clear to see that the practice of singing together, of recalling collectively the detailed information contained within each oriori, positions the idea of knowledge itself as both centralised around children and inclusive of the wider whānau network. In this way both the knowledge itself and the approach to its transmission leaves an important clue as to the values driving our whānau and hapū practices around knowledge and education.

An analysis of oriori shows just how important it was to share all kinds of knowledge with children in order to prepare them for their futures. From celestial knowledge drawn from the old whare wānanga, through to voyaging and birthing practices and approaches – there is no separation of less complex ideas for children. In an oral culture, oriori specifically and mōteatea more generally are like the encyclopedia of our tīpuna, capturing the very essence of their wide range of knowledge and their approach to transmitting it through generations and across whānau groups.

You won't find 'ring-a-ring-a-rosy' sentiments conveyed in the works of our ancestors captured in the form of oriori in *Ngā Mōteatea*. There is no nonsense in these chants, and in some cases no comfort in the messages of despair and concern either. If by some chance we can find a link to the composer or the child for whom it was written, what awaits is a veritable treasure trove of whakapapa knowledge. Failing that, for the eager student of the Māori language, oriori contain the sweetest exemplars of poetic expression, a rich archive of cultural practice, and offer us all a way to re-think the role of children in society at the very least.

An Annotated Bibliography of the Lullabies Contained in *Ngā Mōteatea Volumes 1–4*

We've prepared below a very brief annotated bibliography of all twenty-nine oriori published in *Ngā Mōteatea* through volumes 1-4. It is our hope that this whakarāpopoto will encourage the curious to dig deeper, to engage with *Ngā Mōteatea* again in order to recover what we used to know about tama-ariki, our children.

NGĀ MŌTEATEA PART 1

1. He waiata oriori

Written by Hinekitawhiti for her mokopuna, Ahuahu-ki-te-rangi. They lived at Te Ariuru, Tokomaru Bay. The composer takes her granddaughter to various points on the East Coast from East Cape to Raukokore, an example of oriori specific to geneological/geographical context. This oriori contains four verses.

30. He oriori

This is a waiata oriori written by Nohomaiterangi of Ngāti Kahungunu for his sons Te Hauapu and Pani-toangakore. The author laments the dire fate in store for his sons as they were born during the period when bitter inter-tribal wars were being fought in Heretaunga. This oriori consists of a single verse.

75. He oriori

This is a waiata oriori written by Whakaawe of Ngāti Tuwharetoa for his son. The author empasises how much this child was wanted in the very first line, '*E tama i kimihia*' [*Oh child who was sought diligently*] and goes on to set out his lineage, the taonga that will be bestowed upon him and the territories where he will find shelter and refuge in his life. This oriori is five verses long.

81. He oriori mō te Rangitumua

This is a waiata oriori written by Te Motu of Ngāti Kahungunu for Rangitumua, reflecting on the thinning ranks of their ilk. It is also a lament for the changes afoot upon the land and among the people. This oriori consists of a single verse.

NGĀ MŌTEATEA PART 2

101. He tangi mo Rangiamohia

This is a waiata oriori written by Tokorau of Ngāti Raukawa and Ngāti Whakatere, who was lamenting the death of his daughter, Rangiamohia. Rangiamohia died without having any children; however, the descendants of her sister, Te Rōpiha, also sang this oriori when Wi-Romana, grandson of Te Rōpiha died. The oriori provides instruction for the child in times of hardship, with regret expressed for the distress of the child, as indicated by the first line. Where to go and who to seek is the main theme of this oriori, with the names of ancestors clearly given. This oriori consists of a single verse.

121. He oriori mō Te Ua-o-te-Rangi

This is a waiata oriori written by Ripeka Paiatehau of Ngāti Porou for Te-Ua-o-te-Rangi, who died in infancy. In this beautiful prose the child receives full knowledge of their whakapapa and is guided through the process of crossing over to the realms of Hawaiki. Baby is instructed to listen for the call of Te Aokaui-rangi, a cousin who will be there to meet and guide him on his journey to the dwelling place of the ancestors. This oriori consists of three verses.

127. He waiata tangi mō Te Tihi

This is a waiata oriori written by Te Matapō of Ngāpuhi for his grandson Te Rangi-wahipō, lamenting the death of Te Tihi, who was killed at Mataraua. In this oriori Te Matapō sets out the changing political context of their time, offering insight to his grandson about both the treachery that lurks and the safety that is available to him. He instructs his grandson in the pathway to peace, lamenting the difficulty with which such a state may be achieved. This oriori consists of five verses.

145. He pōpō, arā, he oriori

This is perhaps one of the most well-known and often-sung oriori in the Tairāwhiti. It was written by Enoka Te Pakaru of Te Aitanga-a-Māhaki, an elder and a seer well versed in the mythlogy and traditions of ancient times. The main theme of this oriori is the origins of the kūmara and how it was bought from Hawaiki to Tūranga. This oriori consists of four verses.

158. He whakaoriori

This waiata oriori was written by Taoho of Ngāti Whātua for his son Rairoa. The situation at the time of writing was one of war and, as omens of death seemingly surround them, the oriori bids them to nestle closer together, "Me kōhanga tāua". Taoho paints a desolate picture for his son, one which was to come to pass: Rairoa was to have no descendents. This oriori contains two verses.

162. He oriori mō Te Parekanga

This waiata oriori was written by Hautu for Te Parekanga. First collated by Elsdon Best, there is no reference to the iwi of the writer. The oriori provides a great deal of detail pertaining to the process of weaving fine garments – offered to the child as a gift of knowledge. This oriori contains five verses.

185. He waiata oriori mō Te Rara-o-te-Rangi

This waiata oriori was written by Te Hakeke of Ngāti Apa, who lived at the time of Te Rauparaha. He married Kaiwa of the Muaūpoko and their son was Te Rara-o-te-Rangi, who was also called Kawana Te Hakeke or Kawana Hunia, a Chief of Ngāti Apa, for whom the oriori was written. The oriori provided important information pertaining to the child's whakapapa connections both back to the time of the separation of the primordial parents and across the whenua to his many relations from Wairarapa to Manawatū, Horowhenua and beyond. This oriori contains three verses.

186. He waiata mō Te Tahuri

This waiata oriori was written by Peou of Ngāti Raukawa, a younger brother of Te Ahukaramu, for his cousin, Te Tahuri. Tahuri was a son of the renowned Te Whatanui, whose name appears in many songs (41, 61, 117, 131) in various forms as Tohe, Tohe-a-Pare and Whata. When Te Tahuri went through to the Taranaki district because of a love affair with a woman there, news came back that questions had been asked as to who he was, and as to his parentage. It was on this account the song was composed. The oriori makes clear the ancestry of Te Tahuri, his connections to Taranaki and the feats of his ancestors. This oriori contains one verse.

190. He whakaoriori

This waiata oriori was written for Poutūterangi by someone of Ngāti Porou. In this oriori Poutūterangi is connected to their significant ancestors of noble birth and equipped with knowledge about how they were raised as proof. This oriori contains three verses.

NGĀ MŌTEATEA PART 3

201. He oriori mō Tuteremoana

This waiata oriori was written for Tuteremoana by Tuhotoariki, a high priest of Ngāi Tara, the tribe who inhabited Te Upoko o te Ika. The manuscript containing the song belonged to Ihaka Kuaha, an elder of Wairarapa. Tuteremoana was a mokopuna of Tuhotoariki, descended from his younger sibling. The first verse of this oriori is a karakia to assist with childbirth when the child is overdue, or it is thought that something may be troubling the mother. The karakia properly delivered removes the cause of the trouble. Failing this, the woman, accompanied by her whānau, is taken to the shrine for further karakia, which is contained in the second verse of this oriori. The fourth verse of this oriori is a tohi rite for the child. This is one of the most expansive oriori dealing directly with the process of childbirth and the origins of mankind, offering insight into both the spiritual and physical connections of each child born into the world. The details and insight contained within this oriori are incredible. There are eight verses in total.

209. He oriori mō Ta-maunga-o-te-Rangi

This waiata oriori was written for Ta-maunga-o-te-Rangi by Te Maperetahi, a descendant of Whakarae, who was the son of Te Huka-rere, one of the Chiefs of Ngāti Porou and grandson of Tūwhakairiora. This is a Ngāti Porou oriori from Te Araroa. This oriori has great influence over the investigation of land titles in the district and has determined rights in accordance with the information contained within it. The text was recorded by Apirana Ngata at Hinerupe. This oriori is an exemplar of the Ngāti Porou dialect, and each word is carefully chosen to express an exact shade of meaning. It also gives the highest precepts for the guidance of the child for whom the oriori was composed. Maperetahi, according to some accounts, was a woman, a descendant of Te Ata-haia, wife of Tu-te-rangi-whiu. She married Taku-rangi, a descendant of Whakarae, son of Te Huka-rere, and had Ta-maunga-o-te-Rangi. Maperetahi sang it at Tupuni, a pā near the mouth of Karakatuwhero stream on the southern side. She addresses the child, "You are to climb by the steep ascents within the veil of Te Tawai." Te Tawai is a hill above Waioni, the ascent is on an old trail and over the hill is a fortified place, Te Tawai, above Te Maire. On reaching the summit of the hill, one may "gaze directly at the canoe descending from Taumutu". According to Ngata, the people of Tūwhakairiora had sweet voices throughout their tribal domain; that is at Te Kawakawa, Wharekāhika, Horoera and (the valley of) Te Awatere, and they could sing. In 1948, at the time of writing *Ngā Moteatea*, it had been twenty years since he had heard them sing this song in Hinerupe house; people were alive then who knew the words, the air and the significance of the song; their hands opened and closed to the lilt of the chant and to illustrate the places' names; their eyes, eyebrows and heads emphasised the meaning of the words.

215. Pinepine te kura
This waiata oriori was written for Te Umurangi, and is a famous mōteatea of the East Coast, widely sung by Ngāti Kahungunu. This is an exemplar of the value of these lullabies, which contain valuable sources of history and geneological descent. The people of Heretaunga know the true value of the words contained within this oriori and *Ngā Mōteatea* carries two versions, 215a and 215b, with source information shared for each. Version 215a contains four verses, while 215b contains six verses.

219. He oriori
This waiata was composed by Mumura, a woman of Ngā Ariki, who, because of her childless state, daydreamed about children. She took a hue in her hand and composed the oriori for it, as evidenced in the last line, "Nō te hika anō te aituā, he hue te tamaiti oriori ē!" This oriori contains three verses.

231. He oriori
This waiata is of Ngāti Kahungunu. For whom and by whom it was composed is a subject of controversy, and therefore cannot be accurately determined. There are many variations sung in all corners of the East Coast. This oriori also carries many lines of geneology referenced over the ten verses it contains.

234. He oriori mō Te Whakataha-ki-te-Rangi
This waiata is of Te Whānau a Kai, written by Tupai, a descendant of Kai and Taharakau of the Tūranga District and of Rangiaia of the Tūhoe people. He is also a descendant of Paeko, who is remembered because of his saying, "He karanga riri ka karangatia a Paeko; he karanga kai, tē karangatia." Tupai was the last high priest of the house of learning known as Tokitoki at Waerenga-a-Hika. The greater part of his waiata traces the geneology of the gods, as taught in the house of learning, which is in character with most of the songs of the priesthood. That geneology of the gods traces out to Te Whakataha-ki-te-Rangi, whose name was bestowed upon the child for whom the oriori was composed.

261. He oriori mō Makerewhatu
This waiata was written by Kahutia of Rongowhakaata, a chief of the Tūranga District, for Makerewhatu, his daughter by his first wife, Nikoniko. He later married Uaia and had a

daughter, Riparata, who had Heni Materoa, Lady Carrol. This oriori contains a reference to an incident that saw umbrage taken at the offering of burnt vegetables, which resulted in the death of a visiting party. The oriori encourages Makerewhatu to remind those who may ask of her lineage, and the fact that the burnt vegetables incident has been avenged. This oriori contains only one verse.

269. He oriori mō Te Aokapurangi

This waiata was written by Hemi Maeha of Te Aitanga-a-Māhaki, a grandfather to Te Aokapurangi. There is not a long history to this mōteatea; most of it is a gifting of whakapapa for the mokopuna. This oriori contains three verses.

270. He oriori

This waiata was written by Te Aotarewa of Whanganui for a child fashioned from wood. The oriori contains two verses and begins by saying, "Oh child of mine, emergent are you from the origin of Hawaiki, from your pillow you blossom forth, hauled forth by Māui, what became dry land on shore, and a tree grew to be a child for me."

272. He oriori

This waiata was written by Maikara of Ngāti Manawa, and follows in the fashion of those oriori (219, 270) composed for women who long for a child. In this oriori Maikara sings to a stone; afterwards, that stone was used as a talisman on the upper reaches of the Rangitāiki River. The oriori begins with these words, "Cold to the touch is the skin of this child without a name." This oriori has only one verse.

273. He oriori

This oriori was written by Harehare of Ngāti Manawa, and is similar to that of Maikara. It is composed for a child of stone because Harehare longed to mother children. This oriori contains just one verse.

282. He oriori mō Wharaurangi

This oriori was written by Te Rangitakoru of Ngāti Apa for her female relative and describes the naming of the Whanganui River on the West Coast by the journeys of Haunui-a-nanaia over the lands, and describing the signs of the changing seasons. This oriori contains four verses.

NGĀ MŌTEATEA PART 4

331. He oriori

This oriori was contributed by Mohi Te Ataihikoia, and was written by persons unknown of Ngāti Kahungunu for Niniwa-i-te-rangi. The composition reaches back to Hawaiki and traces events forwards to Te Huripureiata and troubles within Tūranga, which developed once the people crossed into Aotearoa. It was passed down by Rakaihikuroa and his descendants in Heretaunga, who settled the Heretaunga District down to the present time. The composition concludes with the battles within the District from Hastings to Wairarapa. This oriori contains eight verses.

350. He oriori

This waiata was written by Te Takai for his female grandchild, and while no iwi information was collected, the regional references suggest they are of the Ngāti Kahungunu tribal area. This is an oriori in the style of those written in keeping with the teachings of Te Matorohanga, offering his mokopuna the scared learnings of the Atua. Instructions are given for his mokopuna to traverse the very heavens safely and in full knowledge of the path trodden and lessons learned by the Atua. This oriori contains one verse.

370. He oriori

This waiata was written by Te Tahatū-o-te-Rangi for the twins Kupe and Ngake, and pertains to the traditions of the people of Ahuriri and Heretaunga. The instructions tell of the battles fought that led them to settle upon their ancestral lands at Te Whanganui-a-Orotū, Heretaunga. This oriori contains one verse.

393. He waiata oriori

This waiata was written by Te Whatapoto for his granddaughter Ngapuao; they are of Ngāti Pikiao, Te Arawa. Their geneology is contained within song 238. The oriori begins "Oh daughter, cease your begging, for it fills me with shame" and proceeds to lay out the means by which she might be sustained over her lifetime, reminding her that, as a descendant of Apatahi, the drive to grow food is strong within their line. The line, "Come back, oh daughter, inside this house! Here you are a cherished child", positions her within the whānau but cautions her that hard work is necessary to be sustained. This oriori contains two verses.

If you are yet to discover *Ngā Mōteatea* in your local library, we strongly encourage you to make some time to do so. These oriori are only 29 of 393 songs captured at a point in time when our cultural knowledge was held by those who had grown up in it and who navigated the recesses of their minds and hearts in the language of our ancestors. Their lived experience was different to ours and as such they brought a different knowing to the way they expressed their values, habits and practices.

For those of us who dip in and out of these deep pools of Māori knowledge, each time we do there is something else to 'discover', more to marvel at and a great appreciation for the foresight of our ancestors and all those involved in creating such a resource for us, their mokopuna. The translations make each thought completely accessible in both English and Māori, with the notes adding the context for a more complete understanding.

In closing, we leave you with these beautiful lines composed by Te Maperetahi of Te Araroa, Ngāti Porou, an articulation of how we might describe the gift of knowledge through a deep knowledge of whakapapa back to the origins of life itself.

Nā tō Matua rā nāna i waihanga,
Nā Rua-te-pupuke, nā Rua-te-mahara, nā Rua-te-hotahota,
nā Tua-waihanga; Hei kahu rā mō tāua ki te pō.

There is, of course, our cloak. It was woven by your parent,
By Recess-of-knowledge, Recess-of-thought,
Recess-of-enterprise, and by Prodigy-of-learning,
as a robe for us to the realms of night. (Song 209)

References

JENKINS, K., & HARTE, H. (2011). *Traditional Māori Parenting: A historical review of literature of traditional Māori child rearing pratices in pre-European times*. Auckland, New Zealand: Te Kāhui Mana Ririki. Retrieved from http://www.ririki.org.nz/wp-content/uploads/2015/04/TradMaoriParenting.pdf

LEE, J. (2005). *Māori cultural regeneration: Pūrākau as pedagogy*. Paper presented as part of a symposium at the Centre for Research in Lifelong Learning International Conference, Stirling, Scotland, June 24, 2005. Retrieved from http://www.rangahau.co.nz/assets/lee_J/purakau%20as%20pedagogy.pdf

MCRAE. J., & JACOB, H. (2011). *Ngā Mōteatea: An introduction*. Auckland, New Zealand: Auckland University Press.

NGATA, A., & JONES, P. (2004A). *Ngā Mōteatea the songs: Part one*. Auckland, New Zealand: Auckland University Press.

NGATA, A., & JONES, P. (2004B). *Ngā Mōteatea the songs: Part two*. Auckland, New Zealand: Auckland University Press.

NGATA, A., & JONES, P. (2004C). *Ngā Mōteatea the songs: Part three*. Auckland, New Zealand: Auckland University Press.

NGATA, A., & JONES, P. (2004D). *Ngā Mōteatea the songs: Part four*. Auckland, New Zealand: Auckland University Press.

NGATA, W. J. (2009). *Te Hū o te Puoro: Ko te mōteatea ki te pā o te hinengaro Māori ki te ao Māori* (Doctoral dissertation). Massey University, Palmerston North, New Zealand. Retrieved from https://mro.massey.ac.nz/handle/10179/1354

PERE, R. R. (1991). *Te Wheke: A celebration of infinite wisdom*. Gisborne, New Zealand: Ao Ake Global Learning.

PERE, R. R. (1994). *Ako: Concepts and learning in the Maori tradition*. Wellington, New Zealand: Te Kōhanga Reo National Trust.

PIHAMA, L., SIMMONDS, N., & WAITOKI, W. (2019). *Te Taonga o Taku Ngākau: Ancestral knowledge and the wellbeing of Tamariki Māori*. Hamilton, New Zealand: Te Kotahi Research Institute. Retrieved from https://leoniepihama.files.wordpress.com/2019/10/te-taonga-o-taku-ngakau-final-report.pdf

PIHAMA, L., SMITH, K., TAKI, M., & LEE, J. (2004). *A literature review on Kaupapa Māori and Māori education pedagogy*. Auckland, New Zealand: International Research Institute for Māori and Indigenous Education.

REEDY, A. (2008, JULY 25). *Māori lullabies subject of PhD research*. Palmerston North, New Zealand: Massey News, Massey University. Retrieved from https://www.massey.ac.nz/massey/about-massey/news/article.cfm?mnarticle=maori-lullabies-subject-of-phd-research-21-07-2008

Tūī, Tūī, Tuituia: Pūrākau to Keep Us Connected

Jenny Lee-Morgan

CHAPTER 8

This paper is based on a section of Jenny Lee-Morgan's inaugural professorial address delivered at Te Noho Kotahitanga marae, Te Whare Wānanga o Wairaka, 13 November 2019.

Mihi/Introduction

Whakarongo ake au ki te tangi ā te manu nei ā te manu – tūī, tūī, tuituia. Tuia i runga, tuia i raro, tuia i waho, tuia i roto, tuia te here tangata.

Ka rongo te pō, ka rongo te ao. Tuia te muka tangata i takea mai i Hawaiki nui, i Hawaiki roa, i Hawaiki pāmamao. Te hono i wairua ki te whai ao, ki te ao mārama.

Tuia ngā whītau whakarei o te hunga mate, ngā tini aituā puta noa i ngā motu, tuia ki a Hinenuitepō, ki a Hinetītama. Tuia ngā whenu o te hunga ora ki a Tāne whakapiripiri e tū iho nei. Kei ngā mana, kei ngā mātāwaka, kei nga maunga kōrero, kei ngā whakamataku tūī, tūī, tuituia koutou katoa ki raro i te tuanui o tō tātou piringa whare o Ngākau Mahaki – tēnei te whakaāhuru i a tātou i tenei wā.

Tuia hoki tātou me ō tātou tuakiritanga ki ngā maunga tūpuna e tāwharau nei i a tātou, ki ngā wai whakaika ō rātou mā, arā, Te Wai Unuroa o Wairaka e māpuna ake nei ngā kare ā-roto me ngā whatumanawa mōu, mō koutou kua ngaro nei. E rere tonu aku mihi ki te aukaha o Te Auaunga e kōriporipo mai nā ki te awanui o Te Whau, puta atu ki ngā wai kōrikoriko o Ngātoroirangi, e kī ana ko te waiū hoki o Ohomatakamokamo! Ka tae ki te ara whakapekapeka o Ruarangi, te tokaroa o te iwi patupaiarehe! Maranga mai koutou, hoki wairua mai rā!

Te uri o Wairaka, nei rā te mihi o tēnei te uri o Rakatura ki a koutou, Ngāti Whātua mai i Ōrākei, puta atu ki Kaipapa, ā, tae atu ki ngā tini iwi o Tāmaki Makaurau – tēnā koutou. Otirā, tēnā tātou katoa!

I've framed my professorial address around the well-known tauparapara 'Tūī, tūī, tuituia' as a way to talk about some key research strands that I'm really excited about in my current work. More than that, as the tauparapara reminds us, it is the importance of connection that is always critical, so I want to take this opportunity to try and bring some of the strands of my work together, and bring important people in my life together, in this kōrero. This perhaps is one of my most challenging lectures, not because I have been named a professor, but because this occasion has brought together an audience that includes scholars, researchers, activists, students, leaders, whānau, aunties, uncles, friends, tamariki and mokopuna. Therefore, I enlist the pedagogical tool of our ancestors, pūrākau, to engage us emotionally, spiritually and intellectually in the kōrero today.

Indigenous Storywork and Pūrākau

This is the strand of my work that took Eruera (my husband) and I to the University of British Columbia in Vancouver last week. In the Long House, on the traditional ancestral and unceded land of the Musqueam Nation, we launched our co-edited book with Emeritus Professor Jo-ann Archibald (also known as Q'um Q'um Xiiem) and Dr Jason De Santolo (Garrwa and Barunggam).

The book, entitled *Decolonizing Research: Indigenous storywork as methodology* (Archibald, Lee-Morgan, & De Santolo, 2019), features fourteen chapters by Indigenous scholars, community researchers and activists across our countries using our respective storytelling traditions, or what Jo-ann Archibald has termed 'Indigenous storywork'. The emphasis on 'work' calls to attention the deep knowledge systems that De Santolo (2019) refers to as 'Indigenous knowledge pathways' back to the memories of our worlds. It is work, because these stories are purposefully crafted carriers of wisdom that require conscious and considered critique to access the extensive levels of knowledge with which they are imbued. Jo-ann Archibald constantly reminds us that, in order to engage in storywork, first you have to be story-ready. Indigenous storywork does not just require story-talk, but the ability to story-listen, to story-learn and to story-teach. Therefore, readiness is an important part of the storywork and pūrākau process, a state that has many shades depending on the preparation required.

As part of my story-ready journey, in my doctoral work – supervised by Emeritus Professor Kuini Jenkins, Professor Alison Jones and Professor Leonie Pihama – I was able to develop pūrākau as a Kaupapa Māori methodology. Heavily influenced by decolonising methodologies (Smith, 2012), I argued that pūrākau should be repositioned from the mainstream discourse of 'myths and legends' to canons of cultural knowledge that are inherently pedagogical and authentic, and are story-markers of identity. Reframing pūrākau in this way emphasises the pedagogy, provocation and politics implicit in our stories.

By its very assertion, Indigenous storywork is political. Pūrākau are a counter narrative to the dominant and colonising discourses that racialise us, that stereotype us and homogenise us, that constrain us to narrow understandings of our ancestors, our histories, our worlds and peoples. Indigenous storywork shifts the power dynamic so we can not only tell our stories, but insist on the centrality of our values, our knowledge and our worldviews. As such, our stories emphasise our cultural experiences, dilemmas, solutions and innovations. Pūrākau permeate Māori epistemological and ontological constructs of our past, present and future worlds.

Te Tokaroa

This pūrākau, like many traditional pūrākau, is embedded in the place names of the land where we currently live, Te Rangimatarau (Point Chevalier, Auckland), which is an area of significance shared by many tribal groups in Tāmaki Makaurau. Looking out to the north, from the point of the peninsula, you can see Te Tokaroa, also known as Te Ara Whakapekapeka a Ruarangi, but commonly referred to today as Meola Reef. Formed by flowing lava tens of thousands of years ago, the reef stretches two kilometres towards the north. I share this abridged local version here to exemplify the value of pūrākau, the way in which pūrākau can be engaged as an accessible, everyday meaning-making and memory-making whānau activity, and to signal the importance of readiness.

> Patupaiarehe, fairy people, lived in the darkness of the Waitākere bush. One night, on the shores of the Waitematā Harbour, two opposing groups were doing battle. The weaker ones tried to escape by building a stone causeway. They laboured on, unaware of the rising sun. The tree limbs sticking out of the lava of the reef Te Tokaroa are said to be the bones of the patupaiarehe fairy people, petrified by the sun.[1]

As a whānau, we regularly walk in the park close to where we live, and the carving that features this pūrākau frames the vista of Te Tokaroa. Usually we read the story, take a fleeting look at the reef and keep walking. On this day, we returned home and recounted the pūrākau in our own words and took some time out to talk together about what this pūrākau teaches us.

Waioro, ten years old at the time, told us that this pūrākau teaches us "to remember". He said thoughtfully, thinking about the length of the reef, 'This pūrākau tells us that you need to have commitment to "build a bridge" and to "hide from the sun".' With a twinkle in his eye, he proclaimed, "so you don't get caught in sun jail!" Finally, he said (as if he was speaking to himself), "You learn not to do that again."

Eruera and I looked at each other in awe and admiration – we had underestimated the ways in which our son could connect with this pūrākau so quickly. 'Remembering' is at the heart of our decolonising endeavour, and key to growing up as Māori today. His reference to the dangers of the sun are heard in his daily school mantra, "No hat, no play, no fun today" – the sun is searing hot and to be avoided lest you be trapped in 'sun jail' and burnt.

When I reflected on the pūrākau, it immediately made me think about the poor patupaiarehe, who were working so hard that they were completely unaware of the brightness and heat of the sun. To me, it was a warning, to not be so engrossed in my work that I'm oblivious to what is going on around me – to the rhythms of the whānau and the kāinga, to the needs, the issues, the excitement and the joy of the children that are passing me by. Ultimately, should I not heed the cautionary messages to be self-aware and take self-care, at my own peril, I too might shrivel up!

On the other hand, Eruera had a completely different interpretation of the pūrākau. Te Tokaroa, to him, represented unfinished business. The reef was a call to keep pushing forward, to complete the 'bridge'. We had a lengthy discussion about where the bridge might lead; nevertheless, he felt invigorated by the pūrākau, and affirmed he was heading in the right direction.

These three brief whānau responses to the pūrākau serve to illustrate the pedagogy inherent in the stories of our tūpuna, etched into our cultural landscape for those who are ready to receive them. Our momentary engagements are only a few of hundreds of learnings that could be gleaned from this pūrākau, especially if rich in cultural detail that draws on our own tribal knowledge systems and worldviews. Our whānau story-talking

---

[1] This version is carved on a monument by Tim Codyre (2009) that overlooks Te Tokaroa. According to kaumātua Haare Williams, Ruarangi was the rangatira of the patupaiarehe, who were known to have fair skin and red hair, hence the need to be shaded from the sun. Ruarangi and the patupaiarehe resided in the ngahere in Waitākere (personal communication, 18 January 2021).

and story-listening with pūrākau also shows that, while they are ancient, they are not isolated from our contemporary realities. Rather, they always exist in context and have the ability to extend their reach to all areas of our lives.

Who Would Do That?

Alongside our discussion about the pūrākau of Te Tokaroa, we showed the children a picture we took the previous year when affronted by portable wharepaku (toilets) pushed up against the carved tupuna portraying the pūrākau (see Figure 1). The local council was hosting a public festival at the park and had located extra ablutions to service the hundreds of people gathering on the day.

When we showed the photo to our second daughter, Kerera (thirteen years old), she asked incredulously, "Who would do that?" This question acted as the catalyst to think

Figure 1: Wharepaku pushed up against the carving of Te Tokaroa; Coyle Park Point Chevalier.

about pūrākau more broadly, to take the analysis to the next level and keep learning. For many of us, the picture of the wharepaku will not be a surprise – in fact, it is almost a commonplace occurrence. The photo symbolises the everyday desecration of the value of Māori language, Māori culture, Māori knowledge, Māori beliefs and Māori people.

My answer to Kerera was swift, and carried me through time. Who would do that? Unfortunately, I responded, the same people who thought it was okay to strap my kuia, Mata Wihongi (Ngāpuhi), and her generation for speaking Māori. She was a new entrant speaking her first language at Kaikohe Native School, established in 1882 on the land that her father gifted in the name of 'education'. The next generation of teachers in the 1950s thought it was okay to determine that my dad, my uncles and aunties should only be allowed to enter the non-academic subject classes at high school, because they were Māori.

It was the same thinking, I told her, that justified the 720-hectare sewage and oxidation treatment plant that was put in the Manukau Harbour in 1960, adjacent to our papakāinga at Ihumātao, where Makaurau marae is located – the place where my nana, Kahukahu Wehi (Ngāti Mahuta, Ngāti Te Ahiwaru, Ngāti Te Wehi, Ngāti Reko), grew up. The sewage polluted the waters, including our Oruarangi Stream, where my dad used to swim and collect kaimoana. Te Manukanuka o Hoturoa (Manukau Harbour) was described as "clear wide waters and white sand ... a bountiful source of seafood and was renowned for pipi and mullet – the stream led to oyster and scallop beds on the reefs around Puketutu island" (Waitangi Tribunal, 1985, pp. 24–25).

Who would do that? Multinational corporates like Fletcher Building, who naively proposed a housing development on Ōtuataua Stonefields (part of our papakāinga) at Ihumātao, one of our last remaining ancestral landscapes rich with significant cultural and archaeological heritage. It is the same people and the same racist logic that originally denied access to our history in schools by refusing to include the New Zealand Wars in the national curriculum (Price, 2016). Despite the petition lodged at Parliament by Leah Bell, aged sixteen, and Waimarama Anderson, aged seventeen, from Ōtorohanga College, the Ministry of Education (at the time) thought that such a change would "erode the autonomy" (Price, 2016) of school boards to make their own programmes and change the function of the curriculum. I could go on, but you get the gist, and I hope if you remember nothing else about my professorial lecture today you remember the picture of the wharepaku, and the question that Kerera has asked.

To me, the photo is a stark reminder of the modern-day wrath of colonisation that is inflicted on Māori in multi-layered ways. The daily racist microaggressions in our schools, in our workplaces, in our communities are still so commonplace they usually go unnoticed. When challenged, they are often refuted with comments like, "You are being too sensitive", "You are taking it the wrong way", "They didn't really mean it like that". The wharepaku also symbolises the buoyancy of institutional racism that sees the continued disproportionate failure of Māori in education (Education Counts, 2020),[2] the disproportionate rates of Māori incarceration[3] (Department of Corrections, 2020), the highest rate of homelessness in the world (Lee-Morgan, Hoskins, Te Nana, Rua, & Knox, 2019) and one of the most disturbing government practices – the uplifting of hundreds of Māori babies from whānau, as journalist Melanie Reid says, "as if they were repossessing a TV" (in Brettkelly & Donovan, 2020). The same racist ideologies of lies and falsehoods were used to justify the colonisation of Indigenous People (Jackson, 2019). It is racist logic that underpins the ideologies of white supremacy, which saw our Muslim community terrorised by a profoundly disturbing level of violence in March 2019 – purposefully executed on Muslim men, women and children in a state of prayer, while in the sanctity of the mosque in Christchurch.

---

[2] In 2019, the proportion of school leavers attaining at least NCEA Level 2 or equivalent by ethnicity was Asian 89.7 percent, European/Pākehā 82.0 percent, Pacific 73.7 percent and Māori 64.7 percent (Education Counts, 2020).

[3] For example, although Māori make up only 12.5 percent of the general population, 42 percent of all criminal apprehensions involve a person identifying as Māori, as do 50 percent of all persons in prison. For Māori women, it is even worse – we comprise around 63 percent of the female prison population (*Stuff*, 2018).

In all the Kaupapa Māori research work I've been involved in, whether it be in education, te reo Māori, health or housing, I know that if we are going to have an impact on theory, methodology, policy or practices, we have to embark on a process of decolonisation and begin to address ideologies such as race, gender and class. We must recognise and understand the way in which social structures and systems are encrypted with social and institutional racism, the inequitable distribution of power and resources that privileges normative frames of whiteness over others. We must 'remember', and commit to collectively 'building the bridge' and reconnecting.

Connectedness

I titled my inaugural professorial address 'Tūī, tūī, tuituia: Research that keeps us connected', because part of the role of the Kaupapa Māori teacher, researcher, leader, community worker, activist, social worker, council worker, mother, father – wherever you are – is decolonisation and the assertion of our tino rangatiratanga, our sovereignty. Decolonisation and tino rangatiratanga rest on learning, understanding, practising, living our cultural values, our worldviews, our stories. These things are not easy to achieve. There are 'sun traps' that our Kaupapa Māori and Indigenous leaders talk about, that include the seduction of a title or accolade, whether it be a government, a corporate, an iwi or a tertiary appointment, or appointment to the position of professor. There is a danger of becoming complacent, of becoming complicit, without the critical edge or capacity to continue to make a difference for our people. As Graham Smith (1997) wrote many years ago, we must not fall prey to the ivory tower syndrome.

One of the ways we must sustain ourselves is keeping connected. Distinguished Professor Larissa Behrendt (Eualeyai/Kamillaroi) (2019) urges, "Our sovereignty is strongest when we are strongest in ourselves. We are strongest in ourselves when we are with each other" (p. 186). Keeping connected to who you are as a whānau, hapū, iwi, marae remains a challenge, especially in the context of neoliberal ideologies that value individualism and 'freedom of choice'. I feel fortunate and want to acknowledge both my Māori and Chinese whānau. Two distinct groups, one Indigenous and the other a shunned ethnic minority, that came together in the margins of society. Both groups and sides of the family endured the hardships of colonisation and racism, but have also always exemplified resilience, courage and strength. My connections to our tūpuna are kept alive in the shared stories about my grandparents, uncles and aunties that continue to inform me about who I am, and who they wanted us to be in our whānau.

Keeping connected to marae, iwi and community – thank you my whanaunga at Te Puea Memorial marae who have enabled me to reconnect to whānau and the kaupapa through our research project 'Te Manaaki o te Marae',[4] and Makaurau marae for the pending research project with Ihumātao that will strengthen my connections to whānau and kaupapa of the whenua.[5] Finally, to my little family, my husband Eruera, our seven children and mokopuna, who connect me to everyday realities of being mother and a naanaa, and the challenges facing Māori as a rangatahi in our rapidly changing world – E kore e mutu te puna o te aroha ki a koutou.

---

[4] This Kaupapa Māori research project is funded by the National Science Challenge and led by the Ngā Wai a Te Tūī research team. This project examines the Kaupapa Māori work of Te Puea Memorial marae with vulnerable whānau, to investigate how marae can be an integral part of urban housing solutions. See Lee-Morgan et al. (2019).

[5] This Kaupapa Māori research project (2019–2022) is funded by Endeavor and investigates the evolution of marae, and focuses on distinctive challenges and opportunities arising within Māori communities. MOKO provides an opportunity to undertake research by, for and with marae (Makaurau marae, Manurewa marae, Papakura marae, Papatūānuku Kōkiri marae, Mataatua marae) and communities that will contribute to the strategic and collective development of kāinga ora for whānau and community wellbeing in South Auckland, and all New Zealand.

I want to close by telling you that I feel optimistic about the future together. This week Waioro was finishing his own research project, and his research question gives me great hope. Hope for decolonisation, hope for sovereignty, hope that the next generation will keep building the bridge. As he looks deeply at the world around him, the way our ancestors did, he asks: "Me pēwhea au e aroha ki te marama? How do I love the moon?"

Tūī, tūī, tuituia ki te ao mārama.

Postscript: Pūrākau for Te Pā Harakeke

I include a part of my professorial address delivered nearly two years ago as a chapter in this publication not only because of the focus on pūrākau but because it is an example of pūrākau in practice in our whānau. In relation to Te Pā Harakeke, I believe pūrākau are at the heart of growing critical, compassionate and connected children.

In the whānau, pūrākau promote a cultural connectedness in their very engagement. The act of storytelling and story-listening requires a story-space that is based on trust, confidence and quality of relationships. This is a special space within the whānau that must be nurtured and protected. Confronted by the bling and speed of technology, we can easily consume, and become consumed by, the technological devices that constantly surround us. In the fast-paced context of this world, story-time is sometimes seen as less appealing and often challenging for parents, grandparents and caregivers. However, in an effort to become 'story-ready', it's important to recognise and demarcate some 'story-space' that will sometimes be spontaneous, or planned and purposeful. While this space will be filled, at times, with playful and joyful stories, there are also the serious and cautionary stories – each creating new spaces of trust, confidence, connectedness and belonging. Despite the nature of the pūrākau itself, this story-space in a whānau develops a reverence that is marked by listening, as Archibald et al. (2019) say, with heart, mind and spirit. In this sense, we should attempt to keep some story-time and story-space sacrosanct, lest the cultural, pedagogical and spiritual value of our stories, and in turn our own ways of raising our tamariki and mokopuna, be diminished. Our pūrākau also live within our children and mokopuna, waiting for the story-space to be created, nurtured, expressed and heard.

Tūī, tūī, tuituia. Tuia tātou e piri tahi nei ki ngā akoranga a ngā tūpuna kia ora ai te pā harakeke mō ake tonu atu. Haumi ē, hui ē. Tāiki ē!

References

ARCHIBALD, J., LEE-MORGAN, J., & DE SANTOLO, J. (EDS.). (2019). *Decolonizing research: Indigenous storywork as methodology.* (Forthcoming). London, England: Zed Books.

BEHRENDT, L. (2019). Indigenous storytelling: Decolonizing institutions and assertive self- determination: Implications for legal practice. In J. Archibald, J. Lee-Morgan & J. De Santolo (Eds.). (2020). *Decolonizing research: Indigenous storywork as methodology* (pp. 175–186). (Forthcoming). London, England: Zed Books.

BRETTKELLY, S., & DONOVAN, E. (2019). NZ's own stolen generation. Radio New Zealand. Retrieved from https://www.rnz.co.nz/programmes/the-detail/story/2018699080/nz-s-own-stolen-generation

DEPARTMENT OF CORRECTIONS NEW ZEALAND. (2020). Prison facts and statistics – September 2020. Retrieved from https://www.corrections.govt.nz/resources/statistics/quarterly_prison_statistics/prison_stats_s eptember_2020

EDUCATION COUNTS. (2020). *School leavers with NCEA Level 2 or above.* Wellington, New Zealand: Ministry of Education.

JACKSON, M. (2018). In the end "the hope of decolonisation". In: E. McKinley & L. Smith (Eds.), *Handbook of Indigenous education.* Singapore: Springer. https://doi.org/10.1007/978-981-10-1839-8_59-1

LEE-MORGAN, J., HOSKINS, R., TE NANA, R., RUA, M., & KNOX, W. (2019). *Ahakoa te aha, mahingaia te mahi: In service to homeless whānau in Tāmaki Makaurau.* Auckland, New Zealand: Ngā Wai a te Tūī Press, Unitec.

PRICE, R. (2016, MARCH 30). Ministry of Education refuses to include New Zealand Land Wars in curriculum. *Stuff.* Retrieved from https://www.stuff.co.nz/national/politics/78386446/ministry-of-education-refuse-to-include-new-zealand-land-wars-in-curriculum

SMITH, G. H. (1997). *The development of Kaupapa Māori: Theory and Praxis* (PhD thesis). University of Auckland, Auckland, New Zealand. Retrieved from https://researchspace.auckland.ac.nz/handle/2292/623

SMITH, L. T. (2012). *Decolonizing methodologies: Research and indigenous peoples* (2nd ed). London, England: Zed Books.

STUFF. (2018). Crime and punishment. Retrieved from https://interactives.stuff.co.nz/2018/05/prisons/crime.html#/

WAITANGI TRIBUNAL. (1985). *Manukau Report: Report of the Waitangi Tribunal on the Manukau Claim.* Wellington, New Zealand: The Government Printer. Retrieved from https://forms.justice.govt.nz/search/Documents/WT/wt_DOC_68495207/The%20Manukau% 20Report%201985.pdf

Mātauranga-ā-Whānau: Intergenerational Knowledge Transmission through Whānau Pūrākau

Marjorie Beverland

CHAPTER 9

Introduction

As seen in Māori worldviews of Te Pā Harakeke, the whānau (extended family) is considered to be collectively responsible for the wellbeing of its members, with the grandparent generation being essential to the protection and education of tamariki (children) and mokopuna (grandchildren) (Pihama & Cameron, 2012). Pohatu's (2015) article on mātauranga-ā-whānau supports the affirmation of whānau knowledge as critical and his analysis of the politics and discourse of decolonising our approaches to intergenerational knowledge transmission is crucial when working with Māori.

Mātauranga-ā-whānau centres knowledge and practices that are embedded within whānau and focuses on ways of knowing and being that are transmitted intergenerationally. Drawing upon my whānau knowledge, experiences and practices, through pūrākau, this chapter discusses the development of a distinctively Māori approach that centres knowledge and practices embedded within whānau. To explain mātauranga-ā-whānau I will discuss briefly the nature of mātauranga Māori (Māori knowledge), whānau and Kaupapa Māori as it relates to relationships and the transmission of knowledge. This will be followed by a sharing of pūrākau from my own whānau, to highlight the mātauranga that stem from each of the pūrākau and which have guided me in the identification of key principles that form what I refer to as the Mātauranga-ā-Whānau framework.

Mātauranga Māori

Mātauranga Māori is the embodied knowledge, understanding, wisdom and practices that we live as Māori. The role of ancestral knowledge and practices has been well documented as central to mātauranga Māori, Kaupapa Māori and Indigenous methodologies (Mead, 2003; Nepe, 1991; Pohatu, 1995; Smith, 1997; Smith, 1999). The centrality of our grandparent generations in the transmission of mātauranga Māori is also critical to the revitalisation and regeneration of our language and cultural ways of being (Pere, 1994; Pohatu, 2015). Mātauranga-ā-whānau is grounded upon Māori knowledge forms that are handed down through generations and have been sustained for current and future generations. Learning from our Nana is central to this discussion as she holds and unlocks knowledge and practices from the generations before her.

Whatarangi Winiata (2020) emphasises that mātauranga Māori is "a body of knowledge that seeks to explain phenomena by drawing upon concepts handed down from one generation of Māori to another" (p. 1). Furthermore, he highlights the ways in which the process of intergenerational transmission contributes to both the maintenance and growth of mātauranga Māori:

Accordingly, mātauranga Māori has no beginning and has no end. It is constantly being enhanced and refined. Each passing generation of Māori make their own contribution to mātauranga Māori. The theory or collection of theories, with associated values and practices, has accumulated mai i te ao Māori/from Māori beginnings and will continue to accumulate providing the whakapapa of mātauranga Māori is not broken (Winiata, 2020, p. 1).

Hirini Moko Mead (2003) also emphasises the expansiveness of mātauranga Māori and the contribution made to the growth of Māori knowledge by each generation:

> The term 'mātauranga Māori' encompasses all branches of Māori knowledge, past, present and still developing. It is like a super subject because it includes a whole range of subjects that are familiar in our world today, such as philosophy, astronomy, mathematics, language, history, education and so on. And it will include subjects we have not yet heard about. Mātauranga Māori has no ending: it will continue to grow for generations to come (pp. 320–21).

Both Whatarangi Winiata and Hirini Mead are highlighting that each generation needs to contribute to the changing nature of mātauranga and it is the upcoming generation's obligation and responsibility to ensure its growth. The earlier work of Nepe (1991) adds to such understandings and further highlights that we have a "systematic organisation of beliefs, experiences, understandings and interpretations of the interactions of Māori people upon Māori people, and Māori people upon their world" (p. 4).

What is clear here is that to be able to grow mātauranga, contributions must be made at every level, whether they are big or small, for example, through theory, practices, sharing pūrākau and language. My Nana knows this inherently and goes about the business of teaching us and helping us to learn through a Māori lens daily by transmitting important knowledge to us, from rongoā to karakia, raising and caring for children, te reo and pōwhiri, dressing and cleaning and thinking and caring. Mātauranga that is transmitted intergenerationally is highly valued and evolving, and includes Māori being able to explain their world through experiences within whānau.

Whānau

Whānau in this context refers to a Māori model of extended family that is inclusive of at least three or four generations and that stretches across multiple layers of relationships that are grounded within whakapapa (Māori cultural genealogical template). Whānau refers to both extended family and to giving birth. As such, it is both a concept and a practice that affirms intergenerational and intragenerational relationships. For Māori, whānau is a source of knowing and experiences should be drawn from this source of "potentiated power" (Pohatu, 2015, p. 39) to produce frameworks. Pohatu (2015) states:

> When asking the question, "where is the first place that we would go to, to draw experience of mātauranga from?", this small piece proposes that whānau is an obvious 'first place' to turn to. It proposes that for Māori, whānau is an acknowledged rich source of applied knowing and experience to draw from, where there is a willingness to invite it as a highly valued companion (hoa haere) in kaupapa, no matter what it is, where we are and who we are with (p. 32).

This highlights that whānau wisdom offers us well-tried ways of working and that this knowing can be invited into spaces as signposts in any kaupapa. My whānau knowing is invited into my spaces, moving it from the margins to assume its position "in guiding us at all levels of our lives ... so that deep discussion can be invited, reflected upon, endorsed by cultural thought" (Pohatu, 2015, p. 42). The affirmation of whānau as key to Māori approaches is highlighted by the inclusion of whānau as a key principle in Kaupapa Māori theory. Kaupapa Māori gave some urgency to revitalising, validating and inviting intergenerational knowledge into the research space in the 1990s, and continues to do so today (Nepe, 1991; Smith, 1997; Smith, 1999). To place this in context, a brief overview of Kaupapa Māori is now provided.

Kaupapa Māori

Kaupapa Māori is a Māori philosophical foundation that has underpinned the development of the approach discussed in this chapter. Kaupapa Māori requires Māori to have an awareness of, and ground processes and methods upon, te reo and tikanga (Smith, 1998). In its broadest sense Kaupapa Māori refers to Māori knowledge and Māori ways of knowing and doing. Smith (1997) highlights that a Kaupapa Māori foundation for theory and research provides a platform for (i) the validation and legitimation of te reo and tikanga Māori; (ii) the prioritisation of the revitalisation of te reo and tikanga; and (iii) the assertion of self-determination and autonomy for Māori.

Much of the early work in Kaupapa Māori theory and methodology emerged from a direct challenge by Māori to the mainstream Pākehā education system and the assimilation policies and approaches upon which it is based. Education is a particular site of struggle, controlled and determined by dominant interest groups (Smith, 1997). The development of colonial schooling and education systems in Aotearoa has been central to the marginalisation of Māori language, culture and knowledge systems (Simon, 1998; Simon & Smith, 2001). A key component of that was a deliberate process of individualisation within education, to align with wider colonial systems that privileged a nuclear family construct over the collective relationships that were embedded in Māori societal structures of whānau, hapū and iwi (Pihama & Cameron, 2012).

Most specifically, Kaupapa Māori educational sites such as Te Kōhanga Reo, Kura Kaupapa Māori, Wharekura and Whare Wānanga have been central to the design and implementation within the education sector of a Māori-designed response to the erosion of Māori language, knowledge and culture (Hohepa, 1990; Royal-Tangaere, 1997). Our ancestors had clearly defined spaces and pedagogical approaches to learning and teaching, with multiple sites, both formal and informal (Hohepa, 1999; Nepe, 1991; Pere, 1994; Royal-Tangaere, 1997).

Schooling was not the only colonial structure that intentionally contributed to the breakdown of the fabric of Māori society. The breakdown of traditional Māori structures in terms of culture and language through colonisation is described by O'Regan (2006) as a context in which Māori were "systematically alienated from their homelands and livelihoods" (p. 157). The impact of this on whānau and intergenerational knowledge transmission has been significant and for many whānau highly destructive (Durie, 2001).

This included the whānau as the initial site of learning in a context that was inclusive of multiple generations and where the grandparent generation was most critical in the transmission of all aspects of mātauranga (Pere, 1994).

When carried out with integrity, as is its responsibility, Kaupapa Māori is both emancipatory and empowering (Walker, Eketone, & Gibbs, 2006). Furthermore, Kaupapa Māori challenges us to centre te reo, tikanga and mātauranga Māori. In doing so, it not only upholds Māori ways of being and giving full recognition from start to end of Māori cultural values and systems; it also challenges the ways in which knowledge and understanding are constructed in dominant colonising frameworks (Walker et al., 2006). As a culturally defined framework, Kaupapa Māori provides ways in which to organise ideas, views and experiences that are consistent and have integrity (Cooper, 2012). Pohatu (2015) highlights the means by which Māori can engage with integrity through intentional, deliberate and respectful behaviour. He also highlights, through the concept of 'āta', that within the broader discussion of Kaupapa Māori we must be cognisant of the existence of a range of ways that are informed by our own experiences and understandings, grounded upon our whānau, hapū and iwi ways of being.

To construct a Kaupapa Māori framework grounded within whānau, and to build on knowledge transmission within whānau, the recalling and retelling of pūrākau is a crucial component. Pūrākau, a form of Māori narrative, will be shared to illustrate how knowledge is transmitted and thought through. The five pūrākau shared in this chapter will show the pathway to the methodological signposts that form the Mātauranga-ā-Whānau framework.

Mātauranga-ā-Whānau

This discussion is about understanding and making sense of experience, ways of knowing and ways of being that work for Māori. Intergenerational transmission of knowledge through pūrākau is key to mātauranga-ā-whānau. Pohatu (2015) agrees that cultural thought and cultural patterns are readily recognisable through pūrākau. According to Lee (2015), pūrākau have the "potential to unlock philosophical thought, epistemological constructs, cultural codes, and worldviews that are fundamental to our identity as Māori" (p. 98). In this section, the five pūrākau are shared, then a short comment on the theory via a mātauranga-ā-whānau lens follows and finally the key signposts from each of the pūrākau are identified. These signposts are briefly expanded on further. These and other pūrākau have elucidated the key principles and practices that have formed the Mātauranga-ā-Whānau framework shown in Figure 1.

Pūrākau

Nana, my maternal grandmother, is the ultimate philosopher. She was raised among her iwi in Ngāti Maniapoto (King Country, Aotearoa New Zealand) and has spent most of her adult life living in the Waikato region of Aotearoa New Zealand. My Nana is a deep thinker and theorist. She navigates various roles as an agreed leader of our whānau and has provided deep learnings for me as a Māori woman. Her first language is te reo Māori, though she is more than proficient in English. Nana does not change the way she moves and engages with the world, regardless of whether the context is Māori or non-Māori. The way that she engages in her world is naturally occurring, is logical to her and is guided by her lifelong learning in te ao Māori. Further, tikanga underpins her engagement, which includes in part the values and principles of manaakitanga, aroha, ngā ture, tapu and whakapono.

Several pūrākau are now shared to show Nana's engagement and the knowledge transmitted to us in our lives so far. These pūrākau could be teased out and expanded further and for many different contexts. The examples given here are not exhaustive or exclusive.

Pūrākau 1 – Whānau Hui. My upbringing was informed by Māori principles, Māori ways of being and Māori rationales. These areas were particularly noticeable on the marae, in the home or at specific events like tangihanga (funerals). Another of these forums was the whānau hui or family gathering. In my whānau, the hui was a forum specifically used for dealing with any tensions or conflict inherent in the family. There were several uncles who could facilitate the hui, but they would seek advice and guidance from Nana. Children were privy to the tensions within our hui but, importantly, they were also privy to the way that tensions were sorted through and the resolutions that were sought. The hui would start in much the same way every time we met. First, karakia (prayer) by our Nana, then a mihi (informal greeting) regarding the reason we were all there, then each person (including children) would be given the opportunity to speak, moving in the direction of the next person to the left. Finally, after everyone in the family had spoken and resolutions had been obtained, a karakia and mihi to end the hui would be carried out before proceeding to share a meal. Inevitably, however, the hui would take a considerable amount of time, sometimes crossing into two days. During the hui, voices would be raised, comments would be made, crying was inevitable and emotions ran high. In these moments, Nana often used cultural skills and techniques to guide the hui, while gently reminding the family about behaviour and engaging respectfully with one another. This is where I first heard 'āta phrases'. Nana would stand and in te reo Māori discuss the family's ability to āta whakaaro – or think clearly and think deliberately. She would use the term āta korero – the ability to watch tone, speak with clarity and speak in a manner that conveyed respect. In these moments, the atmosphere calmed and the reflection this prompted was evident (Lipsham, 2012, 2016).

Mātauranga-ā-whānau: Hui can be translated to mean a gathering or meeting. Hui can be explained as qualitative in nature and has some similarities with a qualitative approach including studying personal constructs, oral histories and human interaction. However, the inclusion of hui within kaupapa means ensuring tikanga Māori (Māori protocols) are part of the process (Tomlins-Jahnke, 1996). Hui include tikanga or protocols such as karakia (acknowledging sources), whanaungatanga (getting to know one another), sharing intention or kaupapa (reason/topic for hui), addressing the kaupapa in hui, closing rituals and sharing food (Bateman & Berryman, 2008; Salmond, 1975). These processes are key to a successful hui and if one cannot carry out these processes oneself, then a companion can be asked to contribute their time to make sure the hui is carried out with integrity. Hui are important because they carry with them an understanding that in a Māori context a high value is placed on manaaki, whakapapa, aroha, ensuring personal mana and protecting the mauri and wairua within relationships (Mead, 2003). When engaging the signpost of hui, we must know the appropriate tikanga associated with hui. This includes being able to enter, engage with and exit the hui accordingly.

Mātauranga principles: Tikanga, Aro, Hui, Wānanga.

Pūrākau 2 – Raising Mokopuna. Nana shared the responsibility of raising her mokopuna. During my early childhood, at a time when neither of my parents had the capacity to raise us, my eldest brother and I lived with Nana, our middle brother whāngai to my mum's eldest sister, our sister was adopted to our mum's cousin at birth and our youngest brother lived with my mum's youngest sister. Although there came a time when we were returned to our parents during our teenage years, my Nana had already played a significant role in my life, and she still does today at ninety years of age. Nana was raised by different kuia and koroua during her childhood. Sharing the responsibility of raising grandchildren is a normal practice in te ao Māori and being in our grandmother's care as children was an enriching and empowering part of our lives. Why we were in the care of whānau was not focused on and was left for others to sort through.

Mātauranga-ā-whānau: A key epistemological belief within this pūrākau is that the whole whānau is involved in the raising of a child and that whānau operate as a collective. This is true for many other contexts, including engaging in research. As a Māori researcher, for example, you should expect to learn about the whakapapa of the whānau and my experience has been that whānau want to be engaged in kaupapa. My whānau have played a pivotal part in my doctoral journey, from my Nana to my eldest brother, cousins, my son and my niece. Before choosing the topic for my doctoral research I met with Nana to ask her permission – it was at that point that whānau members became involved. Nana wanted my eldest brother and older cousin involved, as she trusted them in terms of taking care of and keeping our whakapapa information safe. I chose another cousin to be involved, as she is a fluent speaker of te reo and would be able to talk with Nana more effectively. My son and my niece were chosen as first cousins to enable them to learn about research and be part of the intergenerational transmission of knowledge. What I know from my experience of having my whole whānau involved is that whakapapa is a central principle and cannot be underestimated. Nana's decision to include others in this research is underpinned by her wanting everyone to be part of a learning and teaching experience to enable mātauranga to be transmitted.

Mātauranga principles: Ako, Whanaungatanga, Tikanga.

Pūrākau 3 – Koha. When I was in Nana's care as a child, I would be allowed to go and stay with my cousins during the holidays. Nana would hand me a $20 note and would say, "Give this to Aunty for letting you stay with her, make sure you work while you are there and do what you are asked." This may not seem like much to the untrained eye; however,

Nana was teaching me how to treat people in terms of respect, behaviour, reciprocation and being thoughtful to the needs of others. This was not a one-off practice; it happened every time I visited someone else's home. There may have been other underlying factors connected with the money in terms of what Aunty would have needed to take care of me for the week. Twenty dollars was a lot of money in the 1970s; however, this practice was not about the money.

Mātauranga-ā-whānau: The practices here are foundational in our whānau and arguably within te ao Māori. Specifically, the principles of āta mahi (to work diligently), āta whakaako (to deliberately instil knowledge and understanding), āta whakaaro (to give time to thought – to be creative and reflective) and āta whakarongo (consciously listening with all the senses) apply in this example. The āta phrases, designed by Taina Pohatu (2004), were expanded on in my Master's research as ethical principles in my methods section, but they are also methodology (Lipsham, 2012, 2016). Nana did not carry out these actions or teach me about them because it was 'the right thing to do'; she was engaging tikanga. Tikanga underpins an approach grounded in Kaupapa Māori theory. Respect, behaviour, reciprocation and being thoughtful to the needs of others as noted in the pūrākau are koha through a Māori lens and play a crucial part in being able to engage with Māori or Kaupapa Māori. The giving of koha is seen on the marae as part of a formal pōwhiri process and it is common today for the koha to be monetary. However, its primary focus is not about recompense, but mutual obligations and strengthening ties (Durie, 2001). It is common for Māori to koha money, food, labour or time to their communities. The practice of koha for Nana does not just belong at the marae during pōwhiri, or at kaupapa. Tikanga extended into all areas for Nana.

Mātauranga principles: Tikanga, Mātauranga, Ako.

Pūrākau 4 – Karanga. A karanga is a Māori ceremonial call or a welcome call that is carried out in many different contexts, which can include the birth of a child, welcoming people onto a marae or an equivalent event of welcome. My cousins and I asked our Nana about the prospect of learning karanga. She replied by asking us what we thought that meant and that if we wanted to have further discussions on the topic we would need to set a date that suited all of us, and that the meeting would need to be held at our whenua (our ancestral land) in Benneydale. It was understood that the meeting held at our whenua might not include the actual teaching of karanga and that there would be reasons why some would be selected for karanga and others might be appropriate in other roles. She didn't say these words; however, as mokopuna we understood her body language, the tone of her voice and the feelings we had as she talked. We understood these things as a collective, but also as individuals. Interestingly, that initial discussion would start to naturally 'weed out' those who were truly interested and those who were not. Although it was not confirmed, Nana's theory of selection was already in play.

Mātauranga-ā-whānau: Nana's strategy in the karanga pūrākau was to offer up the place in which hui (meetings/gatherings) could take place in order that she might see who was interested in karanga. Underpinning the strategy was the idea that the conversations are held at a place that was appropriate and fitting to the context and study of karanga, rather than carrying out karanga proper. The questions that were part of the continuing conversations regarding karanga are cultural markers. For example, learning karanga is steeped in tikanga and, therefore, if possible, researching at one's marae, a place of importance, or on whenua is important. Learning in wānanga is important. Nana knows this, and her questions were based around this thinking. The questions in the pūrākau lend themselves to analysis, processes, hui, inquiry, conditions, place, space and curiosity.

Mātauranga principles: Tikanga, Mātauranga, Aro, Wā, Wāhi, Hui/Wānanga.

Pūrākau 5 – Tapu. Nana considers Māori knowledge to hold aspects of tapu and treads carefully, especially when teaching aspects of te ao Māori that are part of tikanga. This is partly why the conversation regarding karanga developed as it did. Nana would consider karanga to be a ritual steeped in tapu. I recall a time during my early years of study. I was completing a National Diploma of Social Work many years ago and we were asked to research our whakapapa. I returned to the Waikato to ask Nana, very enthusiastically, about who my tūpuna were and what their names were. I had a pen and paper ready to write the information down. She did share information with me, and I wrote everything down. After the conversation, she asked what I'd do with the paper. "Paper?" I asked. "Yes," she said, "that you wrote our whakapapa on." She was worried that it would be thrown away, ripped up or discarded. To her, the paper represented whakapapa, and therefore people who had passed, and the deep respect she held for them meant she worried about their wellness, as well as mine, if I did anything wrong with the paper. The paper held tapu through her lens as Māori, because tūpuna names were written on it.

Mātauranga-ā-whānau: This is an example of how mātauranga is transmitted, and the multiple layers of learning and teaching. The idea of tapu has evolved over generations and Nana is carrying through her knowing into what we might consider today as a contemporary example. Tapu is explained by Rangimarie Rose Pere (1994) as "spiritual restriction, ceremonial restriction, putting something beyond one's power, placing a quality or condition on a person or on an object or place; but whatever the context its contribution is establishing social control and discipline, and protecting people and property" (p. 39). Whether or not it is a contemporary example, the consequence of tapu is still relevant and cannot be disregarded as superstition. Tapu is a means of social control and protection but it often occurs, and is largely a concern, at a whānau level. Tapu is important when thinking about engaging with others, things, knowledge, places or any context. Just because you are Māori, or your topic and/or participants are Māori, it doesn't necessarily mean you are conducting or engaging in Kaupapa Māori (Rautaki Limited, 2016). To engage in mātauranga-ā-whānau you must be able to think about the safety of whānau and self using a Māori lens. Tapu acknowledges those things that exist outside of being human, as well as very practical considerations, and we need to always be aware of our responsibilities to all things physical and metaphysical. Our role as insiders in research is also important here. We should be reflecting on the concept of tapu to uphold the tino rangatiratanga of whānau and mātauranga or the consequences will not just be on us, but on whānau, our whānau and wider communities.

Mātauranga principles: Wā, Wāhi, Tikanga, Mātauranga.

Pūrākau Concluding Comments

The pūrākau presented here illustrate a range of intergenerational teachings and learnings. They are presented using my lens as a mokopuna, though many of my cousins and siblings may have different interpretations of what has been shared here. What we would all agree on, however, is that Nana has been able to transmit knowledge to us all in a way that is positive, caring and nurturing. Nana is a very humble individual, who is very calm by nature. She knows all her mokopuna intimately, all of their names and their habits, and connects to us in terms of our mauri daily. There are many more pūrākau that have served to provide information, learning and guidance to my siblings, cousins and myself as mokopuna. These pūrākau are examples of how, within our whānau, our Nana has continued the practices of our tūpuna (ancestors) in sharing knowledge by actively engaging us, her mokopuna, both as observers and as active participants within tikanga processes.

Mātauranga-ā-Whānau Framework

From the pūrākau and the identification of mātauranga principles, the following framework provides an overview of the key elements within a mātauranga-ā-whānau approach. In the following section I will give a brief overview of each of the framework key principles that I have identified in the pūrākau above and which are illustrated in Figure 1.

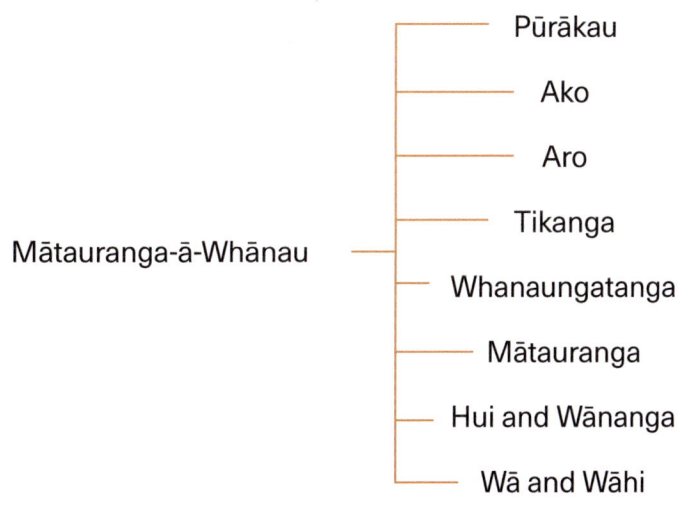

Figure 1: Mātauranga-ā-Whānau Framework.

Pūrākau: A pūrākau approach unlocks philosophical thought, epistemological constructs, cultural codes and worldviews that are fundamental to our identity as Māori (Lee, 2015). Pūrākau is a traditional Māori storytelling approach that engages Māori voice, heart, mind and soul. Pūrākau have inherent power and the potential to create transformation for Māori. Māori value knowledge and value the telling of their own pūrākau for the purposes of sharing, transmission, developing, learning and teaching. Pūrākau is the vehicle through which mātauranga-ā-whānau is transmitted, engaged and understood intergenerationally and provides tamariki and mokopuna with deep understandings and histories of our people.

Ako: Ako is the pedagogy of learning and teaching in the Māori tradition, which includes a range of tikanga. Within te ao Māori it is acknowledged that both the tamaiti (child) and the pakeke (adult) are involved in the teaching and learning; it is a reciprocal relationship (Pere, 1994). This relates to other relationships too, which include the teacher and student, mother and child, father and child, grandparent and grandchild. This includes the consideration of āta and its varying signposts (Pohatu, 2004). Ako is important, as it considers the many relationships and positions within whānau and the place of notions such as mana, tapu and tuakana–teina within the process of sharing knowledge and learning.

Aro: Aro is reflective praxis throughout the process for all involved. As a mokopuna I have come to know that it is important for me to reflect on what is happening around me, and our whānau. This includes the capacity to reflect on both internal whānau relationships and the external influences that impact upon whānau, such as politics, colonisation and wider relationships. Aro indicates that it is important not to restrict time, allowing time to ponder, talk with other whānau, hapū and iwi, and sit with the mātauranga that is presented to us.

Tikanga: Tikanga is the fundamental values, protocols and practices that inform us as Māori. Mead (2003) notes that tikanga provides us with the processes to do things in a way that is tika, or correct. In all forms of relationships, we have learned that one must consider tikanga. Tikanga requires us to be committed to te reo, kawa, karakia, manaaki and ensure that what we do is 'tika'; that is, that we live in ways that are affirming and validating of the cultural relationships, values and practices that are critical to Māori.

Whanaungatanga: Whanaungatanga means to action the process of coming together as a whānau, being relational and connecting to each other's whakapapa. It relates to building relationships, strengthening ties, building rapport and establishing a connection on a physical and spiritual level. Whanaungatanga is at the centre of Mātauranga-ā-Whānau. It is within whanaungatanga that we enact the intergenerational processes of sharing knowledge, learnings, understandings and guidance, and we do that in ways that uplift all our relations and relationships. For our whānau, our Nana is constantly affirming this across three or four generations of her tamariki and mokopuna.

Mātauranga Māori: As discussed briefly above, mātauranga Māori is a broad body of knowledge that seeks to explain phenomena by drawing upon concepts handed down from one generation of Māori to another. Mātauranga "encompasses all branches of Māori knowledge, past, present and still developing ... It is like a super subject" (Mead, 2003, pp. 320–21). Mātauranga is a hoa haere (constant companion) to thinking about pūrākau and drawing on knowledge from the past and present. In my understanding, I am not able to view pūrākau through a Māori lens without first understanding mātauranga.

Hui and Wānanga: Both these processes offer the opportunity, through culturally grounded processes, to gather together to engage with and transmit mātauranga. These processes include traditional welcomes, tributes, ceremony and respect paid to the living and the dead, and to the hosts and food. Both hui and wānanga provide an atmosphere that engages the physical and metaphysical sites of being Māori. Both have survived principally through the activities of the marae, where traditional knowledge is passed down the generations by word of mouth. Both can be explained as qualitative in nature and have some similarities, including studying personal understandings, oral histories and human interaction (Salmond, 1975). As noted above, however, hui and wānanga ensure tikanga Māori is central (Tomlins-Jahnke, 1996).

Wā and Wāhi: My upbringing and the pūrākau in my whānau have taught me that time and place are very important aspects of life. Wā means time, and wāhi, location or place. This signpost takes into consideation when, where and why any kaupapa will take place and must also consider context in a micro and macro way.

Concluding Reflections

The above mātauranga-ā-whānau principles, although only briefly introduced, provide an overview of the way I, as a mokopuna, have come to see the ways in which my Nana has maintained the fundamental practices of her tūpuna to ensure that knowledge is retained and passed down through generations.

The use of Kaupapa Māori has been advocated for by Māori for over thirty years (Smith, 1997; Smith, 1999). This chapter has provided an overview of a methodology not only grounded within mātauranga Māori but within whānau specifically. As Pohatu (2015) states, mātauranga-ā-whānau "is an important site and source where Māori have the daily opportunity to use our own images, sources, people, experiences, words and knowing, locating messages, then interpreting them into our contexts" (p. 37). It is also a critical site in which intergenerational transmission of Māori knowledge takes place. This is widely argued by Māori as being a foundation for wellbeing (Durie, 2001).

Mātauranga-ā-whānau requires us to commit to placing our whānau and broader whakapapa connections at the centre of our ways of being. This aligns with Pohatu (2015), who emphasises that mātauranga-ā-whānau "offers whānau-members opportunities to see and shape its wider usefulness in the many worlds we connect with and move in through our lives" (p. 32). Mātauranga-ā-whānau as an approach brings a focus on Māori knowledge that is learned within whānau intergenerationally and that is affirming and validating of the cultural relationships, values and practices that are critical to Māori.

References

BATEMAN, S., & BERRYMAN, M. (2008). He hui whakatika. Culturally responsive, self determining interventions for restoring harmony. *Kairaranga*, 9(1), 6–12.

COOPER, G. (2012). Kaupapa Māori research: Epistemic wilderness as freedom? *New Zealand Journal of Educational Studies*, 47(2), 64–73.

DURIE, M. (2001). *Mauri Ora: The dynamics of Māori health*. Auckland, New Zealand: Oxford University Press.

HOHEPA, M. K. (1990). *Te Kōhanga Reo hei tikanga ako i te reo Māori: Te Kōhanga Reo as a context for language learning*. Auckland, New Zealand: University of Auckland.

HOHEPA, M. K. (1999). *'Hei Tautoko i te Reo': Māori language regeneration and Whānau bookreading practices* (Doctor of Philosophy thesis). University of Auckland, Auckland, New Zealand.

LEE, J. B. J. (2015). Decolonising Māori narratives: Pūrākau as method. In L. Pihama & S. Tiakiwai (Eds.), *Kaupapa Rangahau: A reader* (pp. 95–104). Hamilton, New Zealand: Te Kotahi Research.

LIPSHAM, M. J. H. (2012). Āta as an innovative method and practice tool in supervision. *Aotearoa New Zealand Social Work Review: Te Komako*, 24(2/3), 31–40.

LIPSHAM, M. J. H. (2016). *He kohinga kōrero ā ngā kaiarataki me ngā kaiako: Student supervision: Experiences and views of kaiarataki and kaiako at Te Wānanga o Aotearoa* (Master of Philosophy thesis). Massey University, Palmerston North, New Zealand. Retrieved from http://ezproxy.massey.ac.nz/login?url=http://search.ebscohost.com/login.aspx?direct=true&db=cat00245a&AN=massey.b3751058&site=eds-live&scope=site/=http://hdl.handle.net/10179/11858

MEAD, H. M. (2003). *Tikanga Māori: Living by Māori values*. Wellington, New Zealand: Huia Publishers.

NEPE, T. (1991). *E Hao nei e tenei Reanga: Te Toi Huarewa Tipuna, Kaupapa Māori, An educational intervention* (Master of Arts thesis). University of Auckland, Auckland, New Zealand.

O'REGAN, H. (2006). State of the reo nation: Māori language learning. In M. Mulholland (Ed.), *State of the Māori nation: Twenty-first century issues in Aotearoa* (pp. 157–168). Auckland, New Zealand: Reed Books.

PERE, R. (1994). *Ako: Concepts and learning in the Māori tradition*. Wellington, New Zealand: Te Kōhanga Reo National Trust Board.

PIHAMA, L., & CAMERON, N. (EDS.). (2012). *Kua tupu te pā harakeke: Developing healthy whānau relationships*. Sante Fe, NM: SAR Press.

POHATU, H. R. (1995). *Whakapapa: A pedagogical structure for the transmission of mātauranga Māori* (Master of Arts thesis). University of Auckland, Auckland, New Zealand.

POHATU, T. (2004). Ata: Growing respectful relationships. *He Pukenga Korero*, 8(1), 1–8.

POHATU, T. (2015). Matauranga-ā-whānau: He Konae Aronui. *Aotearoa New Zealand Social Work*, 27(4), 32–38.

RAUTAKI LIMITED. (2016). Kaupapa Māori analysis. Retrieved from http://rangahau.co.nz/analysis/80/

ROYAL-TANGAERE, A. (1997). *Learning Māori together: Kōhanga reo and home.* Wellington, New Zealand: NZCER.

SALMOND, A. (1975). *Hui: A study of Māori ceremonial gatherings.* Wellington, New Zealand: A. H. & A. W. Reed.

SIMON, J. (1998). *Ngā Kura Māori: The Native Schools system 1867–1969.* Auckland, New Zealand: University of Auckland.

SIMON, J., & SMITH, L. T. (2001). *A civilising mission? Perceptions and representations of the New Zealand Native Schools system.* Auckland, New Zealand: Auckland University Press.

SMITH, G. H. (1997). *The development of kaupapa Māori: Theory and praxis* (Doctor of Philosophy thesis). University of Auckland, Auckland, New Zealand. Retrieved from http://ezproxy.massey.ac.nz/login?url=http://search.ebscohost.com/login.aspx?direct=true&db=cat00245a&AN=massey.b1588237&site=eds-live&scope=site

SMITH, L. T. (1998). *Decolonizing methodologies: Research and indigenous peoples.* Dunedin, New Zealand: University of Otago Press.

SMITH, L. T. (1999). *Decolonizing methodologies: Research and indigenous peoples.* Dunedin, New Zealand: University of Otago Press.

TOMLINS-JAHNKE, H. (1996). *Whaia te iti kahurangi: Contemporary perspectives of Māori women educators* (Master of Education thesis). Massey University: Palmerston North.

WALKER, S., EKETONE, A., & GIBBS, A. (2006). An exploration of kaupapa Māori research, its principles, processes and applications. *International Journal of Social Research Methodology, 9*(4), 331–344. doi:10.1080/13645570600916049

WINIATA, W. (2020). Whakatupu Mātauranga. Retrieved from https://www.wananga.com/te-whakatupu-matauranga.html

Te Kura Mai i Tawhiti: Ancestral Knowledge and Practice in Kaupapa Māori Early Years Provision

Erana Hond-Flavell
Aroaro Tamati
Will Edwards
Ruakere Hond
Gareth J. Treharne
Reremoana Theodore
Richie Poulton
Mihi Ratima

CHAPTER 10

Tātai Whakapapa

Ko Rangi, ko Papa,	*From the supreme parents, Ranginui and Papatūānuku,*
ka puta ko Rongo,	*came Rongomaraeroa,*
ko Tānemahuta, tū ki te rangi e tū iho nei.	*and Tānemahuta, positioning himself heavenwards.*
Whai muri iho ko Tangaroa,	*Following was Tangaroa,*
ko Tūmātauenga, Haumiatiketike,	*Tūmātauenga, Haumiatiketike,*
Tāwhirimātea, i rere ki te rangi, e hai.	*and Tāwhirimātea, who fled to the heavens.*
Tokona rā ko te rangi ki runga ko papa ki raro, ka wehewehea	*The heavens above and land below, separated*
ka puta te whai ao, te ao māramarama.	*so the natural world, the world of light, could be revealed.*
Ka takatū ko te ira tangata	*Humanity then emerged and flourished*
i ngā arearetanga o Papa.	*in every crevice of Papatūānuku*
Hōrapa kau ana ki te matawhenua,	*Spreading out over the face of the earth,*
ki te tuawhenua,	*Populating mainlands*
ki ngā motumotuhanga, e hai.	*and islands.*
Koia rā tēnei e Rongo,	*This is how it should be, Rongo.*
whakairia ake ki runga.	*Uphold and protect it.*
Hohou ko te rongo	*Secure peace and harmony*
ki runga, ki raro,	*above and below,*
ki te hunga tāngata,	*for humankind,*
ki ngā tamariki mokopuna.	*for all descendants.*
Hui ē! Hui ē! Tāiki ē!	*In unity affirm it! In unity secure it!*

Nā Huirangi Waikerepuru (1991)

This karakia, *Tātai Whakapapa*, is frequently recited at Te Kōpae Piripono (TKP), a Kaupapa Māori early years and whānau centre in Taranaki. It speaks of the natural phenomena associated with the creation of the universe and specifically of te ao Māori, alluding to the relationships and ongoing interactions between members of the first whānau, from whom Māori descend. *Tātai Whakapapa* connects our past to the present and to the future. When recited, the karakia reiterates our individual and collective responsibility to ensure that te ao Māori and mātauranga Māori are safeguarded for our children and generations to come. *Tātai Whakapapa* draws on ancestral knowledge and evokes a Taranaki Māori worldview within which the approach of Te Kōpae Piripono to education for tamariki and whānau is located.

Translating Ancestral Knowledge into Practice: The Example of Te Kōpae Piripono

The voices of whānau members of Te Kōpae Piripono, and local Taranaki informants, provide insights into the way ancestral knowledge informs philosophy and practice in Kaupapa Māori early years provision, to enrich the lives of tamariki and their whānau.

Te Kōpae Piripono

Te Kōpae Piripono is a centre for Kaupapa Māori early years provision (KM-EYP) established in Ngāmotu New Plymouth in 1994 as a Taranaki Māori speaker community response to the breakdown of local intergenerational Māori language transmission and the threatened state of the Taranaki dialect and ancestral knowledge (Hond, 2013; Tamati, Hond-Flavell, & Korewha, 2008). At the time, decolonisation wānanga such as Te Pūmaomao (Murphy, 1997) raised community awareness of the processes of colonisation that continued to marginalise Taranaki Māori and undermine the use of Māori language and cultural practices. Amid growing awareness of the colonial antecedents to marginalisation, the community sought ways to reconnect with local culture, reclaim ancestral knowledge/mātauranga Māori, and strengthen local identity and pride. Karakia like *Tātai Whakapapa* provided historical context and inspiration for those seeking to learn from the example of their forebears. Karakia and waiata from critical periods in local histories fed a sense of agency around determining future developments for the region's eight iwi (Waitangi Tribunal, 1996). With growing access to ancestral knowledge and opportunities to learn and practise with others of like mind, people became engaged in the social, cultural and political issues of the time (Hond, 2013).

The early life, education and wellbeing of tamariki in Taranaki was a focus for those of us who were involved in Taranaki-based community action. If lasting change was to come, the founders of TKP believed efforts should target tamariki and mokopuna – the next generations – to re-establish Taranaki reo and tikanga as their base language and culture. Quality kaupapa Māori educational opportunities were understood as a basis for tamariki and whānau wellbeing.

Initially, the goal was to strengthen and improve whānau access to kōhanga reo in the area, including the opening of a new kōhanga reo in 1992 (Te Kōpae Tamariki – Kia Ū te Reo). Kōhanga reo are mokopuna and whānau development centres operated and licensed by Te Kōhanga Reo National Trust (Te Kōhanga Reo National Trust, n.d.). In 1994, TKP opened as a centre for KM-EYP, similar to kōhanga reo but licensed instead as a standalone early childhood centre by the Ministry of Education.

TKP sought to build a whānau-focused early learning centre in which tamariki could grow with Taranaki reo as their first language, mātauranga Māori as their foundational knowledge base, Taranaki region as homeland, a strong local Māori identity and a sense of belonging to whānau. The founders of TKP were confident that such a beginning in life and education, nurtured and actively supported by their parents and whānau, would positively shape the view tamariki held of the world and of themselves, and equip them to lead fulfilled lives as Taranaki Māori. Throughout its more than twenty-five years of operation, TKP has been sustained by its vision of educational success and intergenerational wellbeing for tamariki, whānau and community as Taranaki Māori (Ratima et al., 2019; Tamati et al., 2008). In that time, almost 250 children and their whānau have participated in TKP's tamariki and whānau development programme.

The whānau development emphasis of KM-EYP is a key factor that differentiates the centre from those ECE programmes that focus solely on children's care and learning. The broader focus places an additional financial burden of care on KM-EYP centres like TKP. Still, such an emphasis is crucial. TKP immerses tamariki and whānau in Taranaki reo and tikanga, operationalised in a quality early learning and whānau development programme that emphasises connection with the whānau collective and the wider Taranaki Māori community. In this Kaupapa Māori environment, those involved in TKP believe that tamariki and whanau can flourish as Taranaki Māori. Since 2005, we have undertaken research to obtain evidence of how this can be achieved.

Te Kura Mai i Tawhiti Research Programme

The Ministry of Education recognised TKP as a Centre of Innovation (COI) in 2005, funding a three-year practitioner-led research project exploring whether "whānau development at Te Kōpae Piripono fosters leadership across all levels of the whānau enhancing children's learning and development" (Tamati et al., 2008). The COI research explored TKP's whānau development approach to early education and the impacts of involvement for tamariki and their whānau.

In 2013, Te Pou Tiringa (the governance entity of TKP) partnered with the National Centre for Lifecourse Research (University of Otago, Dunedin) to create our research programme, Te Kura Mai i Tawhiti (TKMT). Building on the findings of the COI study (Tamati et al., 2008), the TKMT research programme seeks to contribute to building an evidence base for what constitutes effective KM-EYP, of which TKP is an example. It examines the effects of KM- EYP on whānau educational success and wellbeing over the life-course (Ratima et al., 2019). The preliminary stages of TKMT have consisted of two projects – He Piki Raukura and Tangi te Kawekaweā.

The first project, He Piki Raukura, has been funded by the Health Research Council Ngā Kanohi Kitea stream and led by Aroaro Tamati (Tamati et al., 2020). It investigates Māori child behavioural constructs. These constructs are tuakiri – a secure local Māori identity; whānauranga – feeling and acting as a member of whānau/community; manawaroa – courage in adversity, persisting despite difficulty and having a positive outlook; and piripono – integrity, commitment and responsibility for a shared kaupapa/purpose (Tamati et al., 2020). These constructs are hypothesised to be associated with positive life outcomes for tamariki Māori (Ratima et al., 2019). As part of the He Piki Raukura project, a study was carried out over the school year of 2016 (Tamati et al., 2020) using tools the TKMT team had developed to measure the Māori child behaviour constructs described previously. Findings from that study and the second project, Tangi te Kawekaweā, are currently being used to design a ten-year prospective study that will examine how KM-EYP may reinforce positive behaviours and characteristics that underpin a secure Māori identity and/or lead to positive lifecourse outcomes (Ratima et al., 2019).

The second project, Tangi te Kawekaweā, funded by the New Zealand Council for Educational Research (Teaching and Learning Research Initiative) and led by Erana Hond-Flavell (Hond-Flavell, Ratima, Tamati, Korewha, & Edwards, 2017) examines whānau engagement in KM-EYP such as Te Kōpae Piripono. This chapter draws primarily on qualitative data collected in the preliminary phase of Tangi te Kawekaweā.

Tangi te Kawekaweā Study

The first phase of the Tangi te Kawekaweā study was conducted in 2015–2016 (Hond-Flavell et al., 2017) and sought to identify and examine the factors associated with whānau engagement in KM-EYP by conducting semi-structured interviews with former parents/caregivers of TKP (n=19), and wānanga discussions with whānau groups (n=5). Expert informants (n=10) were also interviewed to gain insights into the barriers to and facilitators of whānau engagement.

The voices of TKP whānau members interviewed during the Tangi te Kawekaweā study provide real-world insights into the way mātauranga Māori informs practice at this KM-EYP centre, with potential to improve the lives of tamariki and whānau. The Tangi te Kawekaweā dataset was re-analysed inductively for the purpose of writing this chapter, using the six phases of Braun and Clarke's (2006) approach to thematic analysis, and leading to the development of six themes addressing the application of ancestral knowledge: 1) Whānau – the korowai of kinship and connection; 2) Tuakiri Taranaki – securing Taranaki Māori identity; 3) Kaitiaki matatau – expert teachers; 4) Wānanga as learning and development opportunities; 5) Tikanga–Tukanga – principles and processes; and 6) Tirohanga – a shared vision. These themes are presented below and supported with relevant quotes from whānau.

THEME 1: WHĀNAU – THE KOROWAI OF KINSHIP AND CONNECTION

The overarching theme of whānau permeates every aspect of KM-EYP. The wellbeing and development of tamariki is viewed through a whānau lens that is inclusive of their parents and whānau, which means whole-whānau development is the impetus of programming (Tāmati et al., 2008). Māori know that whānau and whakapapa were prime considerations of our tūpuna because we have the instructive messaging in stories, waiata and karakia such as *Tātai Whakapapa*. It may be viewed as characteristically Māori to hold a whānau-oriented worldview that prioritises the needs of whānau over one's own, so it is an attitude that may require cultivation in those to whom it is unfamiliar. In a variety of ways, participants in the Tangi te Kawekaweā study talked about such things as their reliance on and obligation to immediate and wider whānau; the responsibilities and rewards of belonging to the TKP whānau-collective; the processes involved in building supportive whānau relationships; and their heightened awareness of the significance of connections to whānau in the past, present, and in the future, gained through participation in TKP.

Although most of those who have participated in TKP are connected by Taranaki whakapapa, the KM-EYP centre coheres around its Kaupapa Māori and concern for tamariki, whānau and community wellbeing in Taranaki. The Centre provides an opportunity to experience the satisfaction of belonging to the TKP whānau-collective and connecting with others who value similar things and share the same goals, including securing the Taranaki Māori identity of their tamariki and whānau. For younger parents and caregivers, and for those whose families are not near, or are not supportive, the kaitiaki (teachers) and other TKP whānau-collective members act as kuia (female elders), whaene/pāpā (mother/father figures), tuākana (older siblings/mentors) and hoa (friends). The whānau orientation of TKP cultivates in members a worldview that prioritises whānau over the individual and fosters long-term supportive relationships (whanaungatanga), giving effect to the values and practices of tūpuna.

> That's why I moved my whānau from the South to the North because I knew that there was a group doing exactly what I was wanting to do with their family ... it was just great to have the confidence to be with others who felt the same. The growth wasn't only for my children; the growth was for myself as well. (R7 – mother of a former student)

The TKP construct of whānauranga (feeling and acting as a member of whānau/community) describes the TKP disposition of viewing the world, and seeing oneself as a valued and valuable member of a whānau, fostered through engagement in the TKP whānau-collective (Tamati et al., 2020). As such, whānauranga manifests a Māori worldview. The appointment of buddy kaitiaki and whānau to new parents and whānau entering TKP is one mechanism that provides tuakana to teina (senior to junior, experienced to new) support at a time when there are often elevated levels of anxiety due to the unfamiliarity of the reo Māori environment. The tuakana offers an immediate connection to the TKP whānau-collective. These relationships are observed by tamariki, and they learn how whānau members interact through tuakana–teina relationships and support each other within whānau. Through this exposure, they come to value qualities of te ao Māori such as manaakitanga, tautoko and aroha.

> And it really felt like, over time, this was your whānau, and people really genuinely – not just the kaitiaki, I am thinking of other whānau – really cared for your kids and you cared for their kids, and so it's just the strengthening of the relationships. (R31.1 – mother of a former student)

> These [Kōpae graduates] who have all grown up together ... they are still a tight unit ... that gives me a sense of pride to think for a little while we were part of what has evolved for these tamariki. (R8 – mother of a former student)

TKP makes 'warm demands' of parents and whānau, encouraging them to engage in their children's learning and all activities. Parents and whānau indicated that involvement in TKP necessitates a rethink of cultural values, of roles and responsibilities and, for some, changes in lifestyle. The immediate whānau of the tamariki are welcomed and included at TKP, and are pivotal to successful engagement in KM-EYP, often facilitating entry and providing practical and emotional support to parents and caregivers.

> Any time I thought it might have got a bit tough and thought I can't afford it or I can't do this, [Mum] would say, "go back and talk to [the kaitiaki]. You know if you need a real big hand we'll help you," and stuff like that. I think having someone behind us pushing us a little bit was very helpful; otherwise, I think you'd have a reason to back out. (R2 – mother of a former student)

> It's not just an early childhood centre where you can just drop off and go, and pick up. There's a commitment to go and learn te reo Māori. There's a commitment to come in and mihi, to go around and mihi to everybody. There's a commitment to attend whānau hui. If there are any issues, there's a commitment to talk to someone about that. (R3 – mother of a former student, now a kaitiaki)

Some parents struggle with the day-to-day stresses of living, and are preoccupied with making ends meet. Without the practical assistance and emotional support of the TKP whānau-collective, these parents are less likely to engage in the Centre and risk missing te ao Māori learnings and development opportunities that can lead to positive outcomes for their tamariki and whānau.

> Before they can think about putting their kids in early childhood [they've got issues] like kai on the table ... [TKP] taught me how to love myself, to accept, and to forgive ... how to trust; first of all, to trust myself. (R2 – mother of a former student)

TKP participation in events like the Puanga festival in Taranaki (Māori New Year celebrations), the annual Pāhua commemorations (of the government ransacking of Parihaka in 1881) and whānau kai (shared meals) encourage parents and whānau to participate alongside their tamariki. These occasions provide lived experience of te ao Māori and build relationships within the whānau-collective. Recitation of karakia such as *Tātai Whakapapa*, explanatory kōrero and performance of waiata reinforce whakapapa links to ancestors, to historical events, to peers and to future generations.

> Father: So, the events like Matariki and other kaupapa, wānanga reo, the kapa haka nights, all those sorts of things contributed to that feeling [of belonging] and getting to know other whānau ... Mother: Those things forced people to participate ... there is no escaping the interaction that you need to have in the reo. (R31 – whānau of a former student)

THEME 2: TUAKIRI TARANAKI – SECURING TARANAKI MĀORI IDENTITY

The TKP conceptualisation of wellbeing centres on tamariki and whānau living healthy, fulfilled and contributing lives, successfully engaging in te ao Māori, the Taranaki Māori community and wider society, secure in their Taranaki Māori identity. Tuakiri Taranaki requires fluency in the language and culture of tūpuna – ancestral knowledge. It is likely to develop for tamariki in a safe, loving, whānau environment in which local language and culture is fostered to frame their view of the world as they move forward with self-confidence and pride. Secure tuakiri Taranaki for tamariki and their whānau is a primary objective of TKP and central to a broader imperative to heal historical trauma, defined as "cumulative emotional and psychological wounding over the lifespan and across generations, emanating from massive group trauma experiences" (Brave Heart, 2003, p. 7), and reverse the acculturating impacts of colonisation on the Taranaki Māori community.

Participants described how colonisation impacted their tūpuna and continues to negatively impact their whānau and the Māori community today. The legacy of the muru raupatu (government confiscation of lands) in Taranaki has included historical trauma, which perpetuates injustices and undermines the capacity of whānau to engage in te ao Māori and to thrive in wider society.

> [T]hat's why my mum and dad were [disengaged from things Māori], due to colonisation, because of what happened to their parents. Our grandparents didn't want our parents going through the traumas they went through, so they thought that if they did what the Pākehā said, and lived the Pākehā lifestyle, their children would be safe and probably better off in the world. (R3 – mother of a former student, now a kaitiaki)

Participants viewed TKP as part of the solution to addressing the impacts of colonisation, healing historical trauma and facilitating transformation for children, their whānau and ultimately their communities.

> We all want a better life for our tamariki than what we had, and what our parents had ... [TKP] definitely makes a difference. Just in the way we behave, well for me anyway. It's a positive place to be in, you know, when we leave Te Kōpae we're open to a world full of negativity. Sometimes there is negativity in Te Kōpae, but it can be overcome in Te Kōpae. There are opportunities to overcome the negativity, and there are strategies that are shared. (R3 – mother of a former student, now a kaitiaki)

Participants recalled their joy on entering TKP and finding a Kaupapa Māori education setting where their tamariki could receive a culturally validating education.

> One of the things I really enjoyed was the absolute sense of validation of our lives, that here was an organisation and learning environment where [our son's] Taranakitanga and his whanaungatanga and his whakapapa all meant something. (R8 – mother of a former student)

> Our passion has been to instil in our children te reo Māori, tikanga Māori, te ao Māori, so that our children can grow up and understand who they are and where they are from ... citizens of this world who are Māori ... they know who they are and are proud of who they are. (R7 – mother of a former student)

Involvement in TKP was described as having built confidence and fostered skills that enabled whānau members to become more involved in wider Māori contexts.

> [E]verything that we learned at Kōpae ... It's still going on in our lives. It's still very, very relevant, so much to the point that I try to emulate everything that the Kōpae did in the places that I have gone to ... my study ECE, getting involved in the kura, iwi politics, hapū, iwi, marae, hui. Looking back now I don't think that would have been possible if I wasn't at the Kōpae. So they opened a lot of doors for me, in a sense, so that I knew who I was and where I was from, and I [believed that I] actually had a right to be at the hui, that kind of thing. (R20 – mother of a former student, later a kaitiaki)

Participants described being focused on the future and noted that TKP equips their tamariki with the fundamental understandings and skills to do well in life. Some parents also held an intergenerational perspective. For example, one participant had his mind set on ensuring the paepae of his marae will be filled for generations to come.

> For our kids, we wanted them to have that opportunity to be Māori in every sense ... without the reo there was a huge portion missing in that equation, so that was really, really important for us. And it was equally important that they were well rounded, that they got a start to a good education, tikanga and mātauranga. (R20 – mother of a former student, later a kaitiaki)

> I know that later on, she would be on our marae as a kuia, very, very formidable because for me, it was always going to be intergenerational. To retain is one thing, to maintain is another, that's kaitiakitanga, but to sustain it through generation to generation that ... that's the key. (R12 – father of a former student)

THEME 3: KAITIAKI MATATAU – EXPERT TEACHERS

The role of kaitiaki in integrating ancestral knowledge into a contemporary education and care programme for tamariki and whānau cannot be over-stated. Kaitiaki translate Indigenous concepts into practice so they are accessible. They normalise Taranaki reo Māori for whānau members of all ages. Highly trained – or training – teaching professionals, it is significant that the kaitiaki are of the local community and are experienced parents and grandparents who exude aroha, manawanui and manaakitanga for tamariki and their whānau unreservedly. The kaitiaki complement each other in their specific skills and special interests, but each is an exponent of the characteristics and qualities aspired to by whānau members.

The kaitiaki have been described as the 'glue' (Tāmati et al., 2008) of TKP, promoting strong relationships within the whānau-collective and nurturing the positive view of tamariki and whānau that is the foundation for successful interactions and outcomes for whānau. Participants talked warmly about the TKP kaitiaki and the critical role they had in the achievement of outcomes for their whānau. The life experiences of kaitiaki within the local community enable them to relate to whānau, to understand whānau circumstances and empathise with the difficulties many face. Participants reported feeling confident and comfortable in their care.

> [Kaitiaki] probably shaped our parenting style; gave us examples of how to deal with things. They ... would say [tamariki] did this today and they [kaitiaki] dealt with it like this. And we would think, "Oh that's a good way" ... There used to be a lot of tips ... You would sit in karakia and stuff, and you would observe how they would deal with behaviours and then you could follow it. They were always open if you had a question, they were very approachable. (R18.2 – mother of a former student)

Kaitiaki translate ancestral knowledge for tamariki and whānau, weaving cultural principles and practices into quality programming for tamariki, disseminating through wānanga, providing advice and guidance, and modelling desired behaviour. Kaitiaki are the day to day facilitators of learning and development in tamariki and whānau, encouraging positive change for whānau and the community:

> When we were around, [kaitiaki] used simple phrases that were repetitive, just to encourage us to take those baby steps and that is how we started to learn. It was like their [teaching] but with an older group of people, applying the same principles to us. (R10 – mother of a former student)

> There were all those learning type things that you want your under-fives to learn as well as tikanga [and] speaking Māori. (R2 – mother of a former student)

> It is life changing. It builds confidence in families. People look at, and grow, their families differently, I think. Because they've had that guidance and support to be able to do that. It is, it's life-changing, is all I can say really. (R25 – former kaitiaki)

Participants described the kindness, patience and support they and their whānau received from the kaitiaki. The actions of the kaitiaki are not always overt but more an understated way of being and doing that has influence. As one participant described:

> I think that's where its subtle power is. You start looking at things differently, like the belief system ... So you have a different view of the world and what it looks like, how you sense ... mauri, tapu, noa ... It made me want to become more Māori ... I think it did help [me become] more patient and understanding ... it helped me to understand children so that did help me with my daughter's upbringing. (R12 – father of a former student)

THEME 4: WĀNANGA AS LEARNING AND DEVELOPMENT OPPORTUNITIES

Wānanga are forums for sharing and securing knowledge, for the exchange of ideas, and for learning. The poutama whakawhanake (staircase of learning and development) is an inclusive metaphor for the TKP approach to development. Each member of the whānau-collective has a place on the learning staircase, at a step appropriate for them and their journey of learning in each area or skill. This concept unites the whānau-collective in shared commitment to constant improvement and mutual support for each other's development. Wānanga on a range of topics, such as those related to reo and tikanga Māori, sociopolitical consciousness-raising, childrearing and health are critical for whānau development and the support of parents and whānau. An ongoing programme of wānanga is organised for parents and whānau. The whānau development programme sits in and around the progressive daily programme for tamariki and whānau engagement in local days of significance and community events.

> Unless you create those opportunities for [parents and whānau] to participate, in [wānanga] they won't engage. The idea that learning suddenly has meaning is a real key in understanding that they have something to offer the learning as well. (R30 – father of a former student, stakeholder informant)

Wānanga for te reo me ngā tikanga Māori and the kaupapa of TKP are pivotal to the development of whānau in mātauranga Māori.

> [TKP was] life-changing, in terms of developing te reo Māori, providing those supports that would otherwise have been provided by tauheke. Providing a haven where this learning can take place for the whole family, not just for the kids but for the parents as well. (R27 – local community leader and stakeholder informant)

> Discussion in whānau wānanga is so important in allowing people to talk to issues and to reflect and then become closer for it. You can see that … when children and parents … speak Māori and are able to operate according to the tikanga of the whānau of Te Kōpae. (R9 – father of a former student)

Parents and whānau take advantage of the relationships TKP has with community-based organisations and providers. For example, participants described Takawai and Chris Murphy's Te Pūmaomao programme (Murphy, 1997) as a wānanga that opened their eyes, ears and hearts to te ao Māori. Parents and whānau, still grieving the loss of language and land within their communities, found Te Pūmaomao transformational and some credited the programme as the turning point in their lives and in the decision to engage in TKP.

> The Pūmaomao course … was the first time I had actually had that sort of experience of understanding why we as Māori were like we were and I was like I was. So when you start from that sort of awareness … then a whole lot of things fall into place for you … we've followed a lot of that kaupapa really in terms of commitment to speaking Māori in the household, to the girls, and using karakia, the values that we express … and all the things that go with that. (R14 – father of a former student)

Participants described other opportunities for whānau learning and development, such as shared meals, haka practices, working bees and trips to community hui and local kura. Whatever the form, these are learning and development opportunities, and they have the additional benefit of bringing parents and whānau together in the TKP whānau-collective.

> The sorts of things … like outings, wānanga that take place on weekends, going along and doing fundraising, doing those community-building type activities … the good thing about those focused activities is that people … are contributing, [they feel they] are of value because they are doing something. (R30 – father of a former student, stakeholder informant)

The daily TKP programme immerses tamariki aged 0–6 years in te reo me ngā tikanga Māori as they engage in the wide variety of play-based learning activities and experiences. Parents and whānau are encouraged to attend alongside their tamariki when they can. Not only does whānau participation support children's learning, but it also provides the opportunity for whānau to learn language and experience culture, and to be exposed to TKP's way of interacting with children.

> [Y]ou saw at Te Kōpae how the child, if they did something wrong, they would be sat down, spoken to. It affirmed that it wasn't the child, it was the behaviour, and how better could we do this. That was really, really interesting. And when I started practising that … it worked eh! (R4 – mother of a former student)

THEME 5: TIKANGA-TUKANGA – PRINCIPLES AND PROCESSES

KM-EYP is Kaupapa Māori-based and therefore informed by ao Māori principles and values that provide the foundation for the structures of educational best practice within the early-years and whānau programme. TKP employs the pedagogical practice of a highly structured environment (though not always overtly so) in order to provide stability and security for tamariki, their parents and whānau. Agreed processes act as scaffolding, furnishing tamariki and whānau with the tools to accomplish challenging tasks. Parents and whānau learn to employ specific processes as they engage with tamariki and others at home, in TKP and the wider community.

Participants recalled their delight on entering TKP for the first time and experiencing the tau (calm) of the structured tamariki and whānau environment. Some reported instantly feeling this was the early learning setting for their whānau. A collective commitment to Māori language and culture, and the tikanga-based processes of TKP, maintains the quality of the programme and inspires parents and whānau to make personal changes to apply TKP processes in their own homes.

> One of the other things that I really liked was the encouragement of the seamless ways of being and doing ... between Kōpae and home, so that Te Ara Poutama, or that way of negotiating with children, is a really good example ... it's just common sense that it would make it easier for the child if there's consistent expectations at home with what's going on during the day [at TKP]. It really makes sense if you try and instil that in the whole whānau. (R31.2 – father of a former student)

Te Ara Poutama is a structured process for resolving conflict and building relationships that is encouraged for children and adults based on the principle of open, honest and solution-focused communication (Tamati et al., 2008). The process of Te Ara Poutama is practised in the spirit advocated in the teachings of Parihaka leaders Te Whiti o Rongomai and Tohu Kākahi (Tamati et al., 2008) with the wider aim of helping local communities such as TKP to restore their capacity for positive communication and constructive negotiation of issues.

Te Ara Poutama

he tukanga hei whakatau mārire i te take	a process for resolving issues positively
⇨ Me whakaahua tāu i kite ai – kaua mā te pōhēhē te mahi e ārahi	⇨ You describe what you see
⇨ Me āta whakarongo ki ngā kōrero a ērā tāngata whaipānga	⇨ You genuinely listen to others' perspectives
⇨ Me whaiwhakaaro ki te ngākau tangata – kōrerotia ngā kare ā-roto	⇨ You acknowledge feelings
⇨ Me tūtohu te take	⇨ You identify the issue
⇨ Me kimi ētehi ara e tau ai te take	⇨ You explore options to resolve the issue
⇨ Me tūtohu te mahi tika, te ara paiake rānei	⇨ You state the preferred action/behaviour
⇨ Me whakamārama, me tuku kōwhiringa rānei, ina e tika ana	⇨ You clarify and/or provide choices, if required
⇨ Me whai wā, me whai wāhi hoki, ngā tāngata ki te tohu i ō rātou ake whakataunga	⇨ You provide time and space for people to make their own decisions

Figure 1: Te Ara Poutama process (Tamati et al., 2008).

Most adult whānau members will need help to practise Te Ara Poutama to modify long-held attitudes and become comfortable with what may be a novel way of interacting with both tamariki and peers. Because Te Ara Poutama is the accepted process of negotiating social situations at TKP, the tamariki readily communicate in this way and expect the same from those around them.

> I really liked Te Ara Poutama. I really liked the way that kaitiaki were consistent at de-escalating riri and giving children space to explain what's going on for them, and actually learn a way to express dissatisfaction with a situation ... at wā huihui, taking the child out of the heated situation into the corridor and having a kōrero. (R31.2 – father of a former student)

The Ara Poutama process is underpinned by the TKP conception of leadership as Ngā Takohanga e Whā – the Four Responsibilities of Leadership. At TKP, leadership is thought of as four pillars of responsibility and contribution: Te Whai Takohanga – having responsibility; Te Mouri Takohanga – being responsible; Te Kawe Takohanga – taking responsibility; and Te Tuku Takohanga – sharing responsibility (Tamati et al., 2008). The construction of leadership as four responsibilities is an important tikanga at TKP, recognising the inherent ability of all whānau members, including tamariki, to self-manage and demonstrate leadership in their daily lives. Every whānau member contributes to the collective strength and achievements of the centre (Tamati et al., 2008).

Tamariki are not viewed as fledgling leaders but as leaders in their own right. Leadership is fostered through positive communication, and interactions predicated on the presumption of others (especially tamariki) as competent decision-makers who put the interests of the group ahead of their own. With support, both tamariki and pakeke are capable of stepping up to assume roles, take responsibility and peacefully negotiate challenging situations.

> My children [learned] how to be a good friend; for them to communicate well with another child; learn better; their responsibility as well ... I think [kaitiaki] kept a close eye on the children and how they develop ... encouraging them ... watching to begin with and if they needed assistance it was provided for them. (R17 – mother of a former student)

A courageous conversation takes place when one engages positively with others on challenging topics or at challenging times (Davys, 2019). The term is used in TKP in relation to conversations of that nature, such as those that kaitiaki might have with parents/caregivers and whānau about engagement, encouraging whānau development, adult actions that support tamariki learning, development and safety, and so on. Some participants spoke about open and honest communication, which they felt was confronting at the time, but also reassured them that kaitiaki were genuinely committed to their tamariki and whānau.

Conversations of this nature might occur during the programmed uiui whānau (scheduled discussions with parents and whānau), the hui whānau (meetings of the TKP whānau- collective), or opportunistically in and around the TKP activities.

> One thing that worked really well was the expectations and the rules ... they were very clear at the beginning and always reinforced. There weren't many ... but they were clear. And they lived those things, there wasn't any inconsistency. The rules were very clearly enforced, in a kind way so you always knew where you stood. (R10.2 – father of a former student)

THEME 6: TIROHANGA – A SHARED VISION

The primary aim of TKP at establishment was "the retention and enrichment of te reo me ngā tikanga Māori in Taranaki" (Te Kōpae Piripono, 1994) to build a brighter future for our tamariki and mokopuna. More than twenty-five years on, TKP remains intent on the reclamation of ancestral knowledge, practices and all modes of expression in the Taranaki rohe. Through its programme, TKP has the potential to achieve transformative change for Taranaki whānau and contribute to the revitalisation of Taranaki Māori communities. However, this vision can only be realised if consistently shared with and adopted by TKP parents and whānau, so they engage in the whānau-collective and then transmit the learnings to the community through their actions.

> The Kōpae has been good at not wavering from the original kaupapa that it set itself, how they would treat the children, what expectations they would have of parents. They have stayed true all the way through. (R14 – father of a former student)

Participants acknowledged the intergenerational impacts within whānau that could result through involvement in TKP. However, they also noted that transforming the lives of whānau, to counter the impacts of colonisation, is likely to be a gradual process.

> It has allowed us to realise that dream of having something that is right for our kids and for our whānau, that is all about whānau, to be able to shape their education on the back of solid values, core values, and the dreams and aspirations that are similar to their parents', if not wider now because with the next generation coming through ... kotahitanga, manaakitanga, te tiaki a tētehi i tētehi, kotahi tonu te hā o te mokopuna me te kaumātua. All those sorts of things are a way of living, a way of life. And if you change someone's way of life to something that they are not used to then you're talking about a slow and steady transformation, it can't happen overnight. (R9 – father of a former student)

TKP considers tamariki, and all whānau members, as valued and contributing members of the whānau-collective, each capable of demonstrating leadership and having agency in day-to-day interactions. Tamariki are not viewed as passive recipients of adult instruction but as active participants in the functioning of the whānau. This perspective underscores the way kaitiaki engage with tamariki and approach teaching and learning as a multi-directional process between whanaunga, and one in which all whānau members are expected to participate. Kaitiaki facilitate tamariki development by providing opportunities for child-directed learning through play, or real-world experiences such as attendance at local cultural events and days of importance. For example, the Pāhua at Parihaka is an annual event, the experience of which is likely to be later recreated at TKP in the play of tamariki. A former kaitiaki describes how TKP facilitated those experiences and the ensuing learnings, with the potential to shape future educational and development pathways for whānau.

> [Those] who have been grown by their grandparents or their great aunties and uncles … were able to learn experientially. And that is one of the great things I loved about the Kōpae was allowing the kids to be able to live, through play, some of the experiences they were having, like going out to Parihaka every month … You are allowing kids to experiment and experience their emotions through play. To have that fostered by parents who are also learning at the same time … Honestly, I am just so proud of what the Kōpae has done and is doing to support whānau, to support people to become whole, to support families to become whole … I think it will make a difference to them and their futures. How they look at how their kids learn, what they want for their kids, their dreams and aspirations for their kids … I think it is life changing. It builds confidence in families. People look at, and grow, their families differently. (R25 – former kaitiaki)

Conclusion

The voices of TKP parents and whānau have articulated the means by which this KM-EYP in Taranaki gives expression to ancestral knowledge and the teachings of Te Whiti o Rongomai and Tohu Kākahi of Parihaka, Te Ua Haumēne and other Taranaki visionaries, to strengthen whānau and enhance the wellbeing of tamariki and mokopuna. The kaupapa of TKP is captured in the karakia 'Tātai Whakapapa', which implores us to uphold and protect te ao Māori, mātauranga Māori and whānau Māori, to secure the future for tamariki and mokopuna. The Kaupapa Māori approach of TKP combines ancestral knowledge with new insights and innovative practice. It is an advance-to-the-past approach that challenges our colonised thinking about ourselves, our tamariki and the world in which we live.

Like other KM-EYP, including kōhanga reo, TKP promotes whole-whānau learning and development. Tamariki and whānau are immersed in local language and culture as they experience the practical application of ancestral knowledge and wisdom, reinforced by karakia, waiata and other customary practices. This cultural strengthening is critical to whānau development, and to efforts to enrich the lives of tamariki and rebuild Māori communities that have suffered the impact of the tragedy that is Taranaki's historical context of colonisation.

Whānau arrive at KM-EYP from a range of backgrounds, and with varied lived experiences; therefore, specific supports may be required to meet the needs of individual whānau and members. However, based on the experiences of TKP whānau described in this chapter, it appears that it is actual involvement in the whānau-collective and quality programme of KM-EYP that promotes wellbeing and positive whānau development, particularly for those whānau who are needing support.

Taranaki-based centres of KM-EYP have the potential to contribute to a new normal for Taranaki Māori. One where parents, tamariki and whānau are secure in their local Māori identity and have the critical understandings and capacity to engage successfully in te ao Māori, the Taranaki Māori community and wider society. The vision and potential outcomes of KM-EYP should, therefore, be shared widely with Taranaki whānau and community, and beyond, to extend the reach of the programme and enhance whānau access to the long-term benefits of involvement in KM-EYP for tamariki and whānau.

References

BRAUN, V., & CLARKE, V. (2006). Using thematic analysis in psychology. *Qualitative Research in Psychology*, 3, 77–101.

BRAVE HEART, M. Y. H. (2003). The historical trauma response among natives and its relationship with substance abuse: A Lakota illustration. *Journal of Psychoactive Drugs*, 35(1), 7–13.

HOND, R. (2013). *Matua te reo, matua te tangata. Speaker community: Visions, approaches, outcomes* (Doctoral dissertation). Massey University, Palmerston North, New Zealand. Retrieved from https://mro.massey.ac.nz/handle/10179/5439

HOND-FLAVELL, E., RATIMA, M., TAMATI, A., KOREWHA, H., & EDWARDS, W. (2017). *Te Kura Mai i Tawhiti: He Tau Kawekaweā: Building the foundation for whānau educational success and wellbeing; a Kaupapa Māori ECE approach*. Wellington, New Zealand: Teaching and Learning Research Initiative. Retrieved from http://www.tlri.org.nz/tlri-research/research-completed/ece-sector/te-kura-mai-i-tawhiti-he-tau-kawekaweā-building

MURPHY, T. (1997). *Te Pūmaomao: An awakening to rediscover and celebrate*. Ngāmotu/New Plymouth, New Zealand: Te Wānanga Māori, Taranaki Polytech.

RATIMA, M., THEODORE, R., TAMATI, A., HOND-FLAVELL, E., EDWARDS, W., KOREWHA, H., … & POULTON, R. (2019). Te kura mai i tawhiti: A collaborative lifecourse approach to health, wellbeing and whānau development, *MAI Journal*, 8(1), 63–76.

TAMATI, A., HOND-FLAVELL, E., & KOREWHA, H. (2008). Ko koe kei tēnā kīwai, ko au kei tēnei kīwai o te kete. Te Kopae Piripono Centre of Innovation Research Report. Retrieved from http://www.educationcounts.govt.nz/publications/ECE/22551/34830

TAMATI, A., RATIMA, M., HOND-FLAVELL, E., EDWARDS, W., HOND, R., KOREWHA, H., THEODORE, M., TREHARNE, G. & POULTON, R. (2020, UNDER REVIEW). He piki raukura: Understanding strengths-based Māori child development constructs in kaupapa Māori early years provision. *MAI Journal*.

TE KŌHANGA REO NATIONAL TRUST. (N.D.) History. Retrieved from https://www.kohanga.ac.nz/history

TE KŌPAE PIRIPONO. (1994). *Pukapuka Whakamārama: Parent information booklet*. Ngāmotu/New Plymouth, New Zealand: Te Kōpae Piripono.

WAIKEREPURU, H. (1991). *Tātai Whakapapa* (Unpublished composition). Ngāmotu/New Plymouth, New Zealand.

WAITANGI TRIBUNAL. (1996). *The Taranaki Report Kaupapa Tuatahi (Wai 143)*. Wellington, New Zealand: Legislation Direct.

Aro ki te Wairua o te Hā: The Spirituality of Birth

Naomi Simmonds
Teah Carlson

CHAPTER 11

For Māori, the end of night and the beginning of day is an important spiritual time. The first breath of life in a new-born baby, the beginning of a season, the opening of a new meeting house, the start of a new project – all are imbued with a sense of optimism and a sense of unease (Smith, 2012, p. 108).

The spaces between – between day and night, life and death, spiritual and physical, old and new – are significant for Māori. Movement through and between these spaces is facilitated using karakia, tikanga and ceremony. Our cultural traditions enable us to navigate those transitional times and spaces in ways that are culturally and spiritually safe. For Māori women, these transitional or intermediary spaces take on additional meaning – the female reproductive organs are conceptualised as te whare tangata, meaning both the womb and the house of humanity. This highlights the relationship between the maternal body and the collective and connects the maternal body to the creation of the world as Māori understand it. Furthermore, women's maternal bodies have the potential to facilitate movement between space, time and place in both spiritual and physical terms, as described by Ani Mikaere (2003):

> The role of women as whare tangata was highly valued according to tikanga Māori as evidenced by the centrality of the female reproductive functions to Māori cosmogony and the powers attributed to the female organs in mediating the boundaries between tapu and noa. It is also apparent from the pivotal role that women played in preserving the lines of descent, from the gods to present and future generations (p. 90).

The maternal body, in Māori terms, not only demonstrates the intimate entanglement of the material, discursive and spiritual but also speaks to the sanctity and power of the Māori maternal body. This is a powerful thing indeed.

Aro ki te wairua o te hā means to (re)claim what is Indigenous or māori – normal and natural. As our breath enters our bodies and circulates through, enlightening our maternal bodies, so does wairua. To practise, embed and enhance wairua is to transform and command it of the world – to command it of ourselves and our whānau. Reflecting on our atua, we find this worldview that commanding the elements to favour us was a strategy of our tūpuna. In the thousand-year-old karakia, recited on Tainui waka before landing on the shores of Aotearoa New Zealand there are no requests, no please or thank you, to the atua. The karakia commands: "clear the obstacles through your authority and the mana of your tūpuna" (Adams, 2017, p. 33). As Māori women, we have been conditioned to care for others in order to care for ourselves (Simmonds, 2016), but as a māmā to tamariki, sisters, daughters, at times the awareness of wairua does not take precedence. Reclaiming our birthing practices, reciting our creation stories and cosmologies, breathes life back into our tūpuna practices and they become our current realities.

This chapter examines Indigenous spirituality (wairua) and birth for Māori women and whānau in Aotearoa New Zealand. As Māori, we have a unique and enduring spiritual tradition that values the sanctity of the maternal body and the collective approach to raising children, and in turn children 'raising' whānau, which this chapter will discuss. In what follows, we seek to weave together the cosmological and historical narratives of Māori with the contemporary experiences of women today to examine the wairua of birth and of the maternal body in a uniquely Māori way. In doing so, we seek to reveal the transformations to maternities and of maternity care when the inextricability of the physical and spiritual in birth is provided for.

The first part of this chapter discusses the way Māori cosmological histories establish an inseparable relationship between the maternal body and te taha wairua. These (her)stories are replete with legacies about the unique and pivotal role women play in ensuring the survival of Māori whānau, tribes and communities. Following this we briefly discuss the colonial impositions upon the spiritual and embodied spaces of birth for women and whānau. The final section in this chapter provides a discussion of the contemporary understandings of wairua and birth for women and their families. This leads us to the key argument of this chapter: that reclaiming Māori maternities is inextricable from reclaiming language, ceremony and wairua. In this context, it becomes almost impossible to talk about one without reference to the other.[1]

Te Whare Tangata – The Womb Space of Humanity

Te whare tangata has a dual meaning as both the house of humanity and female reproductive organs and more specifically the womb – the place of conception, growth and nurturing. More than the corporeal though, te whare tangata is intimately entangled with whakapapa, whenua and wairua. This understanding of the maternal body as te whare tangata makes inextricable the individual from the collective, the physical from the spiritual, and the present from the past and the future.

We argue that within Māori knowledges, histories and cosmologies is an empowering body of knowledge that destabilises dominant colonial and patriarchal conceptualisations of the maternal body. Further, reclaiming the stories and knowledges of our ancestors has incredible transformative potential for the ways in which the maternal body is understood and treated presently and in the future. Creation stories and cosmologies are not designed to be merely historical accounts but rather can be statements about our current realities. Kirsten Gabel (2013) points out that "we should not be afraid to reconsider the stories of our cosmologies, to reassess them, critique them and to come up with our own relevant interpretations" (p. 56). In doing so, it is possible to connect the past to the ideals and yearnings of the present.

The birth story of Papatūānuku (Earth Mother) is important here. Born from the womb space of Te Pō (the darkness), Papatūānuku made the same journey through

---

[1] We point out that there is only limited space in this chapter to share deep, complex, place-based and contextually bound narratives and knowledges. Furthermore, the stories shared throughout this chapter are not put forward as a totalising account; rather, there are distinct and unique tribal variations. In other words, there are multiple stories and histories. What is presented here is one reading of these stories that seeks to illustrate the centrality of the maternal body and the inextricability of the physical and spiritual from Māori maternities.

the birth canal of darkness and into the world of light that each of us do in our own entry to the world. She travelled through the various phases of the birth canal that in Māori have multiple names[2] and then moved into Te Ao Mārama (the world of light or the world of knowing). The significance of this to understandings of the maternal body and to birth today is reflected in the simple but powerful statement that "the process which brings each of us into being, brought the world into being" (Mikaere, 2011, p. 210). Through our genealogical connection to Papatūānuku, each of us is united in a shared experience of residing in the womb space of our mothers, moving through the various stages of Te Pō (darkness) and finally being born into the world of light.

The entanglement of maternal corporeality with the whenua does not end here. In Māori cosmologies, Ranginui (Sky Father) and Papatūānuku were locked in a tight embrace, which saw the world bathed in darkness. The separation of our ancestral parents to reveal the world we now inhabit is a story with iwi variations. This discussion is significant. It has been said that the experience of Papatūānuku in being separated from Ranginui and her children was like the pains of labour and birth. Ani Mikaere (2003) elaborates: "as the children became restless within her, Papa experienced discomfort such as that felt during labour" (p. 15). When she was turned away from Ranginui, Papatūānuku took her youngest child, Rūaumoko, with her, as he was still breastfeeding; he now resides underneath her and is known as the atua presiding over underground activity (volcanic and seismic movement).

It is in her role as mother to Rūaumoko, to her other children and to us as her descendants that we can look to Papatūānuku as a model. It is in her that we are provided with nurturance and sustenance, and it is from her that we gain wisdom and knowledge about pregnancy, childbirth and mothering. This is reflected in the concept of Te Ūkaipō (the night feeding breast), which is another name used to refer to Papatūānuku and to mothers (Gabel, 2013). Ngahuia Murphy (2011) eloquently expresses this, stating:

> Te Ūkaipō, a beloved name for Papatūānuku, refers to the pre-dawn breastfeeding hours when a mother provides her baby physical, emotional, intellectual, and spiritual nourishment and sustenance through the milk. The use of the term in relation to Papatūānuku speaks to the divinity of the earth in its capacity to nurture and fulfil all the basic needs of humanity (p. 35).

These histories serve as a reminder of the significance and prestige that was accorded to maternal bodies, including perhaps the most important maternal body, Papatūānuku. It is significant also that within the creation stories the first human form created is female – Hineahuone, further serving to entangle maternal bodies with the land, with our ancestresses and their spiritual wisdom.

In this context, maternal bodies are inseparable from a wider politics of land, language and wairua. We return to the concept of te whare tangata and to Ani Mikaere (2003) to further illustrate this point:

> The significance of the whare tangata is rooted in the creation of the world in the overriding tapu, whakapapa ... the inherent tapu of each Māori person is sourced in their connection, through whakapapa, to the rest of humanity, to the gods and to the environment. The role of women, as the bearers of past, present and future

---

[2] Ross Calman (2004) states: "First came Te-Pō-tē-Kitea, Te Pō-tangotango and Te Pō-tē-whāwhā, the unseen, the changing and the untouchable Pō. Then came Te Pō-namunamu-ki-taiao, the night of the narrow passage by which man [sic] enters the world; Te Pō-tahuri-atu, the turning, the movement; and finally Te Pō-tahuri-mai-ki-taiao, the turning, the movement through the narrow passage into the world" (p. 40).

generations is therefore of paramount importance. The survival of the whānau, hapū and iwi is dependent upon the reproductive functions of women (p. 31).

To talk about the maternal body in this way requires deep knowledges that are rooted in tribal lands and te reo Māori. The cosmological histories for Māori establish the inseparable connection between the spiritual and the maternal body and reinforce the pivotal role that women, as te whare tangata, have in ensuring the continuation of our genealogies and the survival of our communities. Our narratives are replete with accounts of the unique and special role women play in sustaining the collective. That said, there is strong evidence that the role of men in pregnancy and birth was significant. In many cases men spoke to the child in the womb, recounted tribal histories and cosmologies to babies in utero, cooked for pregnant women, and assisted with birthing the babies (Mikaere, 2003; Murphy, 2011). The earth is our ultimate mother; our whakapapa tells us this. This is not a metaphor but an embodied and lived reality. There is a political imperative in claiming this. Whakapapa also tells us that unlike Western patriarchal conceptualisations of 'mother' as the self-sacrificing and infinite giver, our relationship with Papatūānuku is reciprocal and highly interdependent and is complemented by our relationships with Ranginui. These relationships are simultaneously material and spiritual, individual and collective, ubiquitous and unique. However, they have not been free from colonial impositions and attacks.

Colonialism: Attacks on Our Bodies and Spirituality

Within Western patriarchal and colonial ideologies, the intimate entanglements of the physical and spiritual as embodied by concepts like te whare tangata are often considered 'messy'. The goal of Western ideologies is to separate, compartmentalise and rationalise (and in many cases, erase) the wairua of our maternal bodies and of birth. It is this wairua that, as Linda Tuhiwai Smith (1996) argues, marks the clearest contrast between Indigenous knowledges and the West. Smith (1996) says, "for Western trained academics the whole area of wairua or 'the spiritual,' unless embedded in Christian theology, cuts across the rationalism and empiricism which is part of their training" (p. 112). A wairua approach, as discussed by Moewaka Barnes et al. (2017), demonstrates that for Māori we cannot and do not 'leave wairua at the door':

> ... a wairua approach places Māori in the centre of a world where past, present and future generations are at the forefront of affect; where wairua is felt as the ability to honour and connect to others, not simply a feeling on the day (p. 322).

In this section we briefly consider the attacks on Māori maternal knowledges caused by colonialism. The worlds and words with which Māori maternities were traditionally known have been marginalised, oppressed and in some cases outlawed, often leaving women and families bereft of a language that speaks to the power and sanctity of the maternal body. More than simply a harmless omission or an innocuous move from 'traditional' to 'modern', we argue that colonialism has systematically and purposefully attacked our wairua, while simultaneously institutionalising and medicalising maternal bodies. Colonialism and patriarchy have denied, and continue to deny, the legitimacy of

Māori women's knowledges and wairua, as well as the sanctity of maternal bodies. The intersection of colonial, racist and sexist oppressions positions many Māori women in in-between spaces and these remain largely unexamined in the academic literature.

The (mis)appropriation and (mis)representation of mana wahine maternal knowledges have impacted Māori women in specific ways. Early colonial ethnographers, usually male and white, 'researched' Māori traditions and wairua. Their research endeavours were framed by imperial epistemologies of 'discovery' and Christian ideologies. They spoke to Māori men, reified male figures in Māori mythology and imposed their cultural mores and values on the knowledges, wairua and bodies of Māori women (Mikaere, 2003; Yates-Smith, 1998).

For the most part, these early ethnographic accounts presented Māori women, in cosmological narratives and mythology, as passive, distant, irrational and polluting, in contrast to male characters who were considered active, present, rational and powerful. Further, Christian missionaries were quick to label Māori women in cosmologies and in our communities as wanton, immoral and undisciplined.

It was through these forms of Christianity that many Māori women were deprived of spiritual knowledge pertaining to maternities. The reproductive power of Māori women was quickly supplanted with ideologies of shame and sin. Furthermore, ethnographers privileged the stories of male deities, while the feminine elements have been misrepresented. Elsdon Best's writing exemplifies this. Discussing the creation of men and women, Best (1924) notes, "On the whole Māori leaned towards agnatic filiation, the male, he possesses greater mana than does the female, for is not man descended directly from the gods, while woman had to be created from earth!" (p. 89). This is a far cry from Māori understandings of te whare tangata and our relationship to Papatūānuku. The ethnographic (re)telling of Māori stories, and thus Māori realities, firmly established a hierarchy of knowledge, and our ancestresses and goddesses were quickly replaced with eurocentric ideologies of God: "God as male, God as ruling, God as natural ... God as white" (Pihama, 2001, p. 155). The impact of this on wairua and thus on Māori maternities is immense, fragmenting the knowledges, traditions and whakapapa of birth. It did not take long before these colonial ideologies became entrenched in legislation.

The Tohunga Suppression Act 1907, which remained unrepealed until 1962, was perhaps one of the most aggressive assaults on spiritual knowledges and it had a direct impact on maternities. At its very core the Act defined what was considered important and credible knowledge. At this point in time, European knowledges were almost entirely theological and scientific understandings were widely understood as heretical and improper. Māori spiritual knowledges were viewed as insufficient and improper, and therefore our ancestors were denied the right to access their own cultural and spiritual experts. Tohunga were often birth attendants or participated, in various ways, in ceremonies pertaining to fertility, pregnancy, birth, and naming and dedication rituals for infants (Yates-Smith, 1998). Preceding this Act was the Midwives Registration Act 1904. The requirements, under the Act, were that birth attendants be registered. Traditional Māori birth attendants could not be registered unless they were trained in Western midwifery under a non-Māori doctor. The outlawing of a whole class of Māori

[3] Tertiary maternity facilities are designed for women with complex maternity needs, who require specialist multidisciplinary care. 'Well women' (women who are not deemed to be 'high-risk' or have any complicating factors in their pregnancy and labour) may use these facilities in the absence of other maternity facilities in their area. Secondary Maternity Facilities are designed for women and babies who experience complications and may require care from an obstetrician, anaesthetist, paediatrician as well as a midwife. Well women may use these facilities in the absence of other maternity facilities in their area. Primary Maternity Facilities account for 9 percent of all births in New Zealand and these are made up of maternity units in smaller hospitals and birthing centres. Home births accounted for approximately 3 percent of all births in New Zealand in 2014 (Ministry of Health, 2014).

[4] 'Te Tuku o Hine-te-iwaiwa' is a karakia that is employed to assist with difficulties during birth. Hine-te-iwaiwa is considered to be one atua who presides over childbirth and the karakia originated during the birth of her son Tūhuruhuru (Yates-Smith, 1998). She is also thought to be the personified form of the moon (Yates-Smith, 1998), therefore solidifying her connection to women's maternal bodies through the monthly 'moon tides' of women and thus her affiliation with childbirth.

intellectuals, healers and carers through the Tohunga Suppression Act and the Midwives Registration Act stripped away many of the spiritual knowledges and practices in birth and further marginalised Māori maternal knowledges.

The post-World War II period saw a push for hospitalisation and the medicalisation of births. Moving Māori from home to hospital birth was the goal and this was largely achieved; over the course of the following three decades, Māori birthing became almost completely institutionalised, so that by 1967, 95 percent of Māori births occurred in the space of the hospital (Donley, 1986), and this has largely remained unchanged, with 87 percent of all births in New Zealand located in a tertiary or secondary maternity facility (Ministry of Health, 2014).[3]

Several mechanisms, through colonialism, have served to marginalise Māori maternities. The role of wairua in birth has been distorted and attacked on a number of fronts by Christianity. Further, birth was moved away from the auspices of family, spiritual experts and traditional birth attendants, to 'registered' midwives (most of whom were not Māori) or doctors (most of whom were white men). This is reiterated in the writing of Ani Mikaere (2003):

> Control over the process was completely in the hands of medical professionals, the doctors and the hospital staff. Husbands were not present, nor it seems, were other members of the whānau. The woman was completely isolated from her whānau and surrounded by strangers. There was no choice of location, nor of method. She was expected to lie on her back with her feet in stirrups and endure regular internal examinations without protest. There was no question of karakia to Hine-te-iwaiwa (the ancestress associated with childbirth),[4] for hospitals were about science, not superstition. And when the placenta eventually came away, it was borne off to the hospital incinerators without question (pp. 92–93).

Māori women are not alone in the forced transition of birth to the confines of the hospital. In Canada, First Nations women had to endure the changing spatiality of birth. Leanne Simpson (2006) writes:

> The birth of a child became something our women had to endure alone, rather than celebrated with the support of her extended family and community. Women were medicated and hospitalised, told that we could not give birth without the assistance of Western medicine. White doctors, who were 'experts' on birth, replaced our midwives and displaced our confidence in our bodies, our reliance on our traditional knowledge and our trust in our clans, our spirit-helpers, and our ancestors. Our midwives, aunties, and grandmothers were not allowed in delivery rooms, and neither were our medicines, our singing, our drumming, and our birthing knowledges. We were strapped flat on our backs on hospital beds, not allowed to use our knowledge of birthing which told us which positions to use, ways of minimising pain, and ways of birthing naturally and safely. Our male partners were stripped of their traditional responsibilities around birth and were relegated to waiting rooms. We were told that for the safety of our babies we needed intervention and to rely on the Western medical system; to do anything else, we were told, would be irresponsible (p. 28).

Both authors cited above highlight the role of the birthplace and the impositions and attacks on Indigenous women's bodily and spiritual integrity. Naomi Simmonds's (2014) research has revealed that these spatial, embodied and spiritual experiences of past generations are both relived and/or resisted in the birthing experiences of women and families today.

It needs to be remembered, however, that colonialism is not the defining feature of Māori women's birthing experiences. It is imperative, therefore, to look beyond colonialism to those knowledges that provide women, families and communities with ways of knowing and being in the world that recognise and celebrate the sanctity and wairua of the maternal body and of women more generally. Leonie Pihama (2012) explains this beautifully:

> Whakapapa remains irrespective of our knowledge of it. Our tūpuna will always be our tūpuna. What is crucial is finding a way of ensuring that all of our people are able to access that knowledge in order to locate themselves and their relationships with their whānau, hapū and iwi. Therefore our agenda cannot be solely one of challenging modernist constructions of identity but it must encompass a process of reclaiming those knowledge bases that have been submerged through colonialism.

Māori knowledges tell us that the integration of the physical and spiritual can be seamless. In a contemporary context, however, it is possible to see the fissures and cracks that have been caused by colonial attacks on the maternal body. Despite this, women continue to make sense of their maternity experiences through wairua and demonstrate new and creative ways to experience and express this.

Aro ki te Wairua o te Hā: Spatial and Embodied Experiences of Spirituality and Birth

This section builds on and extends the arguments already made that the maternal body is inextricable from the symbolic and the spiritual. It is argued that considering wairua as a critical axis of Māori women's subjectivities can radically transform how the maternal body is understood and how birth is experienced and performed. The authors have completed a comprehensive literature review that considers a wairua approach to pregnancy, childbirth and early parenting. Further, Simmonds' PhD thesis (2014) used a mana wahine approach to examine the lived experiences of birth for ten first-time mothers, five midwives and a group sharing space involving seventeen women and their families. These narratives inform this section.

It is significant that all the women discussed the role of wairua in relation to their birthing experiences. In fact, the importance of wairua to Māori maternities cannot be stressed enough. We contend that the spiritual realities of Māori women are inextricable from their physical realities. This is a consistent and unwavering theme that runs through expressions of Māori maternities both inside and outside of the academy (Gabel, 2013; Grace, 1992; Kahukiwa & Potiki, 1999; Mikaere, 2003; Murphy, 2011; Yates-Smith, 1998). Even when pregnancy and birth pathways appear well aligned with mainstream practices, we should not assume whānau experiences are devoid of what it means to be Māori; a key aspect of this is wairua. Wairua is ubiquitous in Māori contexts including, and especially during, pregnancy and birth. Wairua is experienced and enacted in all situations explicitly and implicitly, with profound impacts on the way whānau navigate services and experience this critical life stage (Simmonds, 2014). A wairua approach provides a powerful way of understanding experiences, practices and relationships in the context of Māori pregnancy and birthing, with significant implications for the health and wellbeing of mothers, babies and whānau.

For example, one woman in her late twenties, who birthed her son at home, explained: "During pregnancy and strongly during labour I felt connected to something greater than myself, to something words can't describe you can only feel … I believe that labour is a gift, our chance as women to grow spiritually, gain mana, to prepare us for the journey of parenthood" (Diary entry, December 2009). This significance of the spiritual was also acknowledged by midwives in Simmonds' research. Jacqui, a midwife practising in Rotorua, explains:

> It is really important because whatever is going on for this woman spiritually is going to impact on how well she births and how well she actually enjoys her pregnancy, her birth and her pēpi. (Key informant interview, November 2010)

What these and many other narratives exemplify is that acknowledging and providing for the spiritual side helps women to make sense of their lived, embodied and spatial experiences of pregnancy, birth and mothering. Reclaiming the spirituality of birth, therefore, is a critical site for Māori maternal knowledges and can be transformative for understandings of Māori women's subjectivities, knowledges, bodies, birth and, importantly, for our babies.

The manifestation of wairua varied across women's experiences. For some, wairua was about connecting to ancestors and/or atua such as Hine-te-iwaiwa. Karakia and mōteatea calling on these ancestors were recited. Other women felt a heightened presence and connection to those family members who may have passed away. This is not unusual for Māori, as illustrated by Leonie Pihama (2001) who notes that "in Māori terms the individual never moves alone, we are always surrounded and guided by generations past" (p. 26).

For others, the spatial politics of birth – where birth occurred – impacted and was impacted by their spiritual experiences. Some women focused on creating a space where they could calm their wairua (spirit) and prepare for the arrival of their baby. Wairua was present in various forms across all women's experiences regardless of the place in which they birthed. Some women, however, felt that 'home' enabled a more heightened spiritual experience than the hospital would have allowed. Sarah, mother to one son who was birthed at home, says:

> Just being at home, and our tīpuna (ancestors) they were all around. I don't know if being in hospital in such a sterile atmosphere would enable that. How do you relax when there are bright neon lights or whatever, white jackets and gloves around? (Interview, January 2010)

Midwife Lisa agrees:

> So at home births, the wairua there is really strong in comparison with a hospital birth ... the environment plays a huge part and the people around you at the time. So I always tell them if they are going to have support people make sure they've got positive people, they're calming, they've got a good influence on you and they are people who you want there who make you feel safe and comfortable, and usually that creates a nice wairua. (Key informant interview, June 2010)

It is too simplistic to simply argue that home birth is the only location in which to experience wairua in birth. The expectation that birth is or has to be 'spiritually transformative' given the right conditions and space can lead to some women feeling 'inadequate' if they don't experience birth in this way. It can also serve to isolate those spiritual experiences that do occur in hospitals, birthing centres or elsewhere, which, as Simmonds' doctoral research revealed, are many.

The use of karakia (prayer/incantations) is something that was performed by women and families regardless of the place in which they birthed. The role and form of karakia varied greatly but in many cases these karakia had very real physical implications. For example, one woman discussed the role of karakia in assisting her to birth the placenta:

> When baby was born my partner did a karakia, it was automatic for him. While I was birthing the placenta I had quite a lot of bleeding and it wasn't slowing down so he did another karakia to bring my awareness back to me. I was losing a lot of blood and once he did a karakia it settled down and I was able to focus back on baby. I needed that. (Interview, December 2009)

What this demonstrates is that within this cultural and spiritual context, the function of karakia can have very real corporeal implications. This is reinforced by Aroha Yates-Smith (1998):

> The significance of karakia in people's lives should not be underestimated. Karakia had a very strong impact on the people involved. In the karakia pertaining to birth, the child and family received encouragement. During the birth karakia had a powerful effect on the woman, providing her with a source of strength in at least two ways; first by invoking her forbears to be present to protect her and the child, and second in a hypnotic way, by drawing her out of the pain (p. 163).

For some women, karakia were used as a preventative measure, or perhaps more correctly as a normalised part of their pregnancy, birth and after-birth experiences. This was the case for Karina, aged in her early thirties:

> We did do lots of karakia and we did that often, before we did anything that I thought might be a little bit worrying I said, "Come on," and I asked Dad to prepare a little karakia for us for when we did go into birth. That was probably the main thing was that I wanted to make sure that someone was going to look after me. (Interview, May 2010)

Within the karakia 'Te Tuku o Hine-te-iwaiwa' are numerous references to specific birthing rituals and practices. The weaving of a ceremonial mat; the use of support posts in birth; and the performance of karanga (call) to welcome the new-born baby are all powerful examples of the rituals and ceremony that surrounded birth presented in this karakia. What is more, the after-birth rituals within Māori culture are vast. The most evidenced is the burial of the placenta in the earth, and in fact the word 'whenua' means both land and placenta (for more on this see Simmonds, 2016), but there are also processes and ceremony for naming, traditional cleansing and healing, dedication rituals and many more.

The significance of spirituality, whether through the use of karakia, the presence and/or assistance of a tohunga, the performance of particular ceremonies before, during and after birth, or simply creating a 'calming' atmosphere, makes it clear that te taha wairua is integral to the embodied experiences of birth for many of the women in this research. The spiritual and physical are inextricably linked and the implications of this for understandings of the maternal body should not be underestimated.

A 1998 study of maternity experiences for Māori women (Rimene et al., 1998) recorded that a number of women expressed concern over the lack of personal dignity they were afforded during childbirth. Similarly, a study about Māori perceptions of assisted reproduction found that some women were fearful of in vitro fertilisation treatments because of the potentially invasive techniques that may be used (Glover, 2008). In a broader context, Fiona Cram and Linda Smith (2003) point out that a number of health checks and medical procedures for women are culturally and physically invasive. For example, they explain that many Māori women feel embarrassed about cervical smear testing. It was expressed in the Cartwright Inquiry Report[5] (1988) that for Māori women the "cultural mores of modesty are not understood by, or even recognised by, most health professionals and especially doctors" (p. 115). It is clear that reinstating the sanctity of the maternal body can have very real implications for the treatment of women during pregnancy and birth. The challenge lies in supporting our women, men, families, communities, practitioners and professionals to understand and express within the spaces of birth the wairua of birth and the sacred nature of women's bodies and of te whare tangata.

Conclusion – Rangatiratanga, Birth and Wairua

A Wairua Approach (Moewaka Barnes et al., 2017) is fundamentally about reclaiming what is important to us as Māori, and important to us as Māori researchers who no longer agree (explicitly or implicitly) to 'leave wairua at the door' of the academy, or in fact the hospital or any other part of our lives (Ratima, 2008). Wairua is not static and outside of feelings, emotions and actions but is something we work at and with, shaping and being shaped by us at every turn as we make sense of our lives. Our research approach places wairua at the centre, as everyday practice, not just 'supernatural', ritualistic or organised expressions of experience. An in-depth exploration of wairua will support the development and enrichment of practices that, for example, draw on tradition as well as

---

[5] The Cartwright Inquiry, undertaken in 1987–1988, looked into allegations concerning the treatment of women for cervical cancer at National Women's Hospital. Sylvia Cartwright, an Auckland District Court Judge, was appointed to conduct the inquiry. The report of the Committee of Inquiry into allegations concerning the treatment of cervical cancer at National Women's Hospital and into other related matters was released in 1988.

current understandings, and engage those who do not have equitable access (including access to 'cultural' practices) to the support and services they need.

Te whare tangata, the birth of Papatūānuku and many other concepts, histories and ancestresses provide us with a body of maternal knowledges that is replete with legacies about resilience and the capacity for resistance, the unique place of women, the sanctity of women's bodies, the power of female sexuality, the complementary roles of men and women within maternities and the central role of children within the community. We contend that these 'stories' – our genealogies and histories – have the potential to radically transform the way in which maternal corporeality is read and understood by women, their families and those who are charged with the responsibility to care for maternal bodies (Carlson, 2019). Furthermore, they tell us that the integration of the corporeal, symbolic and spiritual can be seamless. As Ani Mikaere (2003) points out, "this should not be surprising for the logic of whakapapa (genealogies) tells us that in the final analysis, we are our atua and they are us" (p. 319).

This chapter has sought to examine the wairua of birth for Māori women and families. In doing so, we aim to reveal the possibilities of reconceptualising the maternal body through concepts such as te whare tangata. It is argued that such understandings of birth and of maternal bodies can facilitate opportunities for movement toward more positive conceptualisations of maternities for women and families. The impact of colonisation on birth and the attempts to sever maternal bodies from the spiritual have been discussed. Further, contemporary experiences of wairua within the spaces of birth have also been also presented, to demonstrate the enduring nature of Indigenous spiritual and maternal knowledges, and to understand the relevance and significance of them to our contemporary experiences as Indigenous women today.

There is a risk that isolating and analysing aspects of wairua (spirituality) could threaten its very fabric and leave it open to appropriation. Further, it is important that in any attempts to understand the spirituality of birth for Māori, we avoid definitions that are narrow, prescriptive or constrictive. Thus, Māori self-determination over Māori maternal knowledges and spiritualities is important and is in many ways contextually, culturally and spatially bound. There are some important connections to other Indigenous maternities (see Anderson, 2000; Lavell-Harvard & Lavell, 2006; Simpson, 2006). That said, there is great diversity in the ways in which spirituality is understood and performed within tribes and families and there are even individual differences. As such, expressions and experiences of spirituality in relation to birth can range from the extraordinary to the ordinary, from the astonishing to the subtle.

To conclude, we return to those in-between spaces. Experiences and understandings of wairua and the maternal body, and of birth within Māori culture, exist in varying shades of light and dark and all that exists in between. Such is the beauty of our cultural understandings, as Ani Mikaere (2011) explains: "instead of searching for meaning in simplistic dichotomies such as black and white, we expect and even delight in the subtleties of light and shade" (p. 296). We are researchers, but more than this, we are māmā who have birthed our babies at home and experienced wairua as a space to hold trust through vulnerability, which has been facilitated and enhanced by Māori birthing traditions. As wāhine we exist in these in-between spaces, we facilitate movement between them and we can do so in a powerful way by taking heed of the spirituality of breath, of birth and of new life. Me aro ki te wairua o te hā.

References

ADAMS, T. (2017). *Te Kura reo o Raukawa: Kia tika, kia rere, kia Māori* (Paenga Whā). Tokoroa, New Zealand: Raukawa Charitable Trust.

ANDERSON, K. (2000). *A Recognition of being: Reconstructing native womanhood*. Toronto, Canada: Sumach Press.

BEST, E. (1924). *Māori religion and mythology: Being an account of the cosmogony, anthropogeny, religious beliefs and rites, magic and folk lore of the Māori folk of New Zealand*. Wellington, New Zealand: Government Printer.

CALMAN, R. (2004). Introduction. In A. W. Reed (Ed.), *Reed Book of Māori Mythology* (pp. xiii–xvii). Auckland, New Zealand: Reed.

CARLSON, T. (2019). Mana motuhake o Ngāti Porou: Decolonising health literacy. *Sites*, 16(2), 77–103.

CARTWRIGHT INQUIRY. (1988). *The Report of the Committee of Inquiry into allegations concerning the treatment of Cervical Cancer at National Women's Hospital and into other related matters*. Auckland New Zealand: Government Printing Office.

CRAM, F., & SMITH, L. T. (2003). Māori women talk about accessing health care. *He Pūkenga Kōrero: A Journal of Māori Studies*, 7(2), 1–8.

DONLEY, J. (1986). *Save the midwife*. Auckland, New Zealand: New Women's Press.

GABEL, K. (2013). *Poipoia te Tamaiti ki te Ūkaipō* (Doctoral dissertation). University of Waikato, Hamilton, New Zealand. Retrieved from https://researchcommons.waikato.ac.nz/handle/10289/7986

GLOVER, M. (2008). *Māori attitudes to assisted human reproduction: An exploratory study*. Auckland, New Zealand: University of Auckland, Department of Social & Community Health.

GRACE, P. (1992). *Cousins*. Auckland, New Zealand: Penguin Books.

KAHUKIWA, R., & POTIKI, R. (1999). *Oriori: A Māori child is born – from conception to birth*. Auckland, New Zealand: Tandem Press.

LAVELL-HARVARD, D. M., & LAVELL, J. C. (EDS.) (2006). *Until our hearts are on the ground: Aboriginal mothering, oppression, resistance and rebirth*. Toronto, Canada: Demeter Press.

MIKAERE, A. (2003). *The balance destroyed: Consequences for Māori women of the colonisation of Tikanga Māori*. Auckland, New Zealand: The International Research Institute for Māori and Indigenous Education.

MIKAERE, A. (2011). *Colonising Myths – Māori Realities: He Rukuruku Whakaaro*. Wellington, New Zealand: Huia Publishers and Te Wānanga o Raukawa.

MINISTRY OF HEALTH. (2014). *Report on Maternity 2014*. Wellington, New Zealand: Ministry of Health.

MOEWAKA BARNES, H., RAINA GUNN, T., MOEWAKA BARNES, A., MCPHEE, E., WETHERELL, M., & MCCREANOR, T. (2017). Feeling and spirit: Developing an indigenous wairua approach to research. *Qualitative Research*, 17(3), 313–325.

MURPHY, N. (2011). *Te awa atua, te awa tapu, te awa wahine: An examination of stories, ceremonies and practices regarding menstruation in the pre-colonial Māori world* (Master's thesis). University of Waikato, Hamilton, New Zealand.

PIHAMA, L. (2001). *Tihei Mauri Ora: Honouring our voices: Mana Wahine as a Kaupapa Māori theoretical framework* (Doctoral dissertation). University of Auckland, Auckland, New Zealand.

PIHAMA, L. (2012, JUNE 24). *Reconstructing meanings of family: Lesbian/gay Whānau and families in Aotearoa.* Te Wharepora Hou Blog. Retrieved from https://tewhareporahou.wordpress.com/2012/06/24/reconstructing-meanings-of-family-lesbian-whānau-and-families-in-aotearoa-3/

RATIMA, M. (2008). Making space for Kaupapa Māori within the academy. *MAI Review*, 1. Retrieved from https://www.researchgate.net/publication/26508542_Peer_Commentary_1_-_Making_space_for_Kaupapa_Maori_within_the_academy

RIMENE, C., HASSAN, C., & BROUGHTON, J. (1998). *Ukaipo: The place of nurturing.* Dunedin, New Zealand: Te Rōpū Rangahou Hauora Māori o Ngāi Tahu.

SIMMONDS, N. (2014). *Tū te turuturu nō Hine-te-iwaiwa: Mana wahine geographies of birth in Aotearoa* (Doctoral dissertation). University of Waikato, Hamilton, New Zealand.

SIMMONDS, N. (2016). Transformative maternities: Indigenous stories as resistance and reclamation in Aotearoa New Zealand. In M. Robertson & P. Tsang (Eds.), *Everyday knowledge, education and sustainable futures: Education in the Asia-Pacific region: Issues, concerns and prospects, vol 30.* (pp. 71–88). Singapore: Springer.

SIMPSON, L. (2006). Birthing an indigenous resurgence: Decolonizing our pregnancy and birthing ceremonies. In D. M. Lavell-Harvard & J. C. Lavell (Eds.), *Until our hearts are on the ground: Aboriginal mothering, oppression, resistance and rebirth* (pp. 25–33). Toronto, Canada: Demeter Press.

SMITH, L. T. (1996). *Ngā aho o te kākahu mātauranga: The multiple layers of struggle by Māori in education* (Doctoral dissertation). University of Auckland, Auckland, New Zealand.

SMITH, L. T. (2012). *Decolonizing methodologies: Research and indigenous peoples.* London, England: Zed Books.

YATES-SMITH, A. (1998). *Hine! E Hine! Rediscovering the feminine in Māori spirituality* (Doctoral dissertation). University of Waikato, Hamilton, New Zealand.

Raranga Wahakura: Weaving Wellbeing for Mokopuna and Whānau

Tanya White

CHAPTER 12

Wahakura are vessels of wellbeing, providing safe sleeping spaces that give tangible form to applications and processes of Tikanga Pā Harakeke. As such, they are a woven manifestation of whakapapa and an embodiment of mana, mauri and tapu, emanating from the pā harakeke, a site of significance, a wāhi tapu and a repository of taonga raranga. This chapter presents a case study of raranga wahakura. It is an articulation of raranga epistemology from a weaver's perspective. It works to highlight the essentiality that relationships with Papatūānuku have towards achieving hauora outcomes for mokopuna. Tikanga Pā Harakeke provides a tangible model of practice for oranga whānau, serving as a point of access for whānau to connect with te ao Māori, and its fundamental nature as a 'woven universe'.

Whakaahua 1: Wahakura Rangimārie Pā Harakeke.

A Weaver's Perspective

As kairaranga, a weaver, a grandmother, a descendant and a mokopuna from many, I am my own case study. The wahakura I weave are the workings of many. They are data that evidence a woven network of whakapapa relationships to whānau, tūpuna, atua, Papatūānuku and te taiao.

Waiomio is the awa. Miria is the marae.

Te Rapunga is the whare tūpuna. Hahaunga is the whare kai.

Wairere is the urupā.

Hineāmaru is the tupuna wahine.

It was on my mother's marae that I first saw how people are woven together, to each other, to the whenua and to tūpuna.

At the tangi of my nanny Moengaroa, I saw my mother's hūpē, like long strands of translucent muka, stretching down from her nostrils, twisting and twining with the waters leaking from her eyes. Falling, and reaching back. Returning again to the whenua, I learned that the weaving of wai in the flow of hūpē and roimata linked us to our wider selves and to Papatūānuku, as she opened to receive our loved ones.

When I was eleven there was a reunion at Miria marae for the descendants of Poraumati Riki Reihana and Huia Maihi Kawiti, my mother's paternal grandparents. I remember sitting in Te Rapunga, our whare kaumātua, and being in awe of the reams of brown paper covering the walls of our meeting house. Upon this brown paper was written a meticulous account of our whakapapa connections, to each other and to the wider groupings of Ngāti Hineāmaru. I sat for hours, carefully writing with pencil the ancestor names from the paper on the wall into a book of remembrance my parents had given to me. Rows and columns of names were grouped according to the specific branches from the family tree they represented. Interspersed with horizontal and vertical penned lines, the words, the names, the tūpuna were woven, just like the photos of loved ancestors carefully grouped by the aunties and presented on the walls. They exhibited a raranga pattern repeating itself in various ways around the walls of the whare, giving a sense of movement and continuum. This was my first conscious witnessing, as an eleven-year-old, of the whakapapa grid.[1] It is upon these experiences within Te Rapunga that my understanding of whakapapa is planted.

Te Kahu o te Ao: The Epistemological Fabric of Raranga

WEAVING A WORLDVIEW

The universe is woven. Raranga epistemology is grounded in whakapapa relationships to Papatūānuku, to the natural environment, and to the very fabric of the universe. The writings of Reverend Māori Marsden (2003) state that "The whare wānanga sees and interprets the world as a *kahu*, a fabric comprising a fabulous matrix of energies; rhythmical patterns of pure energy, woven together" (p. xiii). After World War II, Māori Marsden returned to the wānanga that had convened in Hokianga, and was questioned by the elders about his war experiences. One of the elders asked him to explain the difference between an atom bomb and an explosive bomb. Marsden (2003, p. xiii) recalled Einstein's concept of the real world behind the natural world as being comprised

---

[1] Dr Pat Hohepa (Henare, Petrie, & Puckey, 2009) talks about the organised arrangement of ancestors: "It is the fixed chart view of the item and the arrangement. You are the item, they are the arrangement. It is a static diagram" (p. 131).

of "rhythmical patterns of pure energy" as essentially being the same as what Māori refer to as 'hihiri' (pure energy). Marsden (2003) relates the following conversation and provides an English translation in his essay on kaitiakitanga:

> Ka tū mai a Toki, ka kī, "E mea ana koe, kua oti i ngā tohunga Pākehā te hahae i te kahu o te Ao?"
> Ka kī atu au, "Ki taku mōhio, āe."
> Ka kī mai a Toki, "E taea e rātou te tuitui?" Ka kī atu au, "Ki taku mōhio, kāo."
>
> "Do you mean to tell me that the Pākehā scientists (tohunga Pākehā) have managed to rend the fabric (kahu) of the universe?"
> I said, "Yes."
> "But do they know how to sew (tuitui) it back together again?"
> "No!" (p. xiii)

Io is the grandmaster weaver, sewing the universe together into a magnificent woven fabric of cosmological purpose and design, Te Kahu o te Ao (the fabric of the universe). Our place within this woven fabric is displayed in rituals of encounter upon the marae, as woven whakapapa relationships between people and cosmological divine order are demonstrated.

In conversation with kaumātua Pat Ruka he told me about whakapapa:

> "Whakapapa is like this," he said, as he spread his arms out wide, stretching them both out to their widest extent. He brought his hands back together, palms facing, and slowly began to extend them out again to their outstretched limits. "Whakapapa is all of your whanaungatanga."

"So, is it all encompassing?" I asked.

"Yes, it is," he replied, moving his outstretched arms from his side, to above his head and then below to the lowest point of their arc, creating a spherical shape. He continued to explain:

"When the kaumātua stood to speak he would encircle himself with his cloak like this [matua Pat demonstrates by crossing his arms close to his chest] because he was encircling himself with his whakapapa. Then he would begin his kōrero.

"Whakaheke is your specific descent from a particular ancestor, like Rahiri, or Māui-tikitiki … and tātai are the short descent lines, like your tātai from Kawiti." Matua Pat again stretched his arms out wide retracing the arc of the sphere around his body, "Whakapapa is the papa of the whaka or haka" (White, 2017a, p. 16).

Wahakura are a Woven Manifestation of Whakapapa

The wahakura is a taonga that articulates fundamental whakapapa relationships between the weaver, the whenua and the wider whānau and hapori. There are links and intrinsic relationships held by a woven vessel (Pā Henare Tate, in Maihi & Lander, 2005). Links to harakeke and Papatūānuku, where rituals are observed. Links to the kairaranga, the one who gathered, worked and caressed the leaves of harakeke to give shape and design. Links to the mokopuna when the wahakura is passed to whānau. And links to tūpuna and atua in applications of tikanga that frame raranga processes. Whakapapa, which is 'all of our whanaungatanga', is the foundation of our being. It encompasses all relationships we experience – not only the relationships between people, but also connections to the whenua, moana, celestial bodies and to atua. It is the connective tissue linking all things from the infinite cosmos to microcosmic organisms.

Ngā Kaitiaki

There are numerous kaitiaki associated with raranga, including Hine-te-iwaiwa, Huna and Rukutia (Harrison, Te Kanawa, & Higgins, 2004). Huna is recognised as the principal atua for the pā harakeke. Harakeke is an offspring of Tāne and Huna.

Whakaahua 2: Whakapapa o te Harakeke.

Another rendition of whakapapa adds Kōuka, Tīkapu and Toi as offspring of Tāne and Huna (White, 2017a).

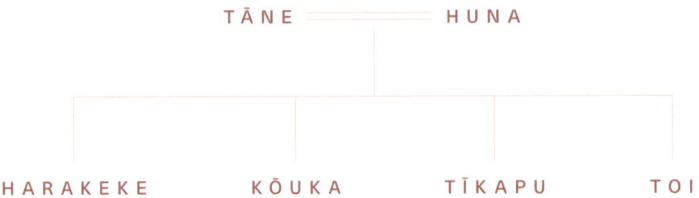

Whakaahua 3: Whakapapa o te Harakeke 2.

Harakeke is also recognised as an offspring of Tāne and Pākoti, as outlined in the following genealogical chart that shows the whakapapa of Poi (Paringatai, 2020).

Whakaahua 4: Whakapapa o te Poi.

Another whakaheke (single-line descent) highlights Raranga-ihi-matua as the essence of harakeke. Raranga-ihi-matua takes Hinemukataiore (harakeke that grows by the sea) as his wife, and from their three children come descent lines containing many varieties of harakeke grouped according to their major uses.

Hine-te-iwaiwa

Hine-te-iwaiwa is the daughter of Tānemahuta and Hinerauamoa.

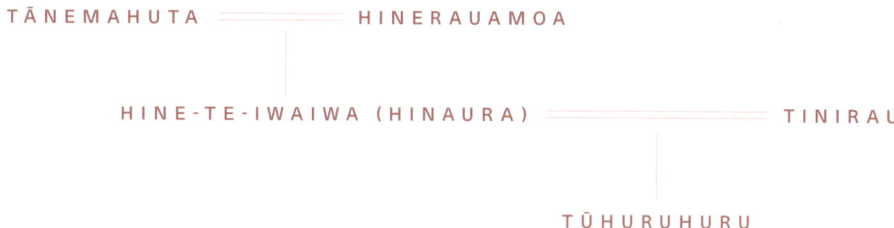

Whakaahua 5: Whakapapa o Hine-te-iwaiwa.

Pūrākau

Hine-te-iwaiwa, who was once known as Hinaura, is the kaitiaki of the whare pora (house of weaving) and childbirth (Jenkins & Harte, 2011). Her story is one of transformation. It speaks of courage, strength and resilience through adversity.

Hinaura, sister (also known by some as cousin) to Māui, had married Irawaru, who was transformed into a dog by Māui-tikitiki. The grieving Hinaura threw herself into the sea, and was washed ashore at the home of Tinirau, whom she eventually married. Hinaura and Tinirau had a child, Tūhuruhuru. They were very happy together for a time, living at the kāinga of Tinirau until Tinirau hit Hinaura, which caused her to leave, taking her son and returning to her whanau village. After months of pleading from Tinirau, Hinaura returned to his kāinga with Tūhuruhuru. They were again happy until one day Tinirau found another woman. Hinaura objected, so Tinirau imprisoned her behind a wall of magic whale ribs. Hinaura was angered and called to her brother Māui-mua for assistance. Māui changed himself into the form of a rupe, pigeon, so Hinaura could ride on his back and escape her prison. Hinaura gathered courage and decided to move on with her life. To mark the event, she changed her named to Hine-te-iwaiwa and became patron of the powers and responsibilities of women in relation to whānau and the arts. She protects and defends women in their work, especially in hapūtanga and the arts of the whare pora. Her pao (song, chant) is used during birthing to assist safe passage for the newborn infant.

Harakeke, Korari

Harakeke, also known as korari, is one of the ancients – fossil pollen dates harakeke at around 21 million years (McGruddy, 2006) – a tuakana and offspring of Tāne and Huna, who was birthed with the eruptions of Rūaumoko and the emergence, or fishing up, of Te Ika a Māui. Harakeke is a long-serving kaitiaki, for millions of years, standing as a natural filter for the waterways it grows beside and sustaining primordial interrelationships in the pā harakeke. It flourishes in the transition zones between land and water, whenua and wai, and assists in the regeneration of mauri. Harakeke is resilient and robust, fast growing and tolerant to extreme conditions including wind, frost and flood (White, 2017a).

Harakeke became essential to wellbeing. Muka (harakeke fibre) became the raw material of whatu kākāhu (cloak making) designs that are unique to Aotearoa. Harakeke was used in the making of nets, all manner of kete (vessels), mats, cordage for fishing and lashings for whare and waka.

Harakeke continues to be a rongoā, used for healing purposes. Harakeke has antifungal, antiseptic and antibacterial properties. At the birth of a child, muka is prepared and tied to the umbilical cord at the pito, as a natural alternative to conventional cord clamps. Muka can also be used as a bandage or sponge to treat infection. Externally, harakeke is used as a poultice to treat boils and ringworm and the take, or firm lower ends of the harakeke, are used to make splints. The liquid from boiling the leaves and roots of harakeke can be used as a disinfectant. Internally, harakeke is a strong purgative to cure intestinal worms, dysentery and other such ailments (Riley, 1994).

Harakeke does not belong to the flax family, but was designated as such by botanists aboard the *Endeavour* because of the similarity between its fibre and that of the 'true linen flax' growing in Europe and other parts of the world. Harakeke is a lily from the botanical Agavaceae family (White, 2017a).

Tikanga Pā Harakeke

A weaver maintains connections to Papatūānuku through tikanga that sustains relationships to te taiao and the gathering of materials in a sustainable way.

Tikanga associated with the gathering of harakeke is expressed in the following well-known whakataukī, composed by Te Aupōuri kuia rangatira, Meri Ngaroto, in the early nineteenth century. It is an intercessory appeal by Ngaroto to prevent the massacre of a group of manuhiri who were visiting Ōhaki marae in Ahipara (Henare, 1995; Henare, Puckey, & Nicholson, 2011; Quince, 1999).

> Hutia te rito o te harakeke Kei hea te kōmako e kō?
> Kī mai ki ahau
> He aha te mea nui o te ao? Māku e kī atu
> He tangata, he tangata, he tangata.

> If you pluck out the heart, the new shoot of the harakeke
> Where will the bellbird sing?
> If you ask me
> What is of most importance in this world? I will answer
> It is the new shoot, the mokopuna, it is people.

Ngaroto draws upon the metaphor of the pā harakeke as a representation of a thriving community and whānau. The long, sword-shaped leaves of the harakeke are joined at their base in the shape of a fan. Each fan represents a whānau. The rito is the central shoot and considered the heart of the pā harakeke. It represents the child, pēpi or mokopuna of the harakeke whānau. It is the new growth.

The paramount objective of Tikanga Pā Harakeke is to protect the rito, because the rito ensures the continuation and longevity of the whānau. The leaves on either side of the rito are mātua, parent leaves, also known as awhi rito because they embrace and nurture the rito. Outer leaves are referred to as tūpuna, ancestors. It is these outer leaves that are generally harvested for weaving purposes. If the central shoot, the heart, or the rito of the harakeke plant is plucked out, the wellbeing of the harakeke whānau becomes severely impaired. Without new growth, or children to sustain its development, a whānau will eventually die. In her plea, Ngaroto is not only asking for the manuhiri who were present to be spared, but all those potential descending generations who are connected to them – those yet to be born.

As an ecological model, the whakataukī speaks about our responsibilities towards care and protection of the whānau harakeke. It is a direct reference to the responsibilities of people to interact with each other and with the environment in a careful and sustainable way. It speaks about manaakitanga and kaitiakitanga and reminds us that our actions will have far-reaching consequences, spanning generations.

Harakeke whānau grow together in clusters. Each cluster is referred to as a pūharakeke (Hiroa, 1911). This can be viewed as a hapū formed by a group of united whānau. A grouping of pūharakeke, however formed (whether cultivated in measured rows, or occurring naturally within the landscape), is known as a pā harakeke. The pā harakeke thus represents a huinga of united hapū or pūharakeke. 'Pā harakeke' is a term that can be used to signify generations, and is a metaphor used to represent the gene pools inherited by children from their two parents (Moorfield, 2005). A pā is also a fortified village and the pā harakeke provides a fort for the thriving ecosystem it supports. It is capable of sustaining a considerable community of varied animal life by providing shelter and a food source. 'Pā' can also refer to connection. Pā harakeke can literally be interpreted as 'being connected with harakeke' and conveys the nature of the pā harakeke as a site of reciprocity and connection, in processes of giving and receiving.

Pūkeko, ducks and other manu find shelter for their nests at the centre of pūharakeke clusters, encircled by the protective fans of individual whānau groups. A multitude of insects live among its leaves, roots and flowers. Nectar-feeding manu including the tūī, korimako and pihipihi (wax-eye) come to pollinate and partake of the sweet liquid produced by the flowering plants. Hutia te rito o te harakeke is a whakataukī that demonstrates an awareness of plant–pollinator relationships and the interconnectedness of ecosystems. The wellbeing of the harakeke ecosystem has a direct effect on the welfare of surrounding ecosystems. This knowledge, imparted through whakataukī, waiata and oriori, influences the collective behaviours of weavers who are assigned to protect the balance and order of natural ecosystems when gathering materials for weaving.

Wahakura

The wahakura kaupapa emerges from the rangahau and work of Dr David Tipene-Leach in the field of SUDI (Sudden Unexplained Death in Infancy) prevention and Safe Sleeping practices. It is a return to a traditional Māori way of sleeping babies that promotes breastfeeding and bonding with baby. Dr Tipene-Leach (2007), as part of the Wahakura Project, notes that Best (1975) records a bassinet-like structure in pre-European times called a porokaraka: "A flax [harakeke] cradle that was slung from a tree or from the rafters of the wharepuni (sleeping house) or wherever the mother went" (p. 6). It was also noted that kuia involved in the 2007 Wahakura Project spoke of babies being laid in kete kūmara to sleep while the parents tended their gardens. The Wahakura Project (Tipene-Leach, 2007) developed a life-saving taonga that was built upon ancient traditions and previous experiences of kairaranga.

The first wahakura I wove was for my daughter Maiarangi, born in 1993. I was a student of Kahutoi Te Kanawa, and part of the weaving programme at Puukenga, Te Whare Wānanga o Wairaka, Unitec. Hundreds of fine-width whenu (harakeke strands) were used. The design was whakatū weave, with three whiri at its foundation. The harakeke was gathered from Waiatarua at the base of Maungarei maunga. We didn't call it wahakura at that time. It was a waka, or pēpi moenga. The components were and are the same: harakeke, or kiekie, and three whiri at the base, to provide integrity and strength in their foundations. This structure also links to the previously mentioned porokaraka, which would have relied on strong foundations in order to be hung from the rafters of the wharepuni.

Whakaahua 6: Plaiting together the whenu.

As the whenu are woven together, there is a plaiting and weaving of whakapapa connections. The mauri of the whenua integrates into the next phase of development and the base of the wahakura begins to develop. There is a sharing of knowledge as interested participants contribute and participate in the shaping of kōrero. The mauri of people present becomes a part of the wahakura (White, 2017a).

From the three-whiri base, connections are solidified, allowing for further development as the sides and embracing body of the wahakura tinana are formed.

He Wahakura, he Wānanga

Every weaving of a wahakura is a wānanga, a learning journey that is specific to the creation of that particular taonga. There is a learning that happens in the relationships between the weaver, the whenua and the whānau. It is an opportunity to take notice of ngā tohu o te taiao, the signs and indicators from the whenua, from the environment. It is these indicators that will guide processes around the timing of when to gather the harakeke, which pā harakeke to gather from, how the harakeke will be prepared and who will participate in the weaving. Ngā tohu o te pā harakeke, signs and indicators from the pā harakeke, are unique on any given day. They reveal relationships to the whenua and can provide understandings about the conditions of whakapapa from which the wahakura emerges. On one occasion, after offering a karakia next to the pā harakeke I intended to gather from, I became aware of a chorus of tātarakihi (cicada) in the trees above. One, who seemed to be the length of the palm of my hand, flew to land directly on the area of my ngākau. I was a little startled by the size, so I did a quick mihi, "Tēnā koe e te rangatira," and then, "Ka kite anō," with a careful brush of my hand. He flew out, about an arm's length away, and then straight back in, landing directly on my nose. The hongi, and direct synthesis of mauri, was acknowledged, as was the role of tātarakihi as kaitiaki in the whakapapa of that wahakura.

On occasion, I have had the opportunity to wānanga with whānau who come together to gather harakeke, to prepare whenu, to learn together and to weave their wahakura. The weaving of the wahakura becomes a weaving of whānau, through many hours of laughter, talking and sharing. It becomes a manifestation of their aroha in the weaving and shaping of a taonga. Below, I am pictured with one such whānau ātaahua, who were expecting their

Whakaahua 7: Greeting the pā harakeke with māmā Mani and her whānau, 2017.
Inset: Papa Hayden gathering harakeke.

first mokopuna. The kuia of the whānau had just arrived from Pōneke. We are greeting Rangimārie pā harakeke, and preparing to place whenu in the awa. Shown in the inset is pēpi's pāpā, who had come two days earlier with pēpi's māmā to gather harakeke. Leaves gathered were prepared with aroha, and the muka released in preparation for whiri.

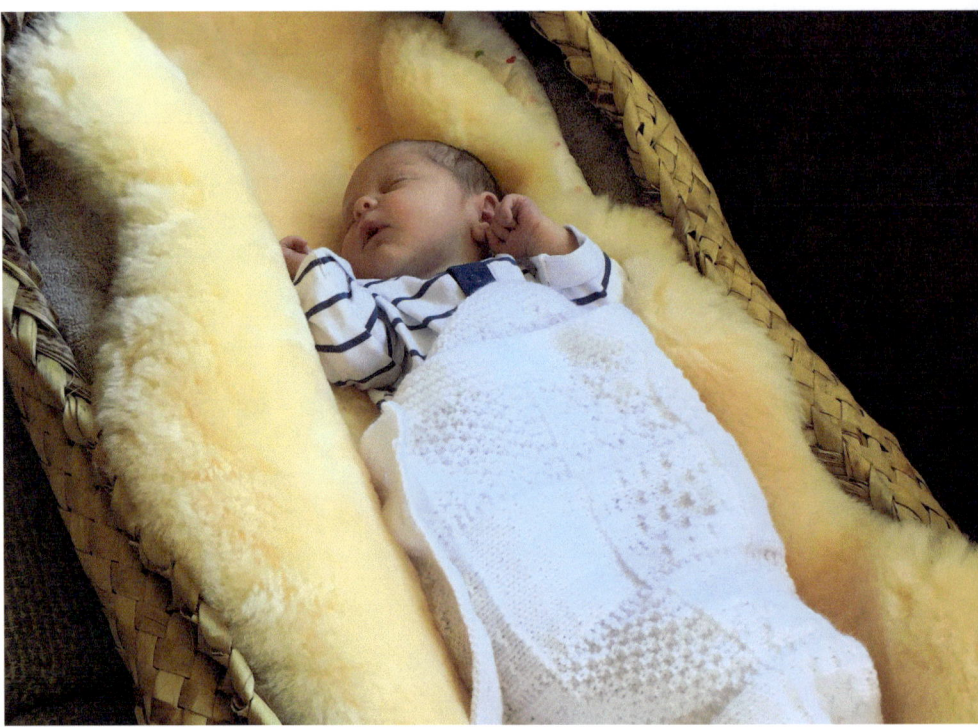

Whakaahua 8: Pikiarero in her wahakura Kotahi te Aroha.

The following kōrero was shared by māmā Mani.

> As a māmā I felt so empowered and inspired by seeing my partner's and whānau's hands weaving something together for the arrival of pēpi and my kōpū felt surrounded by so much aroha. Hapūtanga is a beautiful process but in a modern society where our lives tend to be rushed and busy, I feel it is easy to become disconnected to the sacredness and beauty of growing life. This wānanga enabled me to reconnect with Papatūānuku and bring my focus back to what is important, and a firm reminder of the aroha baby has around her – to me the wahakura is an embodiment of that. (Mani Dunlop, personal communication with the author, 2017)

In recent years, I've been involved with the Weaving Waiora Wānanga, an initiative of Ngāti Whātua Ōrakei Whai Māia. It is a special blessing when I get to meet the parents and whānau who receive the wahakura during the hapūtanga wānanga; then some time later, I often get to meet the mokopuna who have arrived. I feel a connection to them, the pēpi, through the wahakura, the raranga process and the synthesis of mauri.

In 2017 Ngāti Whātua ki Ōrakei came to Te Noho Kotahitanga marae, Unitec, to receive a group of wahakura that had been woven from Rangimarie pā harakeke. While in the whare Ngākau Māhaki, we were able to share experiences and connections to the wahakura kaupapa. Beronia (master weaver) shared a vision of ngā waka o ngā mokopuna: "I'm seeing all the mokopuna in these waka (wahakura) rowing together, and the wake behind them, that is the ancestors." Sariah (weaving waiora facilitator) expressed that the wahakura were taonga tuku iho from our tūpuna: "We're lucky to have that knowledge, skill and expertise still available for us. Not just for us, for our mokopuna."

Whakaahua 9: Wahakura at Ngākau Māhaki wharenui 2017.

Whakaahua 10: Weaving Waiora Ngāti Whātua at Te Noho Kotahitanga marae, 2017.

Whaea Virginia (kuia of Weaving Waiora) stated:

> As wāhine, it is intrinsically within us. We have the knowledge to be able to share to all our hapū māmā, to all our mokopuna. To be able to make them safe through this kaupapa. As each one has shared what they have seen and experienced with the wahakura, I keep seeing that we can keep our babies safe. Keep them close to us, and keep them safe. And we can pass that kaupapa and knowledge on, into our generations (White, 2017b, n.p.).

Matua Toko (Weaving Waiora and Ngāti Whātua kaumātua) began by presenting a cooking analogy, and then returned our focus to connections to Papatūānuku:

> The only time my children enjoy my cooking, is when I enjoy cooking it. When I take my time to cook the meal, I cook it with my heart. Same with the weaving of the wahakura. Every weaver will weave in their own time, at their own pace, and they're getting their own therapy and rongoā, their own mirimiri, and they're weaving their own kōrero into every binding of the wahakura.
>
> You might say that this is the completed weaving from the weaver, yet you still have the weaving with the pēpi inside the wahakura. There is a weave that the pēpi has around the mother and the father, and again with all the siblings. And then you have the weaving of the whānau.
>
> This is the many faces of the weave. It is not just what is in front of us. It is what is inside, and before it. What it actually takes to get the muka. What it takes to grow the harakeke. And again, it all comes back to Papatūānuku. The intent belongs with Papatūānuku. Even for the men (in White, 2017b, n.p.).

Mokopuna

Mokopuna are the rito, they are the new growth and the heart of our pā harakeke, our whānau and communities. They grow between the embrace of awhi rito – parents, grandparents and the wider whānau. Mokopuna are our maintenance plan. They carry our mātauranga pītau ira (DNA knowledge), and our aspirations and ways of being are reflected in them. The wahakura has become part of our legacy left for them. As Tipene-Leach states, "A generation now exists who do not know the times before the wahakura. It is as if the wahakura has always been here and it is woven into the fabric of our family lives" (in Faiers, Rhind-Wiri, & Selby-Law, 2019).

We are all mokopuna. Descendants of ancestors, connected to whakapapa layers that are woven through and from Te Kahu o Te Ao, the woven fabric of the universe.

The process of weaving the wahakura supports the wellbeing of whānau and whenua. Expressions of oranga tangata, oranga whenua are conveyed in Ngā Whenu o te Wahakura (Faiers et al., 2019): "From te ao Māori perspective, the land and the plants sourced from it intrinsically sustain and nourish the wellbeing of whānau and communities" (p. 7). Hāpai te Hauora continues to relate the movement and flow of process from whenua to mokopuna: "Wahakura are made of harakeke, and the process from its inception at the pā harakeke, through to the weaving of each whenu, through to the practical application of the wahakura, inherently sustains the wellbeing of mokopuna" (in Faiers et al., 2019, p. 7).

Pictured below is pēpi Toki, my fourth grandchild. He is only a few hours new, resting peacefully in his wahakura from his journey into Te Ao Mārama. The harakeke for his wahakura was gathered from pā harakeke at Te Noho Kotahitanga marae, Te Whare Wānanga o Wairaka, Unitec. The rui, hāro, hāpine and whiri were completed by his māmā, and the wahakura finished two days before his arrival. The aho muka to tie his pito was sourced from the kohunga pā harakeke that grows outside Te Kōhanga Reo o Te Rongomau, in the grounds of Te Kura Kaupapa Māori o Ngā Maungarongo. When he took his first breath, it took ours away. We gasped and inhaled the light rays that danced around him. They fused to our beating heart, sparking and igniting again and again the whakapapa of aroha and joy.

Every whenu of the wahakura, every weave, every interrelationship threaded through, over and under, is a pathway of woven whakapapa, seeded in sustainable practices, tikanga, that ground us to Papatūānuku. Wahakura articulate a synthesis of mauri – the mauri of Papatūānuku, the mauri of the kairaranga and the mauri of the whānau and mokopuna.

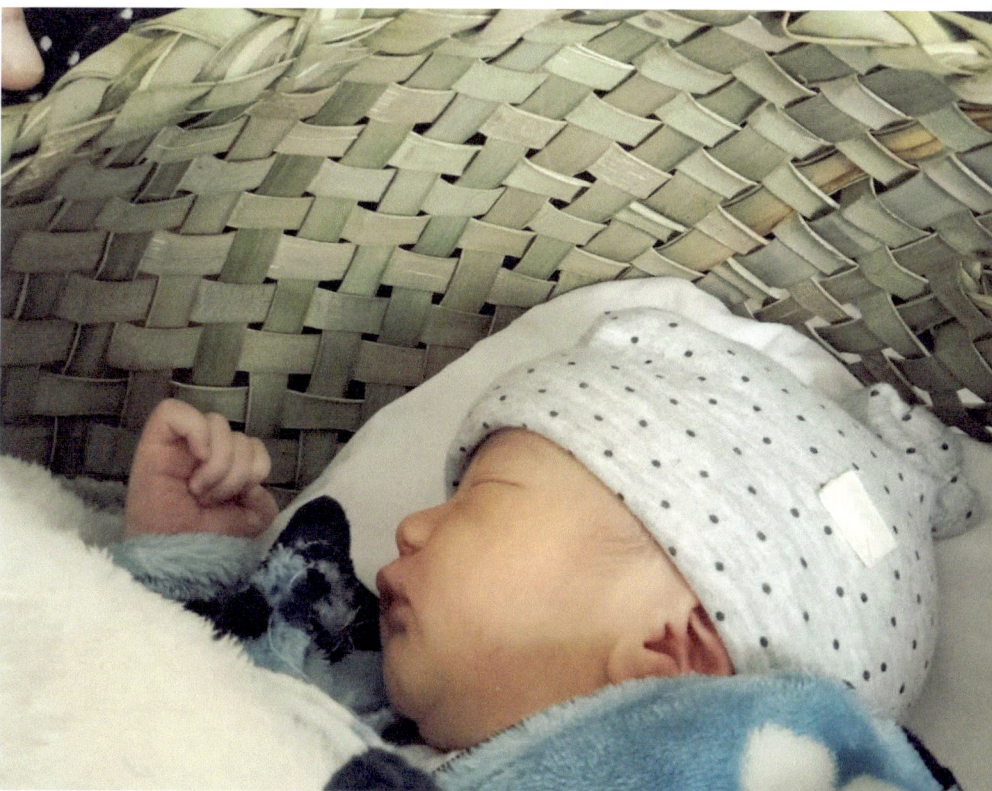

Whakaahua 11: Pēpi in his wahakura.

Wahakura, as the name suggests, waha (gateway, entrance, opening), kura (sacred knowledge), are a point of access to mātauranga Māori and the treasured knowledge handed down from the ancestors. They provide an opportunity for whānau to connect with te ao Māori through tikanga pā harakeke where oranga mokopuna, the wellbeing of mokopuna, is central and essential to oranga whānau, the wellbeing of whānau and whenua. Wahakura are the waka of our mokopuna, waka oranga. They are vessels of wellbeing because they house and embrace ngā taonga tuku iho, the wisdom of the ancestors, while protecting and cherishing the new generation.

Raranga Waiora
Raranga Mauri
Raranga Whakapapa
Raranga
Wahakura

References

BEST, E. (1975). *The Whare Kōhanga (the nest house) and its lore.* Wellington, New Zealand: A. R. Shearer, Government Printer.

FAIERS, N., RHIND-WIRI, H., & SELBY-LAW, F. (2019). Ngā Whenu o te Wahakura: The many strands of Wahakura. The National SUDI Prevention Coordination Service at Hāpai te Hauora. Retrieved from http://sudinationalcoordination.co.nz/nga-whenu-o-te-wahakura

HARRISON, P., TE KANAWA, K., & HIGGINS, R. (2004). Ngā Mahi Toi: The arts. In T. M. Ka'ai, J. C. Moorfield, M. Reilly & S. Mosely (Eds.), *Ki te Whaiao: An introduction to Māori culture and society* (pp. 116–132). Auckland, New Zealand: Pearson New Zealand.

HENARE, M. (1995). Te Tiriti, te tangata, te whānau: The Treaty, the human person, the family. *Rights and responsibilities: Papers from the International Year of the Family Symposium on Rights and Responsibilities of the Family, Wellington, New Zealand, October 14–16.*

HENARE, M., PETRIE, H., & PUCKEY, A. (2009). *He Whenua Rangatira: Northern tribal landscape overview.* Wellington, New Zealand: Crown Forestry Rental Trust.

HENARE, M., PUCKEY, A., & NICHOLSON, A. (2011). He ara hou: The pathway forward: Getting it right for New Zealand's Māori and Pasifika children. Wellington, New Zealand: He Mana tō ia Tamaiti: Every Child Counts/Auckland, New Zealand: University of Auckland. Retrieved from http://www.ririki.org.nz/wp-content/uploads/2015/04/He-Ara-Hou-Report-20112.pdf

HIROA, T. R. (1911). On the Māori art of weaving cloaks, capes, and kilts. *New Zealand Dominion Museum Bulletin, 3,* 69–90.

JENKINS, K., & HARTE, H. (2011). *Traditional Māori parenting: An historical review of literature of traditional Māori child rearing practices in pre-European times.* Auckland, New Zealand: Te Kāhui Mana Ririki.

MAIHI, T. T., & LANDER, M. (2005). *He Kete He Kōrero: Every Kete has a story.* Auckland, New Zealand: Reed.

MARSDEN, M. (2003). *The Woven Universe: Selected Writings of Rev. Māori Marsden.* (T. A. Royal, Ed.) Ōtaki, New Zealand: Estate of Rev. Māori Marsden.

MCGRUDDY, E. (2006). Integrating New Zealand flax into land management systems. Sustainable Farming Fund. Retrieved from https://tararuacropping.files.wordpress.com/2016/08/g0-project-integrating-nz-flax-into-land-management-systems-report.pdf

MOORFIELD, J. C. (2005). *Te Aka: Māori – English: English – Māori: Dictionary and index.* Auckland, New Zealand: Pearson Longman.

PARINGATAI, K. (2020). *Poia mai taku poi: Unearthing the knowledge of the past: A critical review of written literature on the poi in New Zealand and the Pacific* (Master's thesis). University of Otago, Dunedin, New Zealand. Retrieved from https://ourarchive.otago.ac.nz/handle/10523/5181

QUINCE, K. (1999). Māori disputes and their resolution. In P. Spiller (Ed.), *Dispute resolution in New Zealand* (pp. 256–294). Auckland, New Zealand: Oxford University Press.

RILEY, M. (1994). *Māori Healing and Herbal.* Paraparaumu, New Zealand: Viking Sevenseas NZ Ltd.

TIPENE-LEACH, D. (2007). *The Wahakura: The safe bed-sharing project.* Retrieved from http://www.manageme.org.nz/assets/Uploads/446bb620b4/W-Wahakura-book-Sudden-Infant-Death-Syndrome-instructions.pdf

WHITE, T. (2017A). *Mana Mokopuna: Mai i te Waharoa ki te Wahakura: Activating sacred potential through Raranga and Tikanga Pā Harakeke* (Master's thesis). Te Whare Wānanga o Wairaka, Unitec Institute of Technology, New Zealand. Retrieved from https://unitec.researchbank.ac.nz/handle/10652/4219

WHITE, T. (2017B). *Mana Mokopuna: From Waharoa to Wahakura: Applications of Raranga and Tikanga Pā Harakeke for the protection of Papatūānuku (Earth Mother) and Mokopuna.* Transcript of Video Presentation, World Indigenous Peoples Conference on Education, Toronto, Canada.

Wahakura and Te Whare Pora o Hine-te-iwaiwa: Delving Deeply into Te Pā Harakeke

David Tipene-Leach
Sally Abel

CHAPTER 13

Heua, heua, heua ake rā,	Separate it, pull it out, clear it,
kia tū te rangi putuputu ē	so that all parts of heaven can be seen
me te hira mai o te kawa a Tāne te Waiora.	and the wonderment of Tāne te Waiora.
Te whai mutunga a Tāne Matua	The final karakia of Tāne [in]
Te whai mokopuna a Tāne Matua	the pursuit of this particular mokopuna
Parapara tuhi te rangi,	The talents of whom adorn the day
tākina rā te paepae tapu o Tāne	and bring praise for the sacred space.
Hōmai rā kia pikingia, kia kakengia	So allow us to rise
ka makere te whītau.	and let the flax come forth.
Ko wai te wahine o roto o te whare nei?	Who is the goddess of this house?
Ko Hine-te-iwaiwa,	It is Hine-te-iwaiwa,
Te whāriki te takapau	The maker of mats laid down before us
e taka te āhuru ē.	that establish safety and comfort for all.
Uhi, wero,	Cover it, and challenge it,
Tū mai Te Whare Pora.	May the Whare Pora be upstanding.
Haumi ē, hui ē, tāiki ē.	Join together, congregate, progress.

'Tū mai te whare pora o Hine-te-iwaiwa' – a karakia shared by kaumātua Matiu Eru, QSM. First encountered at the opening of a wānanga wahakura at Choices/Kahungunu Health Services, Hastings in 2008. The translation (and the mistakes) are all ours.

Introduction

In recent times the Aotearoa New Zealand health system has seen increasing use of mātauranga Māori (Māori knowledge) employed across a range of health practices and services, particularly mental health (Rangihuna, Kopua & Tipene-Leach, 2018; Wirihana, 2008), and this chapter discusses an approach taken to antenatal and infant care. The aim of the mātaranga Māori approach is to increase access to, and the quality of, services to Māori whānau (extended family) and to decrease a range of inequitable health outcomes, the worst of which, in the case of infant health, is a sudden infant death. This example is of how mātauranga Māori and the use of raranga, the celebrated art of Māori weaving, is deployed in the the quest to prevent Sudden Unexpected Death in Infancy (SUDI).

This chapter illustrates how the notion of 'traditional' (in the sense of 'Indigenous') practice, and its application in modern life, has been fundamental to addressing SUDI – the single biggest cause of preventable post-neonatal mortality in the Māori community. We describe how an intervention based on the mātauranga Māori that belongs to the practice of raranga has helped Māori women to successfully negotiate pregnancy and early infanthood. Using the wahakura (the flax bassinet, a safe sleep device) as a case study, we illustrate how raranga practice and notions of traditional infant care have contributed to SUDI prevention. We then demonstrate how the wider weaving traditions of Te Whare Pora o Hine-te-iwaiwa (the weaving school of learning) are being reclaimed and adapted in an ongoing manner to further address the disproportionately high rate of SUDI among Māori.

What is a Traditional Infant Care Practice?

As stated in a 2001 cross-cultural study of infant care practices in Tāmaki Makaurau Auckland, Aotearoa New Zealand, "the way humans look after infants is invested with moral value, and cultural and personal meaning" (Abel, Lennan, Park, Tipene-Leach, & Finau, 2001, p. 1135). Although infant care practices differ in significant ways across the values, cultures and personal meanings of social groups, the thesis is that they are all predicated upon achieving a similar end – the overall wellbeing of the infant.

Traditional can also mean archaic, customary, accepted, common, normal or usual. For instance, differences in bedsharing and night-time sleeping and feeding patterns across cultural or social groups may reflect different beliefs, but are pathways to the same end. Swedish women justify their bedsharing and overnight on-demand breastfeeding as behaviours that promote independence and emotional wellbeing (Welles-Nystrom, 2005), but these same outcomes are desired by other Western (predominantly Anglo-Saxon) women who may sleep their infants in a different room and may use formula (Owens, 2004). Mayan women (Morelli, Rogoff, Oppenheim, & Goldsmith, 1992), like those in Sweden, value the traditional (customary) practice of extended breastfeeding because of the perceived health benefits to their babies. So too do Indigenous Cameroon Nso women value their traditional (accepted) night-time infant breastfeeding routines and the late weaning of their infant, but in seeking benefits for their infants they have modified these practices to fit around the need for the mother to engage in wage labour (Keller, Voelker, & Yovsi, 2005). Indeed, bedsharing and on-demand extended breastfeeding were also the traditional (normal or usual) infant care practices of Anglo-Saxon women in pre-industrial societies until the requirement for working-class women to do long shifts and night work led to earlier weaning and separate sleeping arrangements (Crook, 2008).

It is not unfair to say, therefore, that traditional infant care practices are invariably the expression of a society's desire for best outcomes for their infants. Although actual practices may differ across cultures and societies, and may change across time, they are all subject to the context in which they exist, adapting as necessary to changing social and cultural imperatives to pursue those best outcomes.

So, what comprises traditional Māori pregnancy and infant care practices? Pre-European or early contact practice is well described by Best (1929). In earlier times, pregnant women, particularly the high born, were given gifts and special foods to acknowledge (and celebrate) their pregnancy. When labour commenced, they became tapu (restricted) and were set aside in the whare kōhanga (a temporary birthing house), also known as whare puhi, whare kahu or whare rauhi, with tapuhi (attendants) for the delivery. The cord was cut with a sharpened rehu or kōrahi (flint) – often a family heirloom – and then tied with the creeping plant mākahakaha, or harakeke (flax) muka (fibre). The pito (umbilical remnant) was then dressed with scraped and oiled houhi (lacebark). To ruia (dangle by the legs and shake) a newborn was to stimulate it to extract secretions from the mouth and nose – similar perhaps to the relatively vigorous stimulation that modern-day infants receive at birth. Both the iho (umbilical cord) and the whenua (placenta) were buried in auspicious places relating to some form of ownership or belonging. All these practices still exist in one form or another. Whare kōhanga, tapuhi, rehu, rui and the houhi dressings have necessarily been modernised; the traditional practice of pito and whenua burial, which has been variable over time, is currently enjoying a renaissance, along with muka umbilical ties. So, while the birthing sites, attendants and instruments have been necessarily modernised, ritual practices around pito and whenua have been either retained (against modern practice) or reclaimed (into modern practice).

Whāngai ū (breastfeeding), providing the best nutrition for infants, was practised universally, along with penupenu (the pre-mastication of solid food), the traditional (archaic) form of the modern complementary feeding and weaning strategy. Penupenu is still practised in some whānau today. Traditionally, Māori infants slept on their back, in what was the common practice across the world until the mid-1900s. But Māori parents would also waha (carry) their infants for extensive periods, as did very early cultures across the world, using slings and creating a means of keeping a watchful eye on the infant while working or food gathering (Taylor, 2010). This is now called 'baby-wearing' and is practised today with modern forms of the sling to maximise closeness and comfort (Russel, 2015). Infant massage was also common in ancient times and tōtō (a particular form of massage) was designed to mould desirable facial features and encourage strong, straight limbs. The pakokori, an infant enclosure constructed of bent semicircles of kareao (supplejack) stuck into the ground that acted as a walking practice frame for the developing infant, was also used to encourage erect posture and robust walking. Expectations of and exhortations to future achievements based on historical precedents were passed on in oriori (historical lullabies) sung repeatedly to infants by whānau. Finally, it seems that while the mother did most of the 'infant' jobs, the father soon took over most duties: "the infant is no sooner weaned than a considerable part of its care devolves upon the father: it is taught to twine its arms round his neck, and in this posture it remains the whole day, asleep or awake" (Cruise, 1824, p. 276).

With colonisation, many of these traditional Māori birthing and infant care practices were lost or marginalised, and Western models of birthing and infant care became more commonly practised. Nevertheless, a few traditional practices, or adaptations of the same, appear to have continued, or have been resurrected, into the modern era. The 2001 infant care practice study of Māori, Pacific and Pākehā families in Auckland (Abel et al., 2001) enabled a comparison of infant care practices across these cultural groups. The study enquired about sources of support and advice, infant feeding, infant sleeping arrangements and traditional practices and beliefs, and found a spectrum of behaviours, which ranged widely across the groups. However, the differences were most pronounced between Pacific caregivers (especially those Island-raised) and Pākehā caregivers (especially those in nuclear families). Bedsharing practices, for example, spanned from the more traditional approach demonstrated by Pacific Island-born mothers (such as adult–infant bedsharing) through to modern practices demonstrated mostly by Pākehā mothers in nuclear families (such as sleeping the infant in a separate room). In general, Māori caregiving practices and beliefs lay in the middle of this spectrum, being more similar to Western practices than those of Pacific caregivers, arguably as a result of the effects of colonisation on loss of land, language and culture. Nevertheless, some Māori traditional practices were evident. Of particular interest here was the use of karakia (prayer) intended to provide protection to the infant, the ritual disposal by burial of the whenua (placenta) and the choosing of a name (not necessarily a Māori name) for its links to tīpuna (ancestors), whakapapa (genealogy) and mana (prestige).

The two decades since that study have seen a resurgence in mātauranga Māori birthing and infant care practices or, at the very least, the use of mātauranga Māori to support best practice. For instance, Ngā Maia o Aotearoa (Māori midwives collective) have, since 2006, promoted Tūranga Kaupapa, which are Māori cultural competence guidelines for midwives formally adopted by the Midwifery Council and the New Zealand College of Midwives (Te Huia, 2019). Some Auckland-based Māori and Pacific providers of care use the Mokopuna Ora: Pregnancy and Parenting Information and Education Curriculum to source appropriate information and guidelines for both pregnant women and their whānau (Mokopuna Ora, 2016). The Hapū Wānanga series of three-day, District Health Board-sponsored, Kaupapa Māori antenatal workshops taught by Māori non-health professionals have spread from the Waikato region across the country. Related programmes, such as Whāngai Ū and Māmā Aroha, are Kaupapa Māori services designed to support Māori women to breastfeed. All these programmes use mātauranga Māori paradigms, ideologies, mythologies, community networks and traditional practices to support innovative approaches in pursuit of the best outcomes for mothers and infants.

The Development of the Wahakura

Innovation in the field of SUDI prevention is another example of the use of mātauranga Māori. In the mid 2000s, after a decade of consistently decreasing sudden infant deaths was followed by a plateau in mortality over a five-year period, a new approach to the prevention of SUDI was demanded (Abel & Tipene-Leach, 2013). A tail of infant mortality, then known as SIDS (Sudden Infant Death Syndrome), persisted stubbornly in conditions of poverty and in Indigenous and other disenfranchised communities (Hauck, Tanabe, & Moon, 2011) and the disparity between Māori and non-Māori rates increased six-fold (Ministry of Health, 2010). The decrease in mortality across the Western world was related to the promotion of back sleeping and the abandonment of the prone infant sleeping position (Dwyer & Ponsonby, 1996). The other risk factors for SIDS were lack of breastfeeding, cigarette smoking (in pregnancy) and bedsharing. Case-control data worldwide was interpreted to suggest a simple causal relationship existed between the risk factors and SIDS. Hence adult–infant bedsharing was strongly discouraged (Spock, 1946) on the understanding that its cessation would decrease SIDS mortality.

It was, therefore, in an anti-bedsharing context across the globe that the wahakura, a Kaupapa Māori approach to SUDI prevention, developed in New Zealand. It had become clear that bedsharing and cigarette smoking in pregnancy were 'confounding' risk factors (Scragg et al., 1993). In other words, these two variables compounded one another but, importantly, eliminating one could significantly decrease total risk even when the other practice continued. It was also clear that Māori mothers objected to the 'do not bedshare' message, claiming that bedsharing was considered a 'traditional' (normal) way to sleep babies. However, Scragg et al. (1993) had also demonstrated that smoking rates among Māori pregnant women were high and efforts over the years to address smoking in pregnancy have been quite unsuccessful (Walker, Graham, Palmer, Jagroop, & Tipene-Leach, 2019). The wahakura was developed to provide a safer shared sleeping arrangement by creating a separate infant sleeping surface that was attractive to Māori mothers, without having to work with the difficulties of smoking cessation (Abel & Tipene-Leach, 2013). This safer shared-sleeping environment was based on the mitigation of the duplex risk factor of bedsharing where there was smoking in pregnancy. Later research provided further compelling evidence that this was a sensible approach; namely, that the combination of these risk practices was demonstrated to be twenty-one times more prevalent among Māori (Tipene-Leach et al., 2010), and the relative risk of SUDI for those exposed to both risk factors compared with those exposed to neither was shown to be thirty-three times greater (Mitchell et al., 2017).

The wahakura is a 72 x 34cm flax bassinet designed to be placed in or on the bed beside or between the parent(s) or caregiver(s) – a walled-off space for the baby that preserves the valued closeness of direct bedsharing. It was promoted as a safe sleep device that drew heavily on the traditional (ancestral) raranga practices of our tīpuna. The name was coined around the two words 'waha' (which also means to 'carry' as in pregnancy) and 'kura' (precious little object). In the public health community, it was promoted as an incorporation of mātauranga Māori into health practice, a Māori-driven initiative. The aspect of returning to a traditional infant care practice was pursued in line with the description of a pōrakaraka as "a swinging cradle ... suspended by a beam from a cord" (Best, 1907, p. 7). While it was not described as being woven from flax, there is little else that it might have been constructed from.

Although there were a number of obstacles to achieving mainstream acceptance of the wahakura as a SUDI prevention strategy (Abel & Tipene-Leach, 2013), in time this acceptance was achieved – not least because of the research that accompanied it. The wide deployment of the wahakura and the plastic Pēpi-Pod (modelled on the wahakura) as safe sleep devices (SSD), and of the Safe Sleep Programmes of various District Health Boards that used these devices, was credited with a 29 percent drop in infant mortality across the years 2009 to 2015 (Mitchell, Cowan, & Tipene-Leach, 2016). In other words, the mātauranga Māori intervention and the reclaimed traditional infant care practice approach was considered effective and gained acceptability in mainstream maternity services. Some timely research projects that clarified issues along the way had facilitated this mainstream acceptability. For example, the 2009 Auckland survey (Tipene-Leach et al., 2010) demonstrated the extent of bedsharing where there was smoking in pregnancy; a retrospective case study of SUDI mortality (Hutchison et al., 2011) demonstrated that two-thirds of the deaths occurred in a shared bed; and a 2014 qualitative study with Māori women using the wahakura (Abel, Stockdale-Frost, Rolls, & Tipene-Leach, 2015) showed that the use of the wahakura was 'acceptable' to Māori women. Finally, randomised controlled trials (RCT) of the wahakura (Baddock et al., 2017a; Baddock et al., 2017b) and the Pēpi-Pod (Tipene-Leach et al., 2018) versus a standard bassinet could demonstrate no difference between these overnight infant sleep environments, indicating that the wahakura had not introduced new risks to the infant sleep space. Finally, the RCT investigating mother–infant behaviours showed that extended breastfeeding was much more likely with wahakura use (Manhire et al., 2018) and that the advent of one traditional infant care practice could facilitate conditions for the extension of another.

Interestingly, but perhaps not surprisingly, the safe sleep environment and the wahakura and Pēpi-Pod as safe sleep devices have become widely popular with non-Māori mothers. Weavers market these items online and anecdotally we know that scores of wahakura are sent to Australia every year. Pēpi-Pods are now being systematically deployed by health authorities in some Aboriginal communities in Queensland (Young et al., 2015). Finally, wahakura have also been sent to a major English university, where their researchers are exploring whether a Māori invention might inform SUDI solutions in deprived British homes.

Te Whare Pora o Hine-te-iwaiwa

The wahakura story does not end here – and neither does the deployment of mātauranga Māori and the reclamation of traditional practices. More recently the decrease in infant mortality attributable to SUDI has plateaued again, raising new questions. Have we come to the natural limit of infant deaths preventable by safe sleep approaches? How do we begin to address the all-important 'smoking in pregnancy' risk? Must we now turn to the more difficult question of access to healthcare services or, indeed, to the social determinants of health?

These questions call for an initiative that addresses access to appropriate antenatal care, smoking in pregnancy and multiple other risks for SUDI labelled by the scientific community as potentially 'not modifiable'. These include access to care; birth risks related to smoking in pregnancy such as low birth weight and early-for-dates birth; and the social determinants of health such as poverty, single and/or young motherhood, younger school-leaving age and younger age at first pregnancy (Mitchell et al., 1992).

Te Whare Pora o Hine-te-iwaiwa is a contemporary re-establishment of the wānanga (school of learning) of the female atua (ancestor-god) Hine-te-iwaiwa (the atua of weaving, pregnancy, childbirth and infant care). In traditional (ancient) times, this was an establishment controlled by Māori women, intellectually separated from the world of male control, with protocols determined by women and with effects that concerned women and infants, but whose outcomes determined the health of the village and the hapū (Best, 1929).

The modern day Te Whare Pora is organised as an antenatal weaving clinic for pregnant women and their whānau, offering as SUDI prevention strategies community networks, mātauranga Māori and contact with health professionals that pertain to best antenatal wellbeing. It teaches karakia and pūrākau (creation stories) and introduces thinking around Hine-te-iwaiwa and her wānanga as cultural touchpoints around pregnancy and motherhood. The initiative, based on the teaching of weaving, aims to create time for the development of the healthy habits of impending motherhood and of the trusting, health-promoting relationships in the community that will last through into infant care, child care and long-term self care.

At its heart, Te Whare Pora has the same principles as the wahakura project: a work programme based on raranga with strategies to address SUDI risk based on Māori knowledges and traditions and thereby attractive to Māori women (and whānau). Te Whare Pora, facilitated by a master weaver, teaches pregnant women how to weave the (Māori) accoutrements of the modern pregnancy; that is, a here (umbilical tie), an ipu pito (pito burial container), an ipu whenua (burial container for the placenta), a waikawa (as a container or an 'easy-form' wahakura) and, finally, a wahakura for the infant. This work programme sits alongside the development of safe and meaningful relationships. Te Whare Pora links participant women into Māori community networks of which they might not presently be a part, creating opportunities and support structures for women who may (or may not) be the younger, socioeconomically poorer, single women with a younger school-leaving age and younger age at first pregnancy (Mitchell et al., 1992). It also links them into health worker networks they might not have otherwise accessed, for example, midwives, practice nurses, breastfeeding advocates, counsellors, navigators, Kaupapa Māori smoking cessation facilitators and others.

At one level the weaving, community networking and the access to professional care are strategies for SUDI prevention. But the mātauranga Māori basis of Te Whare Pora nurtures and encourages the revival of the recitation of karakia, the singing of oriori, the burial of pito and whenua remnants, the return of meaning to the naming of infants, and the gathering together and passing on of these knowledges and practices. The potential, however, is for an even wider remit in Māori women's healthcare that follows through the life course, with a vision of mothers and infants tutored in Te Whare Pora accessing immunisation, contraception and cervical smears, and gaining facilitated access to other intimate healthcare that might be more challenging to reach in other healthcare systems.

Conclusion

The conception in 2005 of the wahakura as a safer shared-sleeping environment to mitigate the risk of sudden infant death was specifically designed to have cultural appeal by framing the intervention within the locus of mātauranga Māori and as a reclamation of a traditional, Indigenous infant care practice. This simple woven flax bassinet, designed to allow an infant to sleep safely alongside its parent(s) or caregiver(s), has been embraced by Māori weavers and women across the country, and the wahakura has become incorporated as a new tikanga (practice) in the pregnancy expectations of Māori women. It is the embodiment of a Kaupapa Māori approach (re)asserting itself in a critical fashion for the wellbeing of tamariki Māori and their whānau. The wahakura tikanga has also been extended to provide a framework for the re-emergence of mātauranga Māori and traditional infant care practices so that collectives of mothers and Māori women knowledge holders can draw upon ancestral understandings and practices to enhance wellbeing. The 2020 iteration of the wahakura story seeks to develop the lessons learned over the past fifteen years into a community-controlled initiative that supports pregnant Māori whānau through the antenatal period with a programme based on those knowledges. It is a modern version of the 'women's-business clinic' of old: Te Whare Pora o Hine-te-iwaiwa – the wānanga of the atua of weaving, pregnancy and childbirth.

References

ABEL, S., LENNAN, M., PARK, J., TIPENE-LEACH, D., & FINAU, S. (2001). Infant care practices in New Zealand: A cross-cultural qualitative study. *Social Science & Medicine*, *53*(9), 1135–1148. https://doi.org/10.1016/S0277-9536(00)00408-1

ABEL, S., STOCKDALE-FROST, A., ROLLS, R., & TIPENE-LEACH, D. (2015). The wahakura: A qualitative study of the flax bassinet as a sleep location for New Zealand Māori infants. *New Zealand Medical Journal*, *128*(1413), 12–19. https://pubmed.ncbi.nlm.nih.gov/26101114/

ABEL, S., & TIPENE-LEACH, D. (2013). SUDI prevention: A review of Māori safe sleep innovations for infants. *New Zealand Medical Journal*, *126*(1379), 86–94. https://pubmed.ncbi.nlm.nih.gov/24045355/

BADDOCK, S. A., TIPENE-LEACH, D., WILLIAMS, S. M., TANGIORA, A., JONES, R., IOSUA, E., MACLEOD, E. C., & TAYLOR, B. J. (2017). Wahakura versus bassinet for safe infant sleep: A randomized trial. *Pediatrics*, *139*(2) e20160162. doi: 10.1542/peds.2016-0162

BADDOCK, S. A., TIPENE-LEACH, D., WILLIAMS, S. M., TANGIORA, A., JONES, R., MĄCZNIK, A. K., & TAYLOR, B. J. (2017). Physiological stability in an indigenous sleep device: A randomized controlled trial. *Archives of Disease in Childhood*, *103*(4), 377–382. dx.doi.org/10.1136/archdischild-2017-313512

BEST, E. (1907). Lore of the Whare Kōhanga, Part V. Miscellaneous items. *Journal of the Polynesian Society*, *16*(1), 1–12.

BEST, E. (1929). *The Whare Kōhanga and its Lore*. Dominion Museum Bulletin No.13, reprinted 1975. Wellington, New Zealand: A. R. Shearer, Government Printer,

CROOK, T. (2008). Norms, forms and beds: Spatializing sleep in Victorian Britain. *Body and Society*, *14*(4), 15–35. https://doi.org/10.1177/1357034X08096893

CRUISE, R. A. ESQ. (1824). *Journal of a ten months residence in New Zealand*. 2nd Edition [Capper reprinted (facsimile) 1974].

DWYER, T., & PONSONBY, A. L. (1996). The decline of SIDS: A sucess story for epidemiology. *Epidemiology*, *7*(3), 323–325. https://pubmed.ncbi.nlm.nih.gov/8728452/

HAUCK, F. R., TANABE, K. O., & MOON, R. Y. (2011). Racial and ethnic disparities in infant mortality. *Seminars in Perinatology*, *35*(4), 209–220. doi: 10.1053/j.semperi.2011.02.018

HUTCHISON, B. L., REA, C., STEWART, A. W., KOELMEYER, T. D., TIPENE-LEACH, D. C., & MITCHELL, E. A. (2011). Sudden infant death in Auckland: A retrospective case review. *Acta Paediatrica*, *100*(8), 1108–12. http://dx.doi.org/10.1111/j.1651-2227.2011.02221.x

KELLER, H., VOELKER, S., & YOVSI, R. D. (2005). Conceptions of parenting in different cultural communities: The case of West African Nso and Northern German women. *Social Development*, *14*(1), 158–180. https://doi.org/10.1111/j.1467-9507.2005.00295.x

MANHIRE, K., WILLIAM, S. M., TIPENE-LEACH, D., BADDOCK, S. A., ABEL, S., TANGIORA, A., JONES, R., & TAYLOR, B. J. (2018). Predictors of breastfeeding duration in a predominantly Māori population in New Zealand. *BMC Pediatrics*, *18*, 299. https://doi.org/10.1186/s12887-018-1274-9.

MINISTRY OF HEALTH. (2010). *Fetal and infant deaths 2006*. Wellington, New Zealand: Ministry of Health. Retrieved from https://www.health.govt.nz/publication/fetal-and-infant-deaths-2006

MITCHELL, E. A., COWAN, S., & TIPENE-LEACH, D. (2016). The recent fall in postperinatal mortality in New Zealand and the Safe Sleep programme. *Acta Paediatrica*, 105(11), 1312–1320. doi: 10.1111/apa.13494

MITCHELL, E. A., TAYLOR, B. J., FORD, R. P., STEWART, A. W., BECROFT, D. M. O., THOMPSON, J. M. D., ... & ROBERTS, A. P. (1992). Four modifiable and other major risk factors for cot death: The New Zealand study. *Journal of Paediatrics and Child Health*, 28 (Suppl 1), S3–S8. doi: 10.1111/j.1440-1754.1992.tb02729.x

MITCHELL, E. A., THOMPSON, J. M., ZUCCOLLO, J., MACFARLANE, M., TAYLOR, B., ELDER, D., ... & FLEMING, P. (2017). The combination of bed sharing and maternal smoking leads to a greatly increased risk of sudden unexpected death in infancy: The New Zealand SUDI Nationwide Case Control Study. *New Zealand Medical Journal*, 130(1456), 52–64. https://pubmed.ncbi.nlm.nih.gov/28571049/

MOKOPUNA ORA: HEALTH PREGNANCY AND BABY. (2016). Connectus, TAHA and Whakawhetū, Uniservices. Auckland, New Zealand: University of Auckland. https://mokopunaora.nz/sites/dev-mkpo/files/2016-03/MokopunaOra-introduction.pdf

MORELLI, G. A., ROGOFF, B., OPPENHEIM, D., & GOLDSMITH, D. (1992). Cultural variation in infants' sleeping arrangements: Questions of independence. *Developmental Psychology*, 28(4), 604–613. https://doi.org/10.1037/0012-1649.28.4.604

OWENS, J. A. (2004). Sleep in children: Cross-cultural perspectives. *Sleep and Biological Rhythms*, 2(3), 165–173. https://doi.org/10.1111/j.1479-8425.2004.00147.x

RANGIHUNA, D., KOPUA, M., & TIPENE-LEACH, D. (2018). Mahi a Atua: A pathway forward for Māori mental health? *New Zealand Medical Journal*, 131(1470), 79–83. https://pubmed.ncbi.nlm.nih.gov/29518802/

RUSSEL, N. U. (2015). Babywearing in the age of the Internet. *Journal of Family Issues*, 36(9), 1130–1153. https://doi.org/10.1177/0192513X14533547

SCRAGG, R., MITCHELL, E. A., TAYLOR, B. J., STEWART, A. W., FORD, R. P., THOMPSON, ... & E. M., BECROFT, D. (1993). Bed sharing, smoking, and alcohol in the sudden infant death syndrome. New Zealand Cot Death Study Group. *British Medical Journal*, 307(6915), 1312–1318. doi: 10.1136/bmj.307.6915.1312

SPOCK, B. (1946). *The common sense book of baby and child care*. New York, NY: Duell, Sloan and Pearce.

TAYLOR, T. (2010, JULY 2). Slings and arrows. Retrieved from https://newhumanist.org.uk/articles/2330/slings-arrows

TE HUIA, J. (2019). Ngā Maia Māori Midwives Aotearoa 1993. Retrieved from https://nzhistory.govt.nz/women-together/nga-maia-maori-midwives-aotearoa

TIPENE-LEACH, D., BADDOCK, S. A., WILLIAMS, S. M., TANGIORA, A., JONES, R., & TAYLOR, B. J. (2018). The Pēpi-Pod™ study: Overnight video, oximetry and thermal environment while using an in-bed sleep device for SUDI prevention. *Journal of Paediatrics and Child Health*, 54(5), 638–646. https://doi.org/10.1111/jpc.13845

TIPENE-LEACH, D., HUTCHISON, L., TANGIORA, A., REA, C., WHITE, R., STEWART, A., & MITCHELL, E. (2010). SIDS-related knowledge and infant care practices among Māori mothers. *New Zealand Medical Journal*, 123(1326), 88–96. http://hdl.handle.net/2292/9480

WALKER, R., GRAHAM, A., PALMER, S., JAGROOP, A., & TIPENE-LEACH, D. (2019). Understanding the experiences, perspectives and values of indigenous women around smoking cessation in pregnancy: Systematic review and thematic synthesis of qualitative studies. *International Journal for Equity in Health*, 18, 74. https://doi.org/10.1186/s12939-019-0981-7.

WELLES-NYSTROM, B. (2005). Co-sleeping as a window into Swedish culture: Considerations of gender and health care. *Scandinavian Journal of Caring Sciences*, 19(4), 354–360. doi:10.1111/j.1471-6712.2005.00358.x

WIRIHANA, R. (2008). Utilising mātauranga Māori to improve the social functioning of tangata whaiora in Māori mental health services. In M. Levy, L. W. Nikora, B. Masters-Awatere, M. Rua & W. Waitoki (Eds.), *Claiming spaces: Proceedings of the 2007 National Māori and Pacific Psychologies Symposium 23rd–24th November 2007* (pp. 103–104). Hamilton, New Zealand: Māori and Psychology Research Unit, University of Waikato.

YOUNG, J., CRAIGIE, L., WATSON, K., KEARNEY, L., COWAN, S., & BARNES, M. (2015). Safe sleep, every sleep: Reducing infant deaths in Indigenous communities. *Women and Birth*, 28(Suppl 1), S31–S32. https://doi.org/10.1016/j.wombi.2015.07.105.

Oranga Mokopuna – Ngā Mōtika Tangata Whenua

Paula Toko King
Donna Cormack
Mark Kōpua

CHAPTER 14

Introduction

The significant inequities in health and disability access to care, quality of care and outcomes for Māori compared with Pākehā are well documented (King, 2019; Ministry of Health, 2015, 2019; Robson & Harris, 2007; Waitangi Tribunal, 2019). The evidence is clear that our pēpi, tamariki and rangatahi, compared with Pākehā babies, children and young people, bear the inequitable impacts of those sociopolitical and economic environments that drive adverse health and disability outcomes in Aotearoa me Te Waipounamu (Craig et al., 2014; Duncanson, Richardson, Oben, Wicken, & Adams, 2019; Simpson, Adams, Oben, Wicken, & Duncanson, 2016; Simpson et al., 2017). The links between colonisation and stark health and disability inequities for Indigenous Peoples compared with non-Indigenous Peoples are well described both internationally (Axelsson, Kukutai, & Kippen, 2016; Czyzewski, 2011; Griffiths, Coleman, Lee, & Madden, 2016; Paradies, 2016; Reading & Wien, 2009; Stephens, Porter, Nettleton, & Willis, 2006) and in Aotearoa me Te Waipounamu (Cram, Te Huia, Te Huia, Williams, & Williams, 2019; Gabel, 2019; Higgins, Phillips, Stobbs, Wilson, & Pascoe, 2012; King, 2019; Lawson-Te Aho & Liu, 2010; Reid, Cormack, & Paine, 2019; Robson & Harris, 2007). Health and disability inequities experienced by our pēpi, tamariki and rangatahi are thus the manifest symptoms of colonisation, coloniality (Cram et al., 2019; Gabel, 2019; Grosfoguel, 2002, 2011; King, 2019; Reid et al., 2019) and racism (Harris et al., 2012; King, 2019; Paine, Harris, Stanley, & Cormack, 2018; Reid et al., 2019).

Colonisation includes:

> ... a range of practices, predominantly historical: war, displacement, forced labour, removal of children, relocation, ecological destruction, massacres, genocide, slavery, (un)intentional spread of deadly diseases, banning of indigenous languages, regulation of marriage, assimilation and eradication of social, cultural and spiritual practices (Paradies, 2016, p. 83).

Coloniality refers to the "continuity of colonial forms of domination after the end of colonial administrations" (Grosfoguel, 2002, p. 205), thereby encompassing an understanding of the ways in which colonial mindsets and conditions endure beyond what is recognised as the formal colonial period (Grosfoguel, 2002, 2011). Coloniality is therefore an ongoing process rendered through a "racist ideology of supposed white supremacy and Indigenous inferiority" (Reid et al., 2019, p. 120). Such racist ideology has been "inscribed into colonial institutions, policies, practices as well as into the values, norms and beliefs of people ... and continues to be reproduced today" (Reid et al., p. 120). Racism is thus defined as:

> ... an organised social system in which the dominant racial group, based on an ideology of inferiority, categorizes and ranks people into social groups called 'races' and uses its power to devalue, disempower, and differentially allocate valued societal resources and opportunities to groups defined as inferior (Williams, Lawrence, & Davis, 2019, p. 106).

Colonisation and coloniality involve the dehumanisation of Indigenous Peoples, by an imperialistic, appropriative and extractive society in which one group – in the case of Aotearoa me Te Waipounamu, Pākehā – retains political dominance and produces a society stratified along racial, ethnic or classist lines (Grosfoguel, 2002, 2011; Stasiulis & Yuval-Davis, 1995). The continuation of these very systems of power "over other people's lands and bodies requires purposeful acts of maintenance" (Ngata, 2019, p. 15). Here, Ngata (2019) refers to the concept of "social programming" as a strategy by which resistance to the system is diminished over time:

> This social programming occurs across multiple platforms – education, media, currency, place names, monuments, national heritage schedules, public holidays and commemorative events – that communicate to us in implicit and explicit ways every day whose perspective is centred, who is important to remember, and how they should be remembered. They uphold colonial fictions that justify European domination, which could also reasonably be described as white supremacy (Ngata, 2019, p. 15).

Though current health inequities identify pēpi, tamariki and rangatahi as having significant unmet health needs, we agree with others who contend that discourses of Māori health that are purely inequities and/or needs-based are fundamentally flawed (Reid & Robson, 2007). Such narratives do not acknowledge the treasured status of our pēpi, tamariki and rangatahi in Māori society, as evidenced by mātauranga Māori such as pūrākau, whakataukī and oriori (Cameron, Pihama, Leatherby, & Cameron, 2013; Jenkins & Mountain Harte, 2011; Pere, 1997; Pihama, Campbell, & Greensill, 2019). Nor do they recognise our pēpi, tamariki and rangatahi as leaders of today, as opposed to the distant future (Tawhai, 2016). Lastly, they do not acknowledge the rights to health and wellbeing of our pēpi, tamariki and rangatahi, as tangata whenua (Reid & Robson, 2007).

In any articulation of Māori rights to health and wellbeing, however, whether they be tangata whenua, or Indigenous, or human rights, it is important to be cautious regarding the discourses that are used. This is particularly so with regard to their potential implications.

Monture-Angus (1995) notes:

> ... in searching for meaning and for language that expresses our experience, we must be careful of the words we choose to embrace our experience. What is also important to understand is that it is not the word that is the problem, but the process by which and by whom it is given meaning (p. 39).

Rights-based approaches to health and wellbeing in Aotearoa me Te Waipounamu have become more prominent in recent years. However, dominant Westernised conceptualisations of rights have been critiqued for their ties to colonialism and individualistic focus. Tensions are intrinsic to the discourses relating to international human rights and their relationship, if any, with tangata whenua rights (Mikaere, 2007; Takitimu, 2015). Maldonado-Torres (2017) has discussed the relationship between coloniality and prevailing Westernised notions of human rights in terms of the potential limitations of human-rights-based approaches for Indigenous Peoples as a response to colonisation. As Maldonado-Torres (2017) notes, human-rights discourses bring into question ideas about what constitutes being 'human' in the first instance, noting that coloniality is embedded in the "notion of the human in the hegemonic concept of human rights" (p. 131).

While acknowledging the particular form of human rights that has become dominant, including in Aotearoa me Te Waipounamu, we also see the the potential for a decolonisation of human-rights narratives, through a disruption of Western hegemonic notions of human rights assumed to have universal application (Maldonado-Torres, 2017). We contend that only when sovereign tangata whenua rights are fully acknowledged and recognised can the useful application of international human-rights instruments be made (Mikaere, 2007). It is in this context that international human-rights instruments further affirm and support the development of sovereign tangata whenua rights.

In the following sections, we describe Oranga Mokopuna as an alternative that disrupts Western notions of rights assumed to have universal application. Building upon mātauranga Māori approaches that foreground the treasured status of our mokopuna in Māori society (Jenkins & Mountain Harte, 2011; Pere, 1997; Pihama, Campbell, & Greensill, 2019; Pihama et al., 2015; Pihama, Simmonds, & Waitoki, 2019), Oranga Mokopuna is also situated within the broader body of policy, theory, praxis and research informed by mātauranga Māori that aims to contribute positively to the health and wellbeing of Māori in Aotearoa me Te Waipounamu (Durie, 1998, 1999; Elder, 2013; Henare, 1988; Kingi, 2002; Lawson-Te Aho, 2013; Matua Raki, 2012; Ministry of Education, 1996, 2017; Ministry of Health, 2014; Murphy, 2011, 2019; Pitama, Huria, & Lacey, 2014; Rangihuna, Kōpua, & Tipene-Leach, 2018; Taskforce on Whānau Centred Initiatives, 2010). Oranga Mokopuna is thus positioned as a counter-narrative to coloniality and an alternative to prevailing Westernised rights-based models, and is thereby a means for resistance, transformation and decolonisation of mokopuna Māori rights to health and wellbeing within Aotearoa me Te Waipounamu.

Definitions of Key Concepts Described in Oranga Mokopuna

Māori as tangata whenua are a collective that encompass many unique and autonomous nations with diverse cosmogonies, genealogies, histories and experiential realities. The term 'Māori' is thus acknowledged as a construct describing the Indigenous Peoples of Aotearoa me Te Waipounamu. The concept of mokopuna is chosen to position pēpi, tamariki and rangatahi within te ao Māori as the sacred reflection of our ancestors and a blueprint for future generations. Pere (1997) translates mokopuna "as the blueprint of the spring of water" (p. 10) and tīpuna/tūpuna as "the spring of water that is continuously being established" (p. 10). Cameron et al. (2013) highlight that "we are all mokopuna and we are all tūpuna ... mokopuna will in future generations take the place of the tūpuna. All grandchildren in time become grandparents ... we are a reflection and continuance of our ancestral lines" (p. 4). In addition, the concept of whānau can be interpreted in many ways – for example, to be born – and is more complex than the often-used translation 'extended family'. Murphy (2019) notes that the term 'whānau', "when broken down to its sacred vowels and associated teachings, can be read as whā – nā – ū – all creatures across the four directions of the planet that seek sustenance from the breast of the mother, Papatūānuku, constitute family" (p. 39).

Walker (2013) observes that the "concept of 'extended family' tends to emphasise an external grouping of people whose connections can be mapped and who are thus related. It is an outsider's view" (p. 86). In contrast, Walker (2013) asserts that the "concept of whānau ... emphasises connections through time and space that are more abstract and amorphous as well as deep. It is an insider's view" (p. 86). Whānau is therefore a multi-faceted and multi-dimensional concept grounded in both te ao Māori and tribal worldviews, whakapapa-based, and interconnected with the living and dead. Whānau thus occurs "on a continuum that is both horizontal and vertical" (Walker, 2013, p. 96).

Developing Oranga Mokopuna as a Theoretical Framework

The development of Oranga Mokopuna sits within the broader context of a Kaupapa Māori PhD research study, and is based on whakataukī, and specifically pūrākau, in its application as a Kaupapa Māori theory and methodology. Pūrākau is described as a "traditional form of Māori narrative contain[ing] philosophical thought, epistemological constructs, cultural codes and worldviews" (Lee, 2009, p. 1). Lee-Morgan (2019) discusses the "conceptual framework of *te pū o te rākau* (the core of the tree) ... *pūrākau*" (p. 152), with the term 'pūrākau' "literally refer[ing] to the pū (base or foundation) of a *rākau* (tree)" (p. 151).

Lee-Morgan and Hutchings (2016) highlight pūrākau as "commonly used to describe ancient and historical stories of our atua, heroes and heroines, well-known people and places" (p. 5). Stories are thus considered "fundamental to our sustenance and growth, as soil and water are to trees" (Lee-Morgan, 2019, p. 151), providing "precious cultural clues to understanding the importance of *pūrākau* in our lives, including our research" (p. 151). Lee-Morgan and Hutchings (2016) emphasise how pūrākau "as a cultural imperative guides us to share our 'stories' in ways that engage with the audience" (p. 5). Use of pūrākau thus elicits a "self-directed process of meaning making, raise[s] questions and provide[s] answers, or quench[es] the thirst to learn more" (Lee-Morgan & Hutchings, 2016, p. 5). Pihama, Campbell and Greensill (2019) describe pūrākau as a telling of those "stories of the histories and traditions of *whānau, hapū,* and iwi, including the formation of personal or tribal relationships, alliances, struggles and battles" (p. 140): "Pūrākau were also treated as treasured and precious teachings, they not only contained valuable knowledge about the environment but were fundamental to our identity – pūrākau provided and informed the uniqueness of us as groups of people" (p. 140).

Pūrākau, as Kaupapa Māori theory and methodology, have been applied in a number of different ways. Seed-Pihama (2019), for instance, describes the concept of "*kōrero ingoa* (naming stories)" (p. 108):

> These are stories behind our names; of how we choose, give, receive, change, and uphold our names throughout our lives ... Kōrero ingoa are an important source of intergenerational knowledge. These stories make an integral contribution to the ongoing maintenance work that is being done to hold onto our history, values and practices ... It was through the telling and sharing of kōrero ingoa across my whānau that examples of our ability to endure, resist, decolonize, and achieve resurgence were revealed (p. 108).

Jones (2019) discusses the development of a "*Kōrero* Analysis Framework" (p. 126) for analysing pūrākau as a means of expressing "Māori legal process and principles ... to understand the relevant aspects of *tikanga Māori* as law" (p. 126):

> The Kōrero Analysis Framework is grounded in the Māori stories to which it is intended to apply and has been developed from a tikanga base, which places key principles (whanaungatanga, manaakitanga, mana, tapu/noa, and utu) at the heart of the Māori legal system (p. 127).

Murphy (2019) describes the recovering of mana wāhine stories, which are "re-read as ritual maps that offer instructions toward inner-transformation and healing" (p. 34), while Pihama, Campbell and Greensill (2019) emphasise the importance of pūrākau "in the teaching and learning of our children ... including both the role of ancestral stories and storytelling from within a contemporary context" (p. 141):

> Recognizing pūrākau as inherently pedagogical is significant in the discussions shared by whānau involved in this research ... Passing down historical knowledge is a practice that aligns to our desire and need to understand our past in order to locate ourselves in the present and shape our dreams for our future ... Our tūpuna actively shared historical knowledge in all contexts where children heard the stories and histories as part of both daily and ceremonial activities (p. 143).

Rangihuna et al. (2018) describe Te Mahi a Atua (the tracing of ancestral footprints) as a therapeutic approach using pūrākau that features creation narratives. Within the context of mental health and wellbeing settings, pūrākau "are explored and used to ... help provide a matrix through which communal, family, and individual challenges can be met without recourse to a 'psychologised' and 'psychiatrised' vocabulary" (Kōpua, Kōpua, & Bracken, 2019, p. 6):

> The idea is to begin to work with Māori patients (tangata whaiora), their families (whānau), and their communities (iwi) from a place that is far from the clinical gaze and the clinical mind-set of psychiatry. Māori culture is socio-centric and puts a very high priority on dealing with problems at the whānau level, always understands personal struggles in relation to whakapapa (genealogy) and refuses to treat te taha wairua (the spiritual realm) as something apart from the rest of existence (p. 6).

Pūrākau are shared with tangata whaiora and whānau through wānanga contextualising the challenges faced by atua within the lived experiences of the tangata whaiora. Here the transformational power of pūrākau is through the privileging of Māori voices (Cherrington, 2003; Kōpua et al., 2019; Rangihuna et al., 2018).

> The practice of Mahi a Atua is centred on the idea of 'wānanga'. Wānanga is not a new concept but instead a 'taonga tuku iho' (gift from the past) and is incorporated into Mahi a Atua as a way of being-with and engaging with whānau in distress … Within a healing context wānanga is referred to as the space, time, and unique exercise where there is a 'meeting of minds' to create meaning. It works based on a shared hope that the outcome will be positive …
>
> Wānanga using Mahi a Atua is based on a special kind of interaction where the way in which Māori ancestors viewed and made sense of their realities within a specific context is shared through learning about and engaging with pūrākau. Regardless of which pūrākau are shared, the basic feature is that each participant can create a shift in awareness both within themselves and within others (Kōpua et al., 2019, p. 6).

Thus, consistent with a Kaupapa Māori theoretical and methodological focus on politicised, culturally responsive and transformative research, application of pūrākau provides the ultimate paradigm for the conceptualisation of mokopuna rights to health and wellbeing within Aotearoa me Te Waipounamu.

Oranga Mokopuna – Ngā Mōtika Tangata Whenua

Figure 1 presents a visual representation of Oranga Mokopuna inspired by the many fan-shaped harakeke plants (*Phormium tenax*/New Zealand flax) in our local surroundings. Even within the midst of an urban landscape setting, the harakeke flourish and thrive together in their own little whānau groups. A taonga within Aotearoa me Te Waipounamu, the harakeke foregrounds the centrality of whānau and relationships, and is used in mātauranga Māori practices of child rearing (Jenkins & Mountain Harte, 2011; Pere, 1997; Pihama et al., 2015; Pihama, Campbell, & Greensill, 2019). Many harakeke varieties are grown for a number of purposes, with specific cultural protocols and practices around harvesting and use. One cannot cut the rito or the inner shoot of the plant, nor the protective shoots that embrace the rito either side, or the harakeke will not survive, nor will the ecosystem the harakeke sustains (McRae-Tarei, 2013; Taituha, 2014; Te Ratana, 2012). When harvesting the outer leaves, one must only harvest "what you need and not what you want" (Te Kanawa cited in McRae-Tarei, 2013, p. 28), replacing all that is left over near the base of the plant in order to contribute nutrients back into the soil. From the layering of nutrients within the soil over time, new life emerges (McRae-Tarei, 2013; Taituha, 2014; Te Ratana, 2012). The fan-shaped harakeke centralises the rito/pēpi as highly prized and pivotal to the sustenance of future generations emerging from, nurtured and protected by the awhi rito/mātua (Pihama et al., 2015). Through "ensuring the rito and mātua are left unplucked … the sustainability of the harakeke plant [is warranted] … a valued reminder to protect and nurture our children, the future generation" (McRae-Tarei, 2013, p. 8). Without this nurturing protective mechanism, future generations will not be sustained. Whakataukī, oriori and pūrākau highlight that our mokopuna were always "favoured as gifts from the atua … from the tīpuna … and preceded those unborn … because of their intrinsic relationship to these spiritual worlds, the children inherited

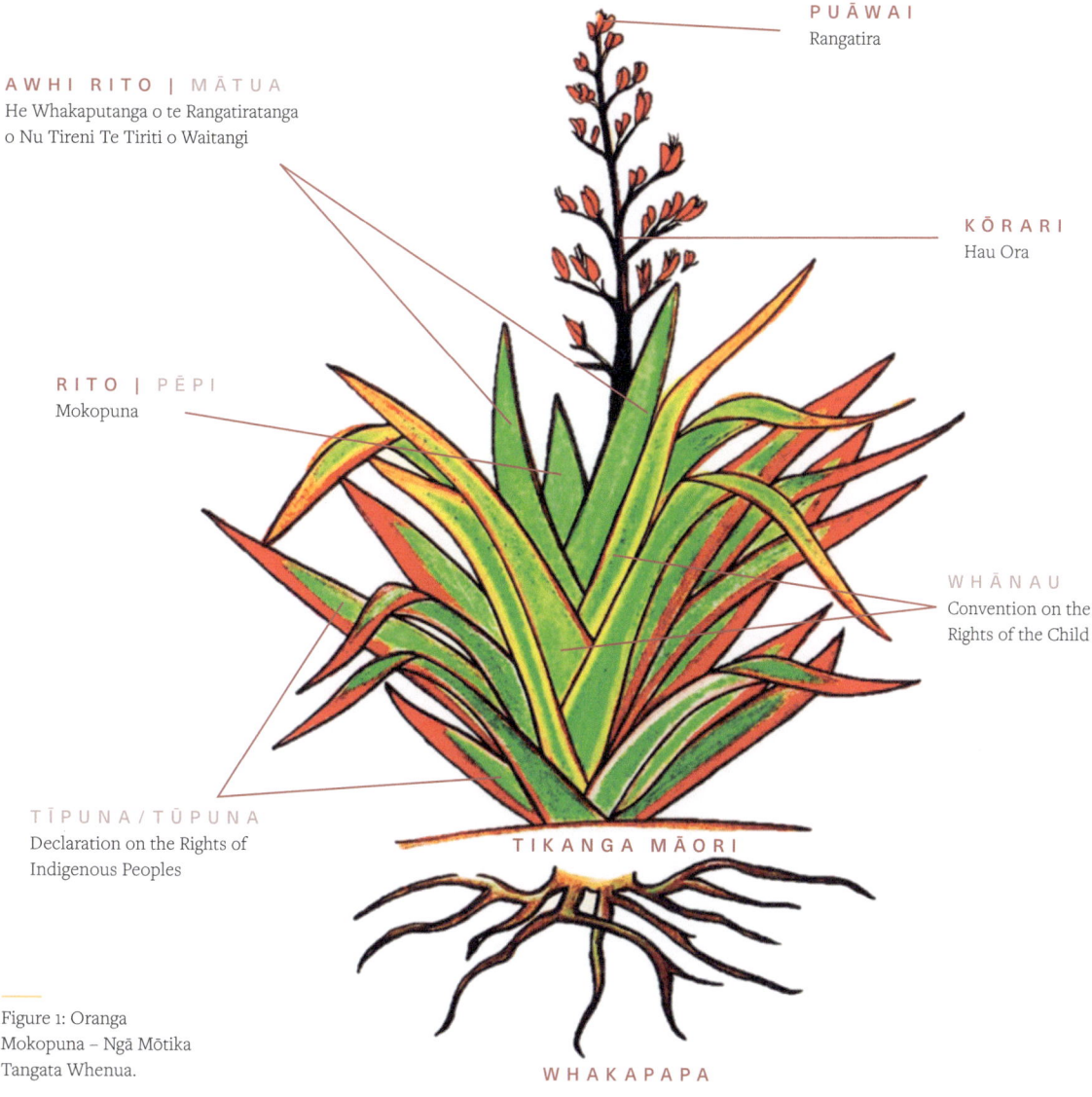

Figure 1: Oranga Mokopuna – Ngā Mōtika Tangata Whenua.

their mana ... they were treated with loving care and indulgence" (Jenkins & Mountain Harte, 2011, p. x).

The following whakataukī reflects the utmost importance of our mokopuna within te ao Māori and, critically, the nurturing and protective role of whānau relationships in the past, present and future. Without this nurturing protective mechanism, future generations will not be sustained:

Hutia te rito o te harakeke
Kei hea te kōmako e kō
Kī mai koe ki ahau
He aha te mea nui o te ao? Māku e kī atu
He tangata, he tangata, he tangata.

Pluck the centre shoot from the flax bush
Where will the Bellbird sing?
You ask me
What is the most important thing in the world
I will say
It is people, it is people, it is people.

Within te ao Māori, relationships are fundamentally based upon "reciprocity, mutuality, responsibility, duties, obligations and the maintenance of balance. These concepts consciously or subconsciously form part of the relationships between whānau, hapū and iwi" (Kahu, 1995, cited in Lawson-Te Aho, 2013, p. 19).

Integral to te ao Māori are our cosmogonies and cosmologies of the universe, and our existence within these, as expressed by our whakapapa. Our relationships with the universe are considered to be:

> ... traced through a series of ordered genealogical webs that go back hundreds of generations to the beginning ... this genealogical sequence, referred to as whakapapa, places Māori in an environmental context with all other flora and fauna and natural resources as part of a hierarchical genetic assemblage (Harmsworth & Awatere, 2013, p. 274).

Royal (2009) elaborates, describing whakapapa as:

> ... genealogies ... and narratives ... about aspects of the world. Through this framework of knowledge, the world is explained and all applications of knowledge and behaviours find their rationale and setting ... there are two aspects of whakapapa: [1] an explanation of and story about the world and its phenomena [2] a paradigm or context of values and perspectives within which actions take place (p. 48).

Lawson-Te Aho (2013) describes whakapapa as "a continuous relationship between the seen and unseen realms of human existence. Thus, it has spiritual, physical and metaphysical qualities" (p. 26). Murphy (2019) emphasises that "every element of creation is inter-related through whakapapa. Humans are teina – the youngest in creation and have a responsibility and obligation to care for their elders. These include the land, oceans, rivers, forests, animal, insect and birdlife" (p. 39).

In Māori cosmogonies, the creation of humankind through the actions of atua (divine beings), Hineahuone and Tānemahuta, is described through pūrākau. It is also within this specific pūrākau that the whakapapa of harakeke becomes interwoven with the whakapapa of humanity (McRae-Tarei, 2013; Mikaere, 2017; Pere, 1982; Taituha, 2014).

As Maldonado-Torres (2017) notes, "for any decolonisation of human rights to occur, there needs to be a decolonisation of the concept of the human" (p. 1). We argue that whakapapa can be considered thus. It is the basis for and the expression of our human existence as tangata whenua of Aotearoa me Te Waipounamu.

With regard to the actions of atua, Hineahuone and Tānemahuta, Lawson-Te Aho (2013) narrates the prelude to the pūrākau we include:

> Tāne and his brothers, the children of Rangi and Papa were ira atua (the divine principle). The divine principle searched the world for the human principle te ira tangata. Their efforts led them to conclude that te ira tangata could not be derived from te ira atua (confirming a two world system of divine and physical existences). There needed to be a separate act of creation (p. 62).

The actions of Hineahuone and Tānemahuta are described in the following pūrākau (McRae-Tarei, 2013; Mikaere, 2017; Pere, 1982; Taituha, 2014):

> Tāne, after forcing apart his primordial parents Papatūānuku and Ranginui, sought the female element to procreate the earth with human beings. In his quest, he procreated with numerous female deities producing offspring of plants and trees with their own Whakapapa. He procreated with Huna and Pākoti, and from these unions came harakeke. He then took the name, Tānemāhuta. Under the counsel of his mother, Papatūānuku, he returned to the female element within, at Kurawaka, the pubic region of his mother Papatūānuku where, from her sacred red soils he sculpted the figure of Hineahuone, and breathed life into her nostrils, the first hongi.
>
> Tānemahuta felt a tremendous force from within Hine, a powerful force, such as he had never experienced before. All that Tāne had sought and hoped for he found in his relationship with Hine; together they brought forth humanity (Pere, 1982, pp. 10–11).

Whenua – Whakapapa

In Oranga Mokopuna, just as humankind was created from the sacred red soils of Kurawaka, the nurturing soils of the whenua that create life for the harakeke symbolise the sovereign tangata whenua rights of our mokopuna. Pere (1997) refers to whenua as depicting "the placenta embracing and cherishing the child in the womb ... the land which is also called whenua offers one the same feeling of warmth, security, nourishment and sustenance, a feeling of belonging" (p. 22). As the whenua continues to be nourished from the nutrients of the older leaves that die, or on harvest are returned to the soil to sustain the harakeke, so do sovereign tangata whenua rights continue to be sustained.

Sovereign tangata whenua rights are derived from the layering of whakapapa, representing genealogical relationships to one another, past, present and future, to the world, across the cosmos and from beyond the origins of the universe. Thus, sovereign tangata whenua rights exist through the very presence of our mokopuna within the universe as described in Māori cosmogonies. They exist regardless of whether we have access to our own whakapapa and histories.

Pakiaka – Tikanga Māori

Tikanga Māori forms the roots (pakiaka) of Oranga Mokopuna. Māori society enjoyed sovereign tangata whenua rights well before Pākehā arrived, under a constitutional framework or governance system based on principles, practices, processes, rituals and traditional knowledge known as tikanga Māori (Jackson, 1988; Jones, 2014, 2016, 2019; Mikaere, 2007, 2011, 2017; Moko Mead, 2003). This framework is sometimes (incorrectly) described as interchangeable with that of 'Māori customary law' (Jones, 2003, 2016; Te Aho, 2007). However, the word 'customary' in the context of rights, titles and laws stems from the common law doctrine of Aboriginal Title. Legal scholars point out that such terminology was developed and defined by the colonisers of Indigenous Peoples. It is therefore not appropriate to use in the context of a discussion around sovereign tangata whenua rights (Mikaere, 2011; Te Aho, 2007). Alfred (1999) argues that "indigenous leaders who engage in arguments framed by a Western liberal paradigm cannot hope to protect the integrity of their nations" (p. 140):

> To enlist the intellectual force of rights-based arguments is to concede nationhood in the truest sense. 'Aboriginal rights' are in fact the benefits accrued by indigenous peoples who have agreed to abandon their autonomy in order to enter the legal and political framework of the state (p. 140).

Thus, we use the term 'tikanga Māori' throughout when referring to the constitutional framework described. Tikanga has been defined as:

> ... the set of beliefs associated with practices and procedures to be followed in conducting the affairs of a group or an individual. These procedures are established by precedents through time, are held to be ritually correct, are validated by usually more than one generation and are always subject to what a group or an individual is able to do (Moko Mead, 2003, p. 12).

In the context of tikanga Māori and its relationship with ngā ture a te Māori (Māori laws), Jackson (1988) explains that:

> ... traditional Māori ideals of law had their basis in a religious and mystical weave, which was codified into oral traditions and sacred beliefs. They made up a system based on a spiritual order, which was nevertheless developed in a rational and practical way to deal with questions of mana, security, and social stability (p. 39).

Thus, the normative guiding principles of tikanga Māori, having withstood the test of time, informed the "values-laden jurisprudence upon which decisions were made to settle disputes, regulate trade, ensure peace after war and reconcile all of the competing interests of human existence" (Jackson, 2010, para.18, cited in Independent Observers Panel, 2012). Although processes and practices have adapted over time to meet changing contexts (and thus requirements), a common set of fundamental core values are considered to underpin tikanga Māori (Barlow, 1991; Benton, Frame, & Meredith, 2013; Jones, 2003, 2014, 2016, 2019; McCully & Mutu, 2003; Mikaere, 2007, 2011; Moko Mead, 2003; Ratima, Durie, & Hond, 2015; Te Aho, 2007; Williams, 2000). One example is mana:

spiritually sanctioned or endorsed influence, power and authority under which one is able to exercise particular rights and obligations. Another is whanaungatanga: grounded in whakapapa genealogical connectivity and embodying the centrality of relationships to individual and collective identity within Māori society, and thus accompanying rights and obligations (Jones, 2016; Moko Mead, 2003).

Like those of other Indigenous Peoples, Māori conceptualisations of health and wellbeing encompass a positive holistic perspective that includes interactions between spiritual, social, mental, emotional and cultural dimensions, and gives prominence to relationships with the universe. Concepts of health and wellbeing are not limited to the individual but include the collective, and traverse generations – past, present and future (Durie, 1998; Moko Mead, 2003; Ratima et al., 2015). Within this context, an example of sovereign tangata whenua rights to health and wellbeing manifest under the constitutional framework of tikanga Māori is that of te tapu o te tangata (the sanctity of the person), where each individual life is considered inherently sacred, with whakapapa links to tīpuna/tūpuna and broader whakapapa networks (Jackson, 1988; Moko Mead, 2003). In relation to rights to health and wellbeing, "if the level of one's tapu is at a steady state, the individual is well in both a physical and psychological state" (Moko Mead, 2003, p. 45).

Jackson (1988) further elaborates on the concept of rights to the sanctity of the person. Whakapapa genealogical links to tīpuna/tūpuna (and thus broader sociopolitical tribal networks) promoted the safekeeping of individuals by establishing "the belief that any harm to [the individual] was also disrespect to that network which would ultimately be remedied" (p. 41). The fulfilling of rights and obligations associated with whakapapa were viewed as "fundamentally important to all ... [I]n the Māori legal system emphasis was placed on the responsibility owed by the individual to the collective" (Jones, 2003, p. 42). Jones (2003) points out, "[t]he corollary of this is that the community accepted responsibility for its members" (p. 42). As an example, the fundamental core value of utu reinforces the importance of balance and reciprocity in the maintenance of whanaungatanga (Jones, 2016; Moko Mead, 2003), underscoring the "centrality of relationships within Māori legal traditions" (Jones, 2016, p. 75).

Kaumātua and legal scholars maintain that Māori did not cede sovereignty to the British Crown in 1840 (Jackson, 1992; Mikaere, 2011; Sadler, 2015). This affirmation, also decreed by the Waitangi Tribunal in 2014 (Waitangi Tribunal, 2014) – the Crown's own introduced and determined mechanism for investigating grievances – leads to the astute observation that "although the Crown was almost indecent in its haste to reject the findings [of the Waitangi Tribunal] ... [it] reaffirms what Māori ... have been saying since 1840" (Matike Mai Aotearoa, 2016, p. 28). Thus, as Māori did not cede sovereignty to the Crown, it is tikanga Māori that forms the foundation for the constitutional framework, and thereby the legal system of laws within Aotearoa me Te Waipounamu, as opposed to the contemporary imported and inflicted Anglo-centric legal positivist system (Jackson, 1985, 1988; Mikaere, 1999, 2011). The existence of the two internationally recognised instruments, He Whakaputanga o te Rangatiratanga o Nu Tireni 1835 (He Whakaputanga), and Te Tiriti o Waitangi 1840 (Te Tiriti) are cited in support of this assertion (Jackson, 1985, 1988; Mikaere, 2007). Sovereign tangata whenua rights to health and wellbeing are thus manifest via the fundamental norms underpinning tikanga Māori. These rights are recognised explicitly in the two international instruments, He Whakaputanga and Te Tiriti (Independent Observers Panel, 2012; Jackson, 1985, 1988; Mikaere, 1999, 2011; Network Waitangi, 2018; Waitangi Tribunal, 2014).

Just as Māori individuals, whānau, hapū and iwi are all unique, tikanga Māori values and practices will vary between whānau, hapū and iwi, or may be described or implemented in different ways depending on the context. Matike Mai Aotearoa (2016) highlights that:

> ... in the hundreds of years prior to 1840 the common land mass that made up the islands of Te Ika a Maui and Te Waka a Maui was occupied by distinct iwi and hapū polities. Each polity exercised its own mana and lived according to its tikanga secure in both its political independence and its whakapapa-based interdependence with others (p. 35).

As the interconnectedness of the roots of each unique harakeke plant supports the collective, so do the values and practices of unique whānau, hapū and iwi interact and interconnect with one another under the constitutional framework of tikanga Māori (Jackson, 1985, 1988; Jones, 2016; Mikaere, 2007, 2011). Mikaere (2017) has written extensively on the adverse impacts of the colonisation of tikanga on Māori, and the particularly negative consequences for wāhine, pēpi, tamariki and rangatahi. Decolonial approaches to tikanga Māori are thus of paramount importance. As Lee-Morgan and Hutchings (2016) highlight:

> ... [a]s is the case for other indigenous peoples, decolonisation here is premised on a belief in our own social, spiritual, economic, political and cultural knowledge systems, traditions, beliefs and practices. These traditions are not seen as a romanticised past, but continue to be a valid source for our sustainability and regeneration as a people, and at the heart of what decolonisation aspires to achieve (p. 4).

Murphy (2019) also states that we "have a responsibility as ancestors of future generations to evolve tikanga that empowers, heals, and decolonises our whānau and uri to come" (p. 227).

Rito – Mokopuna

The rito symbolises the pēpi/mokopuna who, in te ao Māori, are the heart of society. Their very existence within the universe establishes their sovereign tangata whenua rights through whakapapa and tikanga Māori. Yet we are all mokopuna and just as the harakeke leaves become older over time, so do mokopuna become tīpuna/tūpuna.

Awhi Rito/Mātua – He Whakaputanga o te Rangatiratanga o Nu Tireni 1835 and Te Tiriti o Waitangi 1840

The awhi rito, or protectors of the rito, stand on each side. Like the rito, they are never harvested and are seen as ngā mātua, representing the genealogical lines of the parents. In Oranga Mokopuna, they also represent the two internationally recognised instruments, He Whakaputanga and Te Tiriti.

In Oranga Mokopuna, He Whakaputanga affirms existing sovereign tangata whenua rights to health and wellbeing under the constitutional framework and system of laws of tikanga Māori. Te Tiriti then reiterates and further articulates these rights under all three articles as well as the intention of Te Tiriti, based upon its specific phrasing and words of the text collectively. Under Articles 1 and 2 (kāwanatanga and tino rangatiratanga) of te Tiriti, our mokopuna have the right to authority over Māori health development, design, delivery, monitoring and evaluation, and the right to self-determination over their own health and wellbeing. Under Articles 2 and 3 (tino rangatiratanga and ōritetanga), our mokopuna, as taonga, are specifically entitled to protections with the right to equity in all aspects including health and wellbeing. Thus, once sovereign tangata whenua rights derived from whakapapa and implemented under Tikanga Māori are realised through the articulation of He Whakaputanga and Te Tiriti, rights described in international human-rights instruments develop and support these rights to health and wellbeing.

Whānau – Convention on the Rights of the Child

The innermost rau (leaves) represent the whānau. In Oranga Mokopuna, they also represent the articles of the United Nations Convention on the Rights of the Child (the UNCROC) as well as other international human rights instruments ratified by the government (UN General Assembly, 1948, 1966a, 1966b, 1966c, 1979, 1989, 2006). The rights of our mokopuna outlined by the UNCROC can be divided into those of survival, development, protection, participation and provision. For example, Article 24 of the UNCROC stipulates the requirement for governments to recognise the right of the child to the enjoyment of the highest attainable standard of health (UN General Assembly, 1989). The right to the highest attainable standard of health is subject to progressive realisation, and to the maximum extent possible with the resources available (UN General Assembly, 1966c). Article 30 guarantees that collective rights as rights of Indigenous children must be "applied in the context of their unique cultures and histories … the child's right to culture is to be exercised collectively" (Breen, 2017, p. 88). The Committee on the Rights of the Child (2009) notes that:

> … when State authorities including legislative bodies seek to assess the best interests of an indigenous child, they should consider the cultural rights of the indigenous child and his or her need to exercise such rights collectively with members of their group (para 31).

Tīpuna/Tūpuna – Declaration on the Rights of Indigenous Peoples

The outermost rau (leaves) represent our tīpuna/tūpuna. In Oranga Mokopuna they also represent the articles of the UNDRIP (UN General Assembly, 2007), providing the supportive framework for the realisation of both individual and collective rights under the UNCROC and other international rights instruments, for instance, the United Nations Convention on the Rights of Persons with Disabilities (UN General Assembly, 2006). The UNDRIP comprises forty-six articles describing rights and the actions member states must take to respect, fulfil and protect those rights (Erueti, 2017). The most fundamental of these is the right to self-determination contained within Article 3 (Anaya, 2011). This includes meaningful participation in the social, political and economic activities of the state, and free, prior and informed consent. In addition to Article 3, Article 4 (the right to self-government in matters relating to their own affairs), Article 23 (the right to set their own priorities and directions for development such as health), Article 24 (the right to the highest attainable standard of health, the right to traditional medicines and to the maintenance of their health practices and right to access without discrimination all health and social services) and Article 37 (the right to recognition, observance and enforcement of treaties and agreements such as Te Tiriti) relate directly to health and wellbeing (UN General Assembly, 2007).

Kōrari – Hauora

The kōrari, as the stem of the harakeke, represents hauora, the "breath of life [and] … source by and from which mauri (life principle) is mediated" (Marsden, 2003, p. 44). In Oranga Mokopuna, hauora represents the health and wellbeing of our mokopuna – interpretations of which are self-determined and grounded within te ao Māori worldviews. Mokopuna self-determined health and wellbeing will thus thrive when sovereign tangata whenua rights are respected, protected and fulfilled.

Puāwai – Rangatira

In Oranga Mokopuna, the puāwai (flower) centralises our mokopuna as our rangatira of today. Pere (1997) distils the word tamariki as "derived from Tama-te-rā the central sun,

Figure 2: Te Pā Harakeke.

WHAKAPAPA

the divine spark; ariki refers to senior most status, and riki on its own can mean smaller version. Tamariki is the Māori word used for children. Children are the greatest legacy the world community has" (p. 4).

Just as our mokopuna are unique individuals within whānau, and each whānau, hapū and iwi is unique within Aotearoa me Te Waipounamu, so are the harakeke who live together within their collective of interconnected roots. Te Pā Harakeke represents the multiplicity of whānau, hapū and iwi interconnected through whakapapa and interacting with one another under tikanga Māori. Like the formidable obstacle presented by the fortified pā, Te Pā Harakeke speaks to the remarkable strengths we have as a collective of Indigenous Peoples (Figure 2).

Discussion

Oranga Mokopuna builds on mātauranga Māori practices that foreground the treasured status of our mokopuna. Oranga Mokopuna provides a te ao Māori frame of reference for the full realisation of sovereign tangata whenua rights to health and wellbeing for our mokopuna. Oranga Mokopuna also provides an alternative rights-based approach to health and wellbeing in Aotearoa me Te Waipounamu that foregrounds whānau, whakapapa, tikanga Māori, He Whakaputanga and Te Tiriti while incorporating international human rights instruments such as the UNCROC and, specifically, the UNDRIP.

Oranga Mokopuna thus guides the required values, principles, actions and practices for the respect, protection and fulfilment of rights to health and wellbeing for mokopuna Māori, occurring fundamentally through whakapapa and decolonised tikanga Māori, as articulated by He Whakaputanga and Te Tiriti, which stipulate the provisions for rights to health and wellbeing. Sovereign tangata whenua rights are then further developed by individual and collective human rights outlined under the articles of the UNCROC and other international human rights instruments. However, the full realisation of both individual and collective rights is articulated through the UNDRIP.

More broadly, Oranga Mokopuna intends to contribute positively to the health and wellbeing of our mokopuna in Aotearoa me Te Waipounamu through an alternative, decolonial rights-based approach to the realisation of sovereign tangata whenua rights to health and wellbeing. Mahuika (2008) points out that "resistance to colonialism … requires a deeper understanding and 'dismantling' of the 'master's house' [and] a re-programming of the 'oppressors' tools'" (p. 12). It is via such mechanisms that:

> … revitalization and resistance might be made more effective in the ever evolving present and future … it is about empowering Māori, hapū and iwi to carve out new possibilities, and to determine in their own ways, their past, present and future identities and lives (Mahuika, 2008, p. 12).

As a means of resistance, transformation and decolonisation, Oranga Mokopuna proposes a fundamentally different approach and can be conceptualised as both a way to reconfigure and decolonise prevailing approaches, and an alternative that can operate outside of Crown institutions and constraints. Critically, Oranga Mokopuna emphasises that our mokopuna cannot be considered as existing outside the context of whānau.

In addition, the realisation of sovereign tangata whenua rights to health and wellbeing is fundamentally informed by decolonised tikanga Māori. Tikanga will vary between whānau, hapū and iwi, and is thus dependent on context. Rather than a focus on romantic notions of the past, acknowledgement of tikanga Māori systems, processes and practices reiterates mātauranga, te reo and tikanga Māori as the foundation for our resurgence as a decolonised people (Lee-Morgan & Hutchings, 2016). In addition, Māori continue to argue that the growing body of predominantly Crown legislative discourse surrounding Te Tiriti contributes to conflicting reinterpretations leading to further marginalisation of Māori rights (Jackson, 1985; Mikaere, 1999). Thus, the four articles of Te Tiriti and the intention of Te Tiriti based upon its specific phrasing and words, and of the text collectively, must be considered, as opposed to the use of Crown-defined 'principles of the Treaty'. Oranga Mokopuna cannot be employed in a way that disrupts whakapapa or be co-opted in ways that do not align with sovereign tangata whenua rights. Nor can it be fragmented – Oranga Mokopuna must be applied in its entirety.

Conclusion

Oranga Mokopuna challenges prevailing rights-based approaches to health and wellbeing that often assume the primacy of individual rights and leave un-interrogated the coloniality of key notions regarding who defines who is 'human' in human rights discourses (Maldonado-Torres, 2017). Our intent has thus been to recentre decolonised tikanga Māori and local rights instruments in discussions of rights-based approaches, with international human-rights instruments such as the UNCROC, and specifically, the UNDRIP, developing and supporting sovereign tangata whenua rights, rather than being seen as the basis for those rights. The vision of Oranga Mokopuna is for our mokopuna to thrive and flourish as our rangatira of today, through the respect, protection and fulfilment of their sovereign tangata whenua rights to health and wellbeing.

Acknowledgements

The authors would like to thank Dr Moana Jackson for his invaluable comments and feedback during the development of Oranga Mokopuna. Many thanks to Professor Richard Edwards, Department of Public Health, University of Otago, Wellington, for his supportive role in providing PhD supervision for Paula King. Ethics approval was granted by the University of Otago Human Ethics Committee (Category A/Reference code: 17/027). The PhD research study was financially supported by the Health Research Council of New Zealand Clinical Research Training Fellowship Grant, Ngāpuhi Education Scholarship and the Ngā Pae o te Māramatanga Doctoral Bridging Grant.

References

ALFRED, T. (1999). *Peace, power, righteousness: An Indigenous manifesto*. Oxford, England: Oxford University Press.

ANAYA, J. (2011). *Report of the Special Rapporteur on the rights of Indigenous peoples*. Retrieved from https://undocs.org/A/HRC/18/35

AXELSSON, P., KUKUTAI, T., & KIPPEN, R. (2016). The field of Indigenous health and the role of colonisation and history. *Journal of Population Research, 33*(1), 1–7. doi:10.1007/s12546-016-9163-2

BARLOW, C. (1991). *Tikanga whakaaro: Key concepts in Māori culture*. Melbourne, Australia: Oxford University Press.

BENTON, R., FRAME, A., & MEREDITH, P. E. (EDS.). (2013). *Te Mātāpunenga: A compendium of references to the concepts and institutions of Māori customary law*. Wellington, New Zealand: Victoria University Press.

BREEN, C. (2017). The declaration and the implementation of the rights of the Indigenous child in Aotearoa. In A. Erueti (Ed.), *International Indigenous rights in Aotearoa New Zealand* (pp. 86–98). Wellington, New Zealand: Victoria University Press.

CAMERON, N., PIHAMA, L., LEATHERBY, R., & CAMERON, A. (2013). *He Mokopuna He Tupuna: Investigating Māori views of childrearing amongst Iwi in Taranaki*. Retrieved from http://www.communityresearch.org.nz/research/he-mokopuna-he-tupuna-investigating-traditional-maori-views-of-childrearing-amongst-iwi-within-taranaki/

CHERRINGTON, L. (2003). The use of Māori mythology in clinical settings: Training issues and needs. In L. W. Nikora, M. Leby, B. Masters, W. Waitoki, N. Te Awekotuku & R. Etheredge (Eds.), *Proceedings of the National Māori Graduates of Psychology Symposium, 2002: Making a difference* (pp. 117–120). Hamilton, New Zealand: Māori and Psychology Research Unit, University of Waikato.

COMMITTEE ON THE RIGHTS OF THE CHILD. (2009). *General comment no. 11: Indigenous children and their rights under the Convention [on the Rights of the Child]*, CRC/C/GC/11. Retrieved from https://www.refworld.org/docid/49f6bd922.html

CRAIG, E., REDDINGTON, A., ADAMS, J., DELL, R., JACK, S., OBEN, G., ... & SIMPSON, J. (2014). *The health of Māori children and young people with chronic conditions and disabilities in New Zealand – Series 2: Te Ohonga Ake series for the Ministry of Health*. Dunedin, New Zealand: New Zealand Child & Youth Epidemiology Service, University of Otago.

CRAM, F., TE HUIA, B., TE HUIA, T., WILLIAMS, M. M., & WILLIAMS, N. (2019). *Oranga and Māori health inequities – Prepared for the Ministry of Health*. Auckland, New Zealand: Katoa Ltd.

CZYZEWSKI, K. (2011). Colonialism as a broader social determinant of health. *The International Indigenous Policy Journal, 2*(1), Article 5. doi:10.18584/iipj.2011.2.1.5

DUNCANSON, M., RICHARDSON, G., OBEN, G., WICKEN, A., & ADAMS, J. (2019). *Child Poverty Monitor 2019: Technical report*. Dunedin, New Zealand: New Zealand Child and Youth Epidemiology Service.

DURIE, M. (1998). *Whaiora: Māori health development* (2nd ed.). Auckland, New Zealand: Oxford University Press.

DURIE, M. (1999). *Te Pae Mahutonga: A model for Māori health promotion*. Health Promotion Forum of New Zealand. Retrieved from https://www.cph.co.nz/wp-content/uploads/TePaeMahutonga.pdf

ELDER, H. (2013). Te Waka Oranga: An Indigenous intervention for working with Māori children and adolescents with traumatic brain injury. *Brain Impairment*, 14(3), 415–424. doi:10.1017/BrImp.2013.29

ERUETI, A. (ED.). (2017). *International Indigenous rights in Aotearoa New Zealand*. Wellington, New Zealand: Victoria University Press.

GABEL, K. A. (2019). Raranga, raranga taku takapau: Healing intergenerational trauma through the assertion of mātauranga ūkaipō. In C. Smith & R. Tinirau (Eds.), *He rau murimuri aroha: Wāhine Māori insights into historical trauma and healing* (pp. 17–34). Whanganui, New Zealand: Te Atawhai o Te Ao – Independent Māori Institute for Environment & Health.

GRIFFITHS, K., COLEMAN, C., LEE, V., & MADDEN, R. (2016). How colonisation determines social justice and Indigenous health – A review of the literature. *Journal of Population Research*, 33(1), 9–30. doi:10.1007/s12546-016-9164-1

GROSFOGUEL, R. (2002). Colonial difference, geopolitics of knowledge, and global coloniality in the modern/colonial capitalist world-system. *Review (Fernand Braudel Center)*, 25(3), 203–224. Retrieved from https://www.jstor.org/stable/40241548

GROSFOGUEL, R. (2011). Decolonizing post-colonial studies and paradigms of political-economy: Transmodernity, decolonial thinking, and global coloniality. *TRANSMODERNITY: Journal of Peripheral Cultural Production of the Luso–Hispanic World*, 1(1), 1–38. Retrieved from https://escholarship.org/uc/item/21k6t3fq

HARMSWORTH, G., & AWATERE, S. (2013). Indigenous Māori knowledge and perspectives of ecosystems. In J. R. Dymond (Ed.), *Ecosystem services in New Zealand – Conditions and trends* (pp. 274–286). Lincoln, New Zealand: Manaaki Whenua Press.

HARRIS, R., CORMACK, D., TOBIAS, M., YEH, L.C., TALAMAIVAO, N., MINSTER, J., & TIMUTIMU, R. (2012). The pervasive effects of racism: Experiences of racial discrimination in New Zealand over time and associations with multiple health domains. *Social Science and Medicine*, 74(3), 408–415. doi:10.1016/j.socscimed.2011.11.004

HENARE, M. (1988). Ngā tikanga me ngā ritenga o te ao Māori: Standards and foundations of Māori society. In I. K. M. Richardson (Ed.), *The April Report III: Report of the Royal Commission on Social Policy* (pp. 7–41). Wellington, New Zealand: Royal Commission on Social Policy.

HIGGINS, N., PHILLIPS, H., STOBBS, K., WILSON, G., & PASCOE, H. (2012). *Summary of the findings – Growing up kāpō Māori: Accessing paediatric ophthalmology services*. Hastings, New Zealand: Ngāti Kāpō o Aotearoa.

INDEPENDENT OBSERVERS PANEL. (2012). *Ngāpuhi speaks: He Wakaputanga and Te Tiriti o Waitangi – Independent report on Ngāpuhi Nui Tonu claim*. Whangarei, New Zealand: Te Kawariki & Network Waitangi Whangarei.

JACKSON, M. (1985). *The Treaty of Waitangi*. Wellington, New Zealand: Ngā Kaiwhakamarama i ngā Ture.

JACKSON, M. (1988). *The Māori and the criminal justice system – A new perspective: He whaipaanga hou part 2.* Wellington, New Zealand: Department of Justice.

JACKSON, M. (1992). *The Crown, the Treaty, and the ursurpation of Māori rights: Why is the Treaty important.* Auckland, New Zealand: Project Waitangi Tamaki Makaurau & The Mental Health Foundation of New Zealand.

JENKINS, K., & MOUNTAIN HARTE, H. (2011). *Traditional Māori parenting: An historical review of literature of traditional Māori child rearing practices in pre-European times.* Retrieved from http://www.ririki.org.nz/wp-content/uploads/2015/04/TradMaoriParenting.pdf

JONES, C. (2003). *Tino rangatiratanga and sustainable development: Principles for developing a just and effective resource management regime in Aotearoa/New Zealand* (Unpublished Master's thesis). York University, Toronto, Canada.

JONES, C. (2014). A Māori constitutional tradition. *New Zealand Journal of Public and International Law, 12,* 187–203. Retrieved from https://heinonline.org/HOL/LandingPage?handle=hein.journals/nzjpubinl12&div=13&id=&page=

JONES, C. (2016). *New treaty new tradition: Reconciling New Zealand and Māori law.* Wellington, New Zealand: Victoria University Press.

JONES, C. (2019). Indigenous law/stories: An approach to working with Māori law. In J. Archibald Q'um Q'um Xiiem, J. B. J. Lee-Morgan, & J. De Santolo (Eds.), *Decolonizing research: Indigenous storywork as methodology* (pp. 120–136). London, England: Zed Books.

KING, P. (2019). *Māori with lived experience of disability – Part I: Wai 2575, #B22.* Retrieved from https://forms.justice.govt.nz/search/Documents/WT/wt_DOC_150437272/Wai 2575%2C B022.pdf

KINGI, T. K. (2002). *Hua Oranga: Best outcomes for Māori* (Doctoral dissertation). Massey University, Wellington, New Zealand. Retrieved from https://mro.massey.ac.nz/handle/10179/2079

KŌPUA, D. M., KŌPUA, M. A., & BRACKEN, P. J. (2019). Mahi a Atua: A Māori approach to mental health. *Transcultural Psychiatry, 57*(2), 375–383. doi:10.1177/1363461519851606

LAWSON-TE AHO, K. (2013). *Whāia te mauriora: In pursuit of healing – Theorising connections between soul healing, tribal self-determination and Māori suicide prevention in Aotearoa/New Zealand* (Doctoral dissertation). Victoria University of Wellington, Wellington, New Zealand. Retrieved from https://www.otago.ac.nz/wellington/otago059239.pdf

LAWSON-TE AHO, K., & LIU, J. H. (2010). Indigenous suicide and colonisation: The legacy of violence and the necessity of self-determination. *International Journal of Conflict and Violence, 4*(1), 124–133. doi:10.4119/ijcv-2819

LEE, J. (2009). Decolonising Māori narratives: Pūrākau as a method. *MAI Review 2*(3), 79–91. Retrieved from https://oheg.org/decolonising_mori_narratives_prkau_as_a_method.pdf

LEE-MORGAN, J. B. J. (2019). Pūrākau from the inside-out: Regenerating stories for cutural sustainability. In J. Archibald Q'um Q'um Xiiem, J. B. J. Lee-Morgan, & J. De Santolo (Eds.), (2019), *Decolonizing research: Indigenous storywork as methodology* (pp. 151–166). London, England: Zed Books.

LEE-MORGAN, J., & HUTCHINGS, J. (2016). Introduction: Kaupapa Māori in action: Education, research and practice. In J. Hutchings & J. Lee-Morgan (Eds.), *Decolonisation in Aotearoa: Education, research and practice* (pp. 1–18). Wellington, New Zealand: NZCER Press.

MAHUIKA, M. (2008). Kaupapa Māori theory is critical and anti-colonial. *MAI Review*, 3, Article 4. Retrieved from https://www.researchgate.net/profile/Rangimarie_Mahuika/publication/26569994_Kau papa_Maori_theory_is_critical_and_anti-colonial/links/575f300708aec91374b43990/Kaupapa-Maori-theory-is-critical-and-anti-colonial.pdf

MALDONADO-TORRES, N. (2017). On the coloniality of human rights. *Revista Crítica de Ciências Sociais*, 114, 117–136. doi:10.4000/rccs.6793

MARSDEN, M. (2003). *The woven universe: Selected writings of Rev. Māori Marsden*. Ōtaki, New Zealand: Estate of Rev. Māori Marsden.

MATIKE MAI AOTEAROA. (2016). *He whakaaro here whakaumu mō Aotearoa: The report of Matike Mai Aotearoa – The Independent Working Group on Constitutional Transformation*. Retrieved from http://www.converge.org.nz/pma/MatikeMaiAotearoaReport.pdf

MATUA RAKI. (2012). *The Takarangi competency framework*. Retrieved from https://www.matuaraki.org.nz/resources/takarangi-competency-framework-essence-statements–poster/388

MCCULLY, M., & MUTU, M. (2003). *Te whānau moana: Ngā kaupapa me ngā tikanga – Customs and protocols*. Auckland, New Zealand: Reed Publishing.

MCRAE-TAREI, J. (2013). *The sustainability of tikanga practice and values within toi rāranga* (Master's thesis). Auckland University of Technology, Auckland, New Zealand. Retrieved from https://openrepository.aut.ac.nz/handle/10292/5760

MIKAERE, A. (1999). *Challenging the mission of colonization: A Māori view of the Treaty of Waitangi and the constitution*. Retrieved from http://www.gw.govt.nz/assets/council-reports/Report_PDFs/1999_638_2_Attach.pdf

MIKAERE, A. (2007). Tikanga as the first law of Aotearoa. In L. Te Aho (Ed.), *Yearbook of New Zealand Jurisprudence Special Issue: Tikanga Māori me te mana i Waitangi – Māori laws and values i Te Tiriti o Waitangi and human rights* (pp. 24–31). Hamilton, New Zealand: The University of Waikato.

MIKAERE, A. (2011). *Colonising myths – Māori realities: He rukuruku whakaaro*. Wellington, New Zealand: Huia Publishers & Te Tākupu, Te Wānanga o Raukawa.

MIKAERE, A. (2017). *The balance destroyed*. Ōtaki, New Zealand: Te Wānanga o Raukawa.

MINISTRY OF EDUCATION. (1996). *Te Whāriki*. Wellington, New Zealand: Ministry of Education.

MINISTRY OF EDUCATION. (2017). *Te Whāriki*. Wellington, New Zealand: Ministry of Education.

MINISTRY OF HEALTH. (2014). *He Korowai Oranga: Māori health strategy*. Wellington, New Zealand: Ministry of Health. Retrieved from https://www.health.govt.nz/system/files/documents/publications/guide-to-he-korowai-oranga-maori-health-strategy-jun14-v2.pdf

MINISTRY OF HEALTH. (2015). *Tatau kahukura: Māori health chart book 2015* (3rd ed.). Retrieved from https://www.health.govt.nz/publication/tatau-kahukura-maori-health-chart-book-2015-3rd-edition

MINISTRY OF HEALTH. (2019). *Wai 2575 Māori health trends report.* Wellington, New Zealand: Ministry of Health. Retrieved from https://www.health.govt.nz/publication/wai-2575-maori-health-trends-report

MOKO MEAD, H. (2003). *Tikanga Māori: Living by Māori values.* Wellington, New Zealand: Huia Publishers.

MONTURE-ANGUS, P. (1995). *Thunder in my soul: A Mohawk woman speaks.* Halifax, Canada: Fernwood Publishing.

MURPHY, N. (2011). *Te awa atua, te awa tapu, te awa wahine: An examination of stories, ceremonies and practices regarding menstruation in the pre-colonial Māori world.* (Master's thesis). University of Waikato, Hamilton, New Zealand. Retrieved from https://researchcommons.waikato.ac.nz/handle/10289/5532

MURPHY, N. (2019). *Te ahi tawhito, te ahi tipua, te ahi nā Mahuika: Re-igniting native women's ceremony* (Doctoral dissertation). University of Waikato, Hamilton, New Zealand. Retrieved from https://researchcommons.waikato.ac.nz/handle/10289/12668

NETWORK WAITANGI. (2018). *Treaty of Waitangi: Questions and answers* (7th revised ed.). Christchurch, New Zealand: Network Waitangi Otautahi. Retrieved from https://nwo.org.nz/resources/questions-and-answers-booklet/

NGATA, T. (2019). *Kia Mau: Resisting colonial fictions.* Wellington, New Zealand: Rebel Press.

PAINE, S-J., HARRIS, R., STANLEY, J., & CORMACK, D. (2018). Caregiver experiences of racism and child healthcare utilisation: Cross-sectional analysis from New Zealand. *Archives of Disease in Childhood, 103,* 873–879. doi:10.1136/archdischild-2017-313866

PARADIES, Y. (2016). Colonisation, racism and Indigenous health. *Journal of Population Research, 33*(1), 83–96. doi:10.1007/s12546-016-9159-y

PERE, R. (1982). *Ako: Concepts and learning in the Māori tradition.* Wellington, New Zealand: Astra Print.

PERE, R. (1997). *A celebration of infinite wisdom.* Wairoa, New Zealand: Ao Ako Global Learning New Zealand.

PIHAMA, L., CAMPBELL, D., & GREENSILL, H. (2019). Whānau storytelling as Indigenous pedagogy: Tiakina te pā harakeke. In J. Archibald Q'um Q'um Xiiem, J. B. J. Lee-Morgan, & J. De Santolo (Eds.), *Decolonizing research: Indigenous story work as methodology* (pp. 137–150). London, England: Zed Books.

PIHAMA, L., LEE, J., TE NANA, R., CAMPBELL, D., GREENSILL, H., & TAUROA, T. (2015). Te pā harakeke: Whānau as a site of wellbeing. In R. Rinehart, E. Emerald, & R. Matamua (Eds.), *Ethnographies in pan Pacific research: Tensions and Positionings* (pp. 251–256). New York, NY: Routledge.

PIHAMA, L., SIMMONDS, N., & WAITOKI, W. (2019). *Te taonga o taku ngākau: Ancestral knowledge and the wellbeing of tamariki Māori.* Hamilton, New Zealand: Te Kotahi Research Institute.

PITAMA, S., HURIA, T., & LACEY, C. (2014). Improving Māori health through clinical assessment: Waikare o te waka o meihana. *New Zealand Medical Journal*, 127(1393), 107–119. Retrieved from https://global-uploads.webflow.com/5e332a62c703f653182faf47/5e332a62c703f6cd2b2fd78c_NZMJ-1393.pdf#page=107

RANGIHUNA, D., KŌPUA, M., & TIPENE-LEACH, D. (2018). Te Mahi a Atua. *Journal of Primary Health Care*, 10(1), 16–17. doi:10.1071/HC17076

RATIMA, M., DURIE, M., & HOND R. (2015). Māori health promotion. In L. Signal & M. Ratima (Eds.), *Promoting health in Aotearoa New Zealand* (pp. 42–63). Dunedin, New Zealand: Otago University Press.

READING, C. L., & WIEN, F. (2009). *Health inequalities and social determinants of Aboriginal peoples' health*. Prince George, Canada: National Collaborating Centre for Aboriginal Health.

REID, P., CORMACK, D., & PAINE, S-J. (2019). Colonial histories, racism and health – The experience of Māori and Indigenous peoples. *Public Health*, 172, 119–124. doi:10.1016/j.puhe.2019.03.027

REID, P., & ROBSON, B. (2007). Understanding health inequities. In B. Robson & R. Harris (Eds.), *Hauora Māori standards of health IV: A study of the years 2000–2005* (pp. 3–10). Wellington, New Zealand: Te Rōpū Rangahau Hauora a Eru Pōmare, University of Otago.

ROBSON, B., & HARRIS, R. (EDS.). (2007). *Hauora Māori standards of health IV. A study of the years 2000–2005*. Wellington, New Zealand: Te Rōpū Rangahau Hauora a Eru Pōmare, University of Otago.

ROYAL, T. A. (2009). *Let the world speak: Towards Indigenous epistemology*. Porirua, New Zealand: Mauriora-ki-te-Ao/Living Universe.

SADLER, H. (2015). *Ko tautoro te pito o tōku ao: A Ngāpuhi narrative*. Auckland, New Zealand: Auckland University Press.

SEED-PIHAMA, J. E. (2019). Naming our names and telling our stories. In J. Archibald Q'um Q'um Xiiem, J. B. J. Lee-Morgan, & J. De Santolo (Eds.), *Decolonizing research: Indigenous story work as methodology* (pp. 107–119). London, England: Zed Books.

SIMPSON, J., ADAMS, J., OBEN, G., WICKEN, A., & DUNCANSON, M. (2016). *Te Ohonga Ake: The determinants of health for Māori children and young people in New Zealand – Series two*. Dunedin, New Zealand: New Zealand Child and Youth Epidemiology Service, University of Otago.

SIMPSON, J., DUNCANSON, M., OBEN, G., ADAMS, J., WICKEN, A., PIERSON, M., GALLAGHER, S. (2017). *Te Ohonga Ake: The health status of Māori children and young people in New Zealand – Series two*. Dunedin, New Zealand: New Zealand Child and Youth Epidemiology Service, University of Otago. Retrieved from https://www.health.govt.nz/publication/te-ohonga-ake-health-status-maori-children-and-young-people-new-zealand-0

STASIULIS, D., & YUVAL-DAVIS, N. (EDS.). (1995). *Unsettling settler societies: Articulations of gender, race, ethnicity and class*. London, England: SAGE.

STEPHENS, C., PORTER, J., NETTLETON, C., & WILLIS, R. (2006). Disappearing, displaced, and undervalued: A call to action for Indigenous health worldwide. *The Lancet, 367*(9527), 2019–2028. doi:10.1016/S0140-6736(06)68892-2

TAITUHA, G. (2014). *He kākahu, he korowai, he kaitaka, he aha atu anō? The significance of the transmission of Māori knowledge relating to raranga and whatu muka in the survival of korowai in Ngāti Maniapoto in a contemporary context* (Master's thesis). Auckland University of Technology, Auckland, New Zealand. Retrieved from https://openrepository.aut.ac.nz/bitstream/handle/10292/8233/TaituhaG.pdf?sequence=3&isAllowed=y

TAKITIMU, D. (2015). He manawa whenua, he manawa taketake. In L. Pihama, H. Skipper, & J. Tipene (Eds.), *He Manawa Whenua. Proceedings of the Inaugural Indigenous Research Conference of Te Kotahi Research Institute* (pp. 22–33). Hamilton, New Zealand: Te Kotahi Research Institute.

TASKFORCE ON WHĀNAU CENTRED INITIATIVES. (2010). *Whānau Ora: Report of the Taskforce on Whānau-Centred Initiatives – Report produced for Hon Tariana Turia, Minister for the Community and Voluntary Sector*. Wellington, New Zealand: Ministry of Social Development. Retrieved from https://www.msd.govt.nz/documents/about-msd-and-our-work/publications-resources/planning-strategy/whanau-ora/whanau-ora-taskforce-report.pdf

TAWHAI, V. (2016). The power of youth-led decolonisation education. In J. Hutchings, & J. Lee-Morgan (Eds.), *Decolonisation in Aotearoa: Education, research and practice* (pp. 86–100). Wellington, New Zealand: NZCER Press.

TE AHO, L. (ED.) (2007). *Yearbook of New Zealand Jurisprudence Special Issue: Tikanga Māori me te mana i Waitangi – Māori laws and values i Te Tiriti o Waitangi and human rights*. Hamilton, New Zealand: The University of Waikato.

TE RATANA, R. (2012). *Ritual in the making: A critical exploration of ritual in te whare pora* (Master's thesis). Auckland University of Technology, Auckland, New Zealand. Retrieved from https://openrepository.aut.ac.nz/handle/10292/4787

UN GENERAL ASSEMBLY. (1948). *Universal Declaration of Human Rights*. Paris, France: United Nations. Retrieved from https://www.un.org/en/universal-declaration-human-rights/index.html

UN GENERAL ASSEMBLY. (1966A). *Convention on the Elimination of All Forms of Racial Discrimination*. New York, NY: United Nations.

UN GENERAL ASSEMBLY. (1966B). *International Covenant on Civil and Political Rights*. New York, NY: United Nations.

UN GENERAL ASSEMBLY. (1966C). *International Covenant on Economic, Social and Cultural Rights*. New York, NY: United Nations.

UN GENERAL ASSEMBLY. (1979). *Convention on the Elimination of All Forms of Discrimination Against Women*. New York, NY: United Nations.

UN GENERAL ASSEMBLY. (1989). *Convention on the Rights of the Child*. New York, NY: United Nations.

UN GENERAL ASSEMBLY. (2006). *Convention on the Rights of Persons with Disabilities.* New York, NY: United Nations.

UN GENERAL ASSEMBLY. (2007). *United Nations Declaration on the Rights of Indigenous Peoples.* Washington, DC: United Nations.

WAITANGI TRIBUNAL. (2014). *He Whakaputanga me te Tiriti – The Declaration and the Treaty: The Report on Stage 1 of the Te Paparahi o Te Raki Inquiry.* Retrieved from https://forms.justice.govt.nz/search/Documents/WT/wt_DOC_85648980/Te%20RakiW_1.pdf

WAITANGI TRIBUNAL. (2019). *Hauora: Report on Stage One of the Health Services and Outcomes Kaupapa Inquiry, WAI 2575.* Wellington, New Zealand: Legislation Direct. Retrieved from https://forms.justice.govt.nz/search/Documents/WT/wt_DOC_152801817/Hauora%20W.pdf

WALKER, T. W. (2013). *Ngā pā harakeke o Ngati Porou: A lived experience of whānau* (Doctoral dissertation). Victoria University of Wellington, Wellington, New Zealand. Retrieved from https://researcharchive.vuw.ac.nz/xmlui/handle/10063/2724

WILLIAMS, D. R., LAWRENCE, J. A., & DAVIS, B. A. (2019). Racism and health: Evidence and needed research. *Annual Review of Public Health*, 40, 105–125. doi:10.1146/annurev-publhealth-040218-043750

WILLIAMS, J. (2000). *He aha te tikanga Māori.* Paper presented at the Mai i te Ata Harapa Hui, 11–13 August 2000. Te Wānanga o Raukawa, Ōtaki, New Zealand.

Whiti-te-Rā:
A Māori-centred Therapeutic Approach to Wellbeing

Andre McLachlan
Waikaremoana Waitoki

CHAPTER 15

The incorporation of Māori cultural beliefs, values and practices in mental health therapies has grown since the early 1980s. Primary features of Māori health models recognise the importance of strengthening language, identity and cultural practices; kin relationships; engagement with the environment; and connection to the world of wairuatanga (spirituality) (Durie, 1994, 1999; Henare, 1998; Pere, 1984). These Māori concepts of health and wellbeing are recognised as deriving from te ao Māori (a Māori worldview). Despite some uptake of Māori models of health in mainstream health and mental-health settings, Western models continue to dominate. Māori models are often relegated to facilitating engagement, rather than being the governing framework. In addition, Māori models of health have evolved very little in the last thirty years (for example, Te Whare Tapa Whā; Durie, 1994). Possible reasons are that Māori cultural concepts are misunderstood, are used as a supplement to practice and/or they have been misappropriated for mainstream practice (Durie, 2003; McLachlan, Wirihana, & Huriwai, 2017; Pitama et al., 2007). The concern with cultural appropriation without a Māori cultural base is that Māori values, beliefs and experiences become de-Māorified and applied superficially (Love, 2004; McLachlan et al., 2017; Pitama et al., 2007).

In the face of colonising influences of cultural appropriation and marginalisation of Māori values, knowledge and practice, Māori models of health continue to offer pathways to wellbeing that aspire to good health, connected relationships, economic prosperity, high educational achievement, self-determination, living as Māori and a healthy environment. Mason Durie's (2003) Paiheretia model incorporates these philosophical dimensions of wellbeing in conjunction with the Te Whare Tapa Whā model. However, Paiheretia goes further, encouraging practices that enhance wellbeing for Māori, including a secure cultural identity and improved quality of relationships with people and the environment. Durie (2003) notes the importance of opportunities for exposure to culture, by guiding these encounters and increasing understanding for whānau to "integrate the new knowledge and new experiences into a coherent emotional, spiritual and psychological map" (p. 56).

Although there is recognition that working with Māori requires knowledge of cultural concepts and practices, there has been a lack of clarity on how to apply these practically to clinical assessments and/or treatment (Pitama et al., 2017). Within the field of psychology in New Zealand, there is also little evidence of Māori models being applied in practice (Muriwai, Houkamau, & Sibley, 2015). These limitations may be because of epistemic racism, practitioner lack of confidence when engaging with Māori worldviews and/or a dearth of Māori practitioners who might more readily use Māori models (Waitoki, 2016). Growing inequities for Māori require that mental health services offer Māori-centred approaches that include Māori values, beliefs and practices. Māori approaches also include a focus on the social determinants of wellbeing that offer important information to guide engagement, assessment, diagnosis and treatment/healing.

This chapter is a response to the need to update and contribute to Māori health models of wellbeing. The chapter is written for experienced practitioners who are confident working with Māori cultural concepts. We begin by outlining the process of assessment and formulation using the Meihana model and the *Hauora Clinical Guide* (Pitama et al., 2007; Pitama et al., 2017). We then introduce a new model, Whiti-te-Rā, to guide healing and evaluation with Māori clients (McLachlan, Waitoki, Harris, & Jones, 2020). A case study is used to describe how to integrate the models to develop a comprehensive, culturally informed psychological formulation, an interactive treatment/healing plan and processes to evaluate that plan.

The Meihana Model: A Clinical Assessment Framework

The Meihana model was developed by Suzanne Pitama and colleagues at Otago University (Pitama et al., 2007; Pitama, Huria, & Lacey, 2014). The model built upon the Te Whare Tapa Whā model (Durie, 1994) to create a guide for clinical assessment and intervention with Māori clients and whānau accessing mental health services. The Meihana model was developed further into the *Hauora Māori Clinical Guide for Psychologists* (see Pitama et al., 2017 for the full guide), which outlined an adapted, comprehensive psychological assessment framework. The Meihana model is based on four key components:

Te Waka Hourua (WH, double-hulled canoe) relates to the two hulls of a waka. The first hull represents the client and the second hull represents their whānau. The two hulls remind practitioners of the importance of engaging with Māori individuals and their whānau, and the interrelationship between presenting needs, context and support systems when creating plans to address these needs. The two hulls are joined together by six factors that practitioners need to explore. These include the four factors in the Te Whare Tapa Whā model (Durie, 1999): whānau (family), tinana (physical body), hinengaro (psychological/emotional) and wairua (connectedness). The additional two factors include taiao (physical environments) and ratonga hauora (access to quality health services).

Ngā Hau e Whā (NHW) represents the four winds of Tāwhirimātea (god of the wind elements). This factor uses the metaphor of the wind to explore the impact of colonisation, racism, migration and marginalisation on the lives of Māori and their whānau.

Ngā Roma Moana (NRM), representing the four ocean currents, focuses on four cultural components that influence a person's view of themselves, their challenges and their preferences for treatment. These include āhua (personalised indicators of te ao Māori important to the individual and their whānau), tikanga (Māori cultural principles), whānau (relationships, role and responsibilities of the client within te ao Māori including whānau, hapū, iwi and other organisations) and whenua (specific genealogical or spiritual connections).

Whakatere (W, navigation) is a synthesis of the information gathered using this framework to develop a comprehensive formulation to aid diagnosis and treatment planning.

Whiti-te-Rā: An Interactive Wellbeing Guide

Whiti-te-Rā was developed following a systematic narrative literature review and wānanga with Māori psychologists (see McLachlan et al., 2020). The scope of the review was to identify research articles that include any Māori cultural concepts or activities that contributed to wellbeing and/or health for Māori. Studies were excluded if they focused solely on eliminating a health disorder or problem. The review produced 146 research studies, and a further eighty-two studies from a bibliography of Māori and psychology research were assessed (Hyde et al., 2017). The final results yielded thirty-six studies that were analysed using a thematic analysis (Braun & Clark, 2006).

A thematic analysis produced six themes or pathways towards wellbeing for Māori. The six themes were 1. Te reo Māori: Māori language; 2. Taiao: connection with the environment; 3. Wairua: Māori spiritual beliefs and practices; 4. Mahi-a-toi: Māori expressive art forms; 5. Take pū whānau: Māori relational values; and 6. Whakapapa: intergenerational relationships. A subject matter expert wānanga (group discussion) was held to discuss the six themes identified in the literature review. Approximately forty practising Māori psychologists and psychology students provided examples of practice in which each of the themes was used in some way. This process provided verification that the themes resonated with Māori psychologists and that Māori psychologists used mātauranga Māori despite not being taught to do so in their training (Waitoki, 2016).

Mauri Ora

Whiti-te-Rā is a reflection of the concept of mauri ora, a strong cultural identity and the mātauranga Māori-informed pathways that contribute to a flourishing mauri. Mauri is described as vitality, a living force, or the essence of life that is present in all living and natural things (Barlow, 1991; Durie, 2001; Marsden, 2003). Mauri is a dynamic force influenced by the interactions between relationships within an ecosystem (Durie, 2001). Mauri ora (ora: health) is an interactive energy between people and the ecosystem that reflects a healthy balance between hinengaro (emotional), wairua (spiritual) and tinana (physical). Whiti-te-Rā as a Māori health model is premised on enhancing the quality of those interactions through engagement in meaningful, culture-affirming pathways.

Figure 1 represents the Whiti-te-Rā interactive guide. The six themes (pathways/ara) identified in the literature review are represented by hihi (sunbeams). Each hihi is labelled with a theme from the literature review: Te reo Māori, Taiao, Wairua, Mahi-a-toi, Take pū whānau and Whakapapa. Tamanuiterā (the sun) in the Whiti-te-Rā image (Figure 1) represents wellbeing as a strong cultural identity, Mauri ora and the innate potential Māori have. Culture in this respect refers to a self-determined culture – which may be Māori, LGBTQI+ and/or rangatira, for example. Clients decide the culture they wish to engage with. However, engagement with Māori culture can occur on a continuum, from a small amount to full immersion. It is important that choice and safety for clients is maintained at all times.

Each hihi is separated down the middle to enable discussions about knowledge and comfort (labelled 'Mahuru') with culture and active participation (labelled 'Hono'). Houkamau and Sibley (2010) term this process "active identity engagement" (p. 8). Each side of the hihi (Mahuru and Hono) has five poutama (ascension lines) representing the pūrākau (traditional narrative) of Tāne, god of the forests, birds and people, and his ascent to the heavens to bring down the three baskets of knowledge (Waitoki, 2016). The poutama journey provides a mātauranga metaphor of actively seeking wellbeing, enhanced by active engagement in learning and participating in culture. Practitioners work with clients/whānau to identify their level of knowledge and comfort with cultural concepts (Mahuru) and their level of engagement (Hono). This allows for more effective planning of learning and guided activity tasks. The six hihi developed from the thematic analysis are outlined below as Ngā Ara – pathways.

Figure 1: The Whiti-te-Rā interactive guide.

NGĀ ARA REO MĀORI: MĀORI LANGUAGE

Ngā Ara Reo Māori reflects speaking the Māori language informally or formally (for example, with family, peers, in the workplace or on the marae/ancestral home). The literature review identifies the role of the Māori language in developing a strong cultural identity (Durie, 2001; Gibson, 1999; Higgins, 2004; Penetito, 2011; Te Huia, 2015) and contributing to wellbeing (Dyall et al., 2014; Muriwai et al., 2015; Simmonds, Harre, & Crengle, 2014). The findings also show the role of Māori language in healing and its relationship with traditional healing practices (Durie, 1998; Pihama, 2001; Marsden, 2003).

NGĀ ARA TAIAO: CONNECTION WITH THE ENVIRONMENT

Ngā Ara Taiao reflects knowledge of and engagement with the environment, including returning to whenua tūpuna (customary lands), moana (oceans), awa (rivers), ngahere (bush) and maunga (mountains), and the application of traditional Māori roles and values related to kaitiakitanga (stewardship, guardianship and protection). The literature identifies a strong relationship between engagement in the environment and wellbeing (Durie, 2006; Harmsworth & Awatere, 2013; Kingi, Russell, Ashby, & the Youth Wellbeing Study Team, 2017; Palmer, 2004; Reid, Varona, Fisher, & Smith, 2016; Salmond, 2014) and taiao as an important part of the development of individual and collective wellbeing and identity (King, Hodgetts, Rua, & Whetu, 2015; Moeke-Pickering et al., 2015).

NGĀ ARA WAIRUA: MĀORI SPIRITUAL BELIEFS AND PRACTICES

Ngā Ara Wairua reflects beliefs and practices related to Māori spirituality. These include engagement in beliefs and practices associated with ngā atua Māori, formal religions and the environment. The literature identifies the role of wairua in creating a strong cultural identity (Houkamau & Sibley, 2010; Moeke-Maxwell, Nikora, & Te Awekotuku, 2014; Rameka, 2016), and rituals associated with wairua as important aspects of healing and wellbeing (Ihimaera, 2004; Mark & Lyons, 2010; O'Hagan, Reynolds, & Smith, 2012; Paenga, 2008).

NGĀ ARA MAHI-A-TOI: MĀORI EXPRESSIVE ART FORMS

Ngā Ara Mahi-a-toi reflects the different arts and practices that transmit a range of physical skills, Māori knowledge, Māori values and historical narratives (Anderson, 2009; Ministry for Culture and Heritage, 2014; Rawson, 2016). This includes a range of pursuits: kapa haka (Māori performing arts), whakairo (Māori carving) and tukutuku (Māori weaving), Māori sports such as waka ama and kī-o-rahi, taonga pūoro (traditional Māori instruments) and tā moko (Nikora, Rua, & Te Awekotuku, 2007). These activities have been identified as strengthening connection and knowledge related to te reo Māori, whakapapa, identity and physical and relational wellbeing (Henwood, 2007; Hollands, Sutton, Wright-St Clair, & Hall, 2015; Huriwai, Sellman, & Potiki, 1998; Mato, 2011; Puketapu-Hetet, 1989).

NGĀ ARA TAKE PŪ WHĀNAU: MĀORI RELATIONAL VALUES

Ngā Ara Take Pū Whānau reflects the values (take pū) that underpin and are actioned within tikanga Māori (Māori practices) that strengthen whānau wellbeing (McLachlan et al., 2017; Waitoki, Nikora, & Harris, 2014). Tikanga Māori embody traditional messages and knowledge that have been passed down from generation to generation through customs, norms, protocols and lore (whakapapa kōrero) (Baker, 2010; Boulton, Tamehana, & Brannelly, 2013; Kenney, Phibbs, Paton, Reid, & Johnston, 2015; Love, 2004; Rawson, 2016). Wellbeing connections also occur between tikanga and cultural identity, family wellbeing, relationships and connection to the wider community and environment (Boulton & Gifford, 2014; Love, 2004; Panelli & Tipa, 2007).

NGĀ ARA WHAKAPAPA: INTERGENERATIONAL RELATIONSHIPS

Ngā Ara Whakapapa reflects the importance of knowledge of whānau narratives, connections and relationships across generations, both living and deceased. This can include accessing traditional lands, sites of significance and marae; visiting whānau; and learning traditional waiata (songs) or your pepeha (introducing where and whom you are from). The literature finds strong connections to a strong identity (as referenced above) and the activities associated with whakapapa as important aspects of healing and wellbeing (Jahnke, 2002; McCormack, 2014; McLachlan et al., 2017).

Case Study: Tamarere

The following information is synthesised from the application of the Meihana model as outlined in the *Hauora Māori Clinical Guide for Psychologists* (Pitama et al., 2017). The case study in this chapter highlights the factors from the Meihana model as applied to the case of Tamarere. For example, 'Ngā Hau e Whā, colonisation' is abbreviated to 'NHW, colonisation' and is placed alongside relevant case information.

REFERRAL

Tamarere is an eighteen-year-old male of Tainui descent. He was referred for a comprehensive psychological assessment by a pastoral support worker at his training course. The referral indicated that Tamarere preferred a Māori practitioner, preferably someone who could speak te reo (Māori language). Primary concerns over the two months leading up to the referral included low mood, thoughts of suicide, chronic feelings of hopelessness, withdrawal from activities previously enjoyed, poor attendance and low achievement in his tertiary study. He had also reported to his pastoral care worker that he had experienced some events in life that had made him feel bad about himself.

PRESENTATION AND PRIMARY CONCERNS

Tamarere attended two psychological assessment appointments (WH, ratonga hauora). He was engaged in the assessment process, and was oriented to time, person and place; however, he presented as somewhat withdrawn, with flat affect. His sister-in-law accompanied him to his first appointment (WH, whānau). He was living with his older brother and sister-in-law in a four-bedroom house in town (WH, whānau; NHW, migration). He reported that their whare (house) was warm (WH, taiao) and made him feel safe (WH, hinengaro). He was a student who received a student living allowance. He had been having some conflict with his brother, as his brother wanted Tamarere to attend a local church. However, Tamarere reported not believing in "this Pākehā stuff" (NHW, colonisation).

He reported that for the last two months he had been feeling "wainuku" (NRM, āhua), which he described as a sense of being overwhelmed (WH, hinengaro), of drowning, as if Tangaroa was "smothering" him (WH, wairua) and having chronic feelings of hopelessness (WH, hinengaro). He also reported thinking about taking his life (WH, hinengaro) after he was told by his tutor that he might be discharged from his carpentry course. He said that he no longer returned to his whānau in a rural town at the weekends, as he was too tired at the end of the week (WH, whānau; NRM, whānau). He also no longer went to the gym, which he previously enjoyed (WH, tinana).

Tamarere completed the Beck Depression Inventory – II (BDI-II; Beck, Steer, & Brown, 1996). A score of 53 indicated severe depression (WH, hinengaro). Tamarere was also administered the WHOQOL-BREF Quality of Life measure (World Health Organization, 1996). His total scaled score of 15 reflected significant dissatisfaction with his quality of life. His subscale scores reflected general dissatisfaction across all four domains: physical health, psychological health, social relationships and environment. The sister-in-law of Tamarere said that he had lost up to 8 kgs in the last two months (WH, tinana). She reported changes to his sleeping pattern (often sleeping away half the day), which were impacting on his normal functioning ("not attending his tertiary education"; WH, tinana). She also said that she and her partner (the brother of Tamarere) had heard him crying in his bedroom at night (WH, hinengaro).

BACKGROUND INFORMATION

Tamarere was brought up in a rural community (NRM, whenua). His whānau were actively involved on the marae and in hapū affairs (NRM, āhua, whānau and tikanga). He was fluent in te reo Māori (NRM, āhua), and enjoyed attending whakapapa wānanga on his marae (NRM, āhua and tikanga). He enjoyed eeling, collecting kareao and pikopiko from the ngahere (bush) and hunting (NRM, whenua; NHW, taiao; WH, tinana; WH, wairua). He was known in his whānau for his knowledge of "all the good spots for gathering kai and hunting" (NRM, tikanga and āhua).

Tamarere was brought up by his mother and grandfather at their whānau homestead (NRM, whānau). His parents separated when Tamarere was ten years old. His father Thomas lived 25 km away. He saw his father when he returned home on weekends, and often talked to his father on the phone (WH, whānau). His father sometimes talked about his own experiences of depression (WH, whānau), but had been unable to provide advice, having previously said to Tamarere that "nothing the docs have done for me has changed anything" (WH, whānau and ratonga hauora).

FAMILY HISTORY

The father and grandfather of Tamarere had a history of depression (WH, whānau; NHW, Ngā Hau e Whā). The whānau did not like doctors or mental health services as the grandfather was in a mental health institution, Tokanui hospital, in the late 1960s after returning from the Vietnam War. Tamarere said that his grandfather did not talk much about this time. His grandmother (Nan) said that Koro was "never the same" after returning from the war. She further stated that Koro was sent to Tokanui hospital by a doctor and that the family "didn't get to see him for months" (NHW, colonisation and marginalisation; WH, ratonga hauora). The whānau of Tamarere are engaged in the local marae community. His maternal grandmother was the kaikaranga (ceremonial caller) and known for her knowledge of tribal stories and genealogies, song composition and as a traditional healer.

CHILDHOOD HISTORY

Tamarere had several close friends from childhood (WH, whānau). Most worked on farms close to his hometown, although one of his friends studied mechanics at the same institution (WH, whānau). Tamarere did not have a partner, saying he preferred to be single. He had a history of struggling with reading, writing and comprehension (NHW, colonisation). He said that he would always listen to the teachers and find ways to learn so others did not know he struggled to learn. He said his mother or grandfather would read his homework for him. He worked hard to get passing grades and his teachers always encouraged him to "try harder". He said he did not receive any additional support or assessments at school (NHW, racism and marginalisation).

Currently, Tamarere was struggling with his carpentry training. He had aspirations of being helpful to his whānau and hapū. However, he found it difficult navigating the tertiary environment. He felt he was going to "let everyone down", that he was "stupid" and that he would never achieve in life (WH, hinengaro). He said his tutors thought he was being lazy and suggested he needed to party less on the weekends (NHW, racism; WH, hinengaro). He did not consume drugs or alcohol and did not go to parties (WH, hinengaro and tinana).

PREVIOUS TREATMENT AND CURRENT GOALS

Tamarere stated that he only went to the GP if he was injured, and that he did not think a doctor could help him with his feelings or his learning difficulties (NHW, marginalisation; WH, ratonga hauora). He appeared concerned about engaging with a mental health service, saying: "I didn't think I'd ever go to a mental health service! You're not going to send me away are you?" (NHW, colonisation).

WHAKATERE FORMULATION

Tamarere presented as an intuitive young man with strong connections to his whānau, culture and community. He was hardworking and committed to the tasks he set himself. The primary source of wellbeing and identity for Tamarere came from his engagement in tikanga, taiao and his roles within whānau and hapū. Having a strong, stable and supportive upbringing provided access to a wide range of options for identity development and wellbeing. This provided a secure base for him to learn culturally embedded strategies for managing and maintaining his wellbeing and healing. At the time of assessment, Tamarere presented with severe depression in the context of being in an environment that was foreign to his upbringing, and separation from his core attachments and source of wellbeing: whenua, tikanga, te reo Māori and whānau. His childhood experiences suggested a learning disorder and a paternal history of unresolved intergenerational trauma.

His grandfather's experience of the trauma incurred during military service and the subsequent isolation and psychiatric hospitalisation created a 'soul wound', or patu ngākau, that had been left unhealed. This wound subsequently impacted on his grandfather's ability to engage fully with his whānau. His experience of conventional non-Māori treatment for this patu ngākau created a deep sense of mistrust in mainstream mental health treatment. The father of Tamarere also had episodes of depression that were not treated appropriately. These combined experiences contributed to the grandfather, father and therefore whānau being unable to acknowledge, describe or discuss painful and negative events and their effects.

This unhealed soul wound appeared to have been passed to the following generations. The intergenerational transmission of mamae (pain), and the coping strategies of silence and avoidance to manage this pain, impacted on the ability of Tamarere to understand how his current situation, thoughts and feelings led to his depression. His ability to create or find solutions for his present challenges in his everyday activities and values had also been impaired. While the male figures in his life offered a positive, stable and culturally involved upbringing, they did not model how to talk about struggles, disappointment or sadness as a whānau, in a way that would help to acknowledge, validate or ameliorate his low mood.

Socially sanctioned male values of 'being tough, strong and in control of emotions' formed a message Tamarere learned. The effect on him was that he was unable to talk to his whānau about his loneliness and learning difficulties, which compounded his feelings of mokemoke (sadness, loneliness) and isolation. Although he lived with his brother, he was uncomfortable with the pressure to attend church.

The precursor to Tamarere's depression was the move from his secure rural base to an urban setting and starting a tertiary training course. Moving into an urban centre reduced his connection to his source of stability. This tipped the balance between struggle (challenges learning) and resilience (fulfilling his role and maintaining his identity within whānau, collective and the environment).

Tamarere felt overwhelmed by the strain of learning in a new environment without culturally meaningful support. In the context of a pre-existing undiagnosed and untreated learning disorder, Tamarere felt a sense of failure, which is likely to have reinforced a sense of something being fundamentally wrong with him. Tamarere was also not able to adapt to his new environment, which he previously had been able to do at his own pace (for example, hiding his learning disability, while also knowing how to catch eels).

Tamarere also experienced racism and marginalisation that he felt was related to being Māori. His tutor had also criticised and minimised his struggles, which further reinforced and exacerbated his thoughts of failure and feelings of hopelessness.

Tamarere had a desire to provide for others and took pride in showing manaakitanga to others (helping on the marae, gathering and distributing kai, looking after elders in his community). It was apparent that his sense of failure in his studies reflected the values he placed on contributing to the collective (whānau and hapū). This created a reinforcing cycle of further self-critical thought that was likely maintaining his low mood and compounding his sense of being overwhelmed. Tamarere had access to cultural knowledge from home; however, he struggled to engage with local cultural elements (community groups, sports, hunting and fishing, or local marae). His goals were to "have energy and believe in myself" and to finish his course so he could contribute to his community (which would enhance his positive self-concept). He also wanted to be able to talk to his father and grandfather about his experiences. He had a range of strengths and resources to guide and support his choices about wellbeing for himself and his broader whānau networks.

WHAKATERE RECOMMENDATIONS

1. Whānau hui with Tamarere and whānau members to discuss recommendations.
2. Referral for specialist learning assessment. Identify funding options for assessment.
3. Referral to GP for assessment of suitability for antidepressant medication.
4. Identify the relevant dimensions of Whiti-te-Rā cultural pathways framework to locate healing within Tamarere's identified strengths and preference for wellbeing.

WHITI-TE-RĀ AND TAMARERE

The Whiti-te-Rā Framework was discussed with Tamarere to explore activities he felt comfortable with, including the four steps of Whiti-te-Rā (see Appendix): orientation, exploration, planning and review. During the orientation phase, Tamarere acknowledged an understanding of mauri and mauri ora. He struggled with the concept of cultural identity as a term, as he felt the psychologist was just describing what was normal for him and his whānau.

Tamarere was able to identify several activities in each hihi that he had either witnessed, was familiar with or had engaged in. He was invited to identify where he felt he was in relation to first Mahuru and then Hono on these hihi. He did this by drawing a line from the edge of Tamanuiterā up the poutama of each side, rating where he felt he was on his journey (starting on the first step of the poutama). As Tamarere moved further up the poutama, the stronger the rating and the stronger the mauri associated with this hihi.

He identified his wellbeing hihi as Ngā Ara Whānau, Ngā Ara Taiao, Ngā Ara Mahi-a-toi and Ngā Ara Whakapapa. In relation to mauri ora, Tamarere chose being mauri tau (settled) as a priority. He identified seeking mauri tau as a stage of creating stability, safety and a foundation of confidence. In discussion with his psychologist, he was aware that as he grew more confident and his energy increased, he would be asked to consider other hihi that related to his wellbeing. Tamarere said he wanted to talk to his grandfather to learn (using the concept of Mahuru) how he became well, and his experiences of when he was unwell.

Tamarere saw his grandfather as his mentor and believed that a shared experience would enhance their joint healing. He also felt that an enhanced relationship naturally incorporated Ngā Ara Take Pū Whānau as a part of his healing and feelings of stability. He said that he felt the best in recent months when sitting outside looking at the stars and naming those he could remember, or walking along the river near his training course. He identified the importance of Hono in Ngā Ara Taiao as an important part of his wellbeing, physically, spiritually and mentally. Finally, he said that he wanted to relax his mind and do things he enjoyed. He said he used to do whakairo as a twelve-year-old and still had whao (chisels) back at his grandfather's home. He believed having projects to work on that he could gift to whānau would give more immediate feelings of competence and tauutuutu (reciprocity).

Tamarere was supported within psychological sessions over the next eight weeks through a stage of ongoing review (Step Four of the Whiti-te-Rā interactive guide; see Appendix) to reflect on being present in the activities he was doing and to identify unhealthy thoughts early. He was encouraged to engage in more helpful and positive responses to these thoughts, and finally to identify the social, physical and spiritual experiences associated with each activity – in essence, absorbing the healing when engaged in these activities as opposed to just being there as an observer. He eventually disclosed that he often talked to his paternal grandmother, who visited him, although she had passed away before he was born. He identified the hihi Ngā Ara Wairua as a future wellbeing goal.

In reviewing his engagement with his chosen hihi (Step Four of the Whiti-te-Rā interactive guide; see Appendix), Tamarere reported that he had experienced a lift in energy and felt tau (settled), as he reported that he had started walking three times a week along the river (Ngā Ara Taiao). He said this was meaningful as his grandfather had told him that the river touches the shores of both towns (where his whānau resided and where he was studying). He reported that once a week, he went for a walk with a friend from his training course for an hour. He noted that he also ate more and had more energy. He has started carving a small papahou (treasure box) for his grandfather/koro during his visits home. Spending time with his grandfather allowed him to fulfill his wellbeing goals (Ngā Ara Whakapapa; Ngā Ara Take Pū Whānau) and he asked questions about his grandfather's experience when he returned from the war, and about his grandmother and their relationship. He said that engaging in whakairo brought back feelings of competence and confidence and he was looking forward to gifting what he had made to his koro (Ngā Ara Take Pū Whānau).

Tamarere engaged in a formal review of his goals using the Whiti-te-Rā interactive guide. He showed an increase in the poutama steps on all three hihi, with even increments in hono and mahuru for each hihi. He decided to maintain focus on these three hihi again, and added Ngā Ara Wairua for the next eight-week period. In the session, they planned how to extend his learning and engagement in each hihi (Steps Three and Four of the Whiti-te-Rā interactive guide; see Appendix). The WHOQOL-BREF Quality of Life measure (World Health Organization, 1996) and the BDI-II were readministered. His total scaled score of 30 on the WHOQOL-BREF indicated improvement in satisfaction in quality of life across all four domains: physical health, psychological health, social relationships and environment. Tamarere's score of 13 on the BDI-II indicated a significant reduction in severity.

Discussion

The Whiti-te-Rā model provides what Durie (2003) describes as a coherent emotional, spiritual and psychological map for integrating culture within healing. Tamanuiterā, the image of the sun in the model, is an established atua involved in many oral and visual art traditions (pūrākau, carvings, tukutuku, pakiwaitara whaikōrero), providing an effective metaphor for understanding illness (in this case extended mauri noho) and wellbeing through building upon culturally centred strengths and interests. The Whiti-te-Rā model provides a needed reinvigoration of Paiheretia and is well suited to the therapeutic tasks outlined in the model, such as gaining understanding and guiding encounters in te ao Māori and day-to-day life. Tamarere sought out a Māori practitioner who, preferably, could speak Māori. Despite his deep depression at the time, he understood that he needed a Māori practitioner who aligned with his cultural values. While there are very few Māori psychologists in the mental health workforce, and fewer still who speak te reo Māori, the use of Māori-centred models ensures that tikanga and mana for clients is maintained. Furthermore, the Meihana model and Whiti-te-Rā remove the tendency to see Māori cultural concepts as an engagement process that creates a whāriki (mat) on which to lay Western psychology.

The Meihana model (Pitama et al., 2017) provides a culturally centred assessment framework that enables practitioners to identify and explore strengths and challenges facing whānau. Looking beyond pure symptoms is imperative if we are to understand and explore the strengths and resources that underpin a Māori worldview, and to assess the role and impact of social and cultural determinants of wellbeing. The Meihana model is well suited to this task as these factors are inconsistently applied in mainstream assessment. In considering the issues that affected Tamarere, the lens provided by the Meihana model enabled a deeper picture of cultural strength and resilience to emerge and take a central place in his wellbeing journey. Furthermore, a shift towards a strengths-based approach captures examples of cultural taonga that inform the structure of the Whiti-te-Rā.

By harnessing, honouring and respecting the preference of Tamarere to remain connected to his ūkaipō, a distinctive shift occurred. While the narrative of intergenerational trauma could be applied as central to his healing/treatment plan, the transformative, mana-enhancing approach disrupted deficit thinking. The Meihana model and the Whiti-te-Rā recognise intergenerational taonga, the gifts handed down by ancestors to ensure that successive generations flourish. By examining trauma, and the role of colonisation, racism and marginalisation within the context of resilience and strength across generations, pathways for healing appear.

Tamarere chose to focus his healing on learning about his grandfather's experience as a returned serviceman. He felt that it was important to know how his grandfather survived the war, and managed the effects of stigma on returning from the war, being placed in a psychiatric hospital and being disconnected from his whānau, whenua and tikanga. Tamarere was also aware of the racism towards Māori returned soldiers, and he understood why his grandfather 'bottled up' his emotions. The impact of military service is known to have had a detrimental effect on Māori communities, as soldiers were denied the right to practise tikanga Māori, to speak te reo or to have their spiritual, emotional, social and economic wellbeing properly cared for on their return (Waitangi Tribunal, 2018). Returned veterans were therefore unable to transmit knowledge about Māori cultural practices, customs and traditions, as they were likely to be experiencing Post Traumatic Stress Disorder (PTSD) (McGibbon, 2010; Soutar, 2008).

Wirihana and Smith (2014) note that the New Zealand military now use Māori cultural concepts and practises whakapapa kōrero (oral traditions), whakanoa (ceremony of cleansing), marae encounters and cultural reframing (deprograming) of experiences to support recovery from the trauma of war. In addition, examining notions of hypermasculinity for Māori men enables positive conversations to occur about what it means to be a tāne (man) (Hokowhitu, 2004). In doing so, tāne are able to wholeheartedly experience and share the full range of take pū whānau (Māori relational values) important for healing and strengthening relationships and intergenerational bonds. Strengthening these values within the Whiti-te-Rā model includes taurite (balance and harmony), aroha (giving and receiving love), manaakitanga (caring and being cared for), murunga hara (forgiveness) and tūmanako (optimism).

The role of colonisation, marginalisation and racism in education settings was identified in the assessment and incorporated within his formulation and recommendations, as Tamarere's sense of self-worth was tied to his learning issues. In particular, the course tutor had accused him of being lazy and unmotivated, which was antithetical to Tamarere's core value system. The racialisation of Māori learning outcomes and dismissal of learning needs is documented in the literature (Milne, 2013). Smallbone (2019) found that some teachers tended to look 'outwards' for social and cultural causes (socioeconomic status, transiency, home background and oral language development) when working with Māori who have learning challenges. Unconscious bias (Fiarman, 2016; Staats, 2016) also results in lower expectations of Māori students and reduced access to educational learning assessments (Rubie-Davies, Hattie, & Hamilton, 2006).

As Māori culture is placed at the centre of the Whiti-te-Rā model it is important that practitioners who use this model are familiar with the different practices represented in each hihi (sun ray/pathway) of Tamanuiterā. A practitioner must be able to explore cultural values, beliefs and practices, understand barriers both externally and internally to the person (such as whakamā) and have established connections within the community to connect with and guide encounters. A good grounding in and understanding of Māori worldviews is needed before attempting to use Whiti-te-Rā to avoid 'lost in translation' effects (Mika & Stewart, 2017). Furthermore, Māori are not a homogenous group with classic Māori values, and care must be taken not to potentially offend or traumatise a client by insisting on a Māori cultural pathway.

This chapter examines an integration of Māori models of health and wellbeing practice that centres culture as an essential part of a healing journey. The Meihana model provides a metaphor for the journey (Waka hourua) and the context (Ngā Roma Moana and Ngā Hau e Whā), whereas the rising and setting of Tamanuiterā (Whiti-te-Rā) reflects the passage of time and signposts for navigating pathways to wellbeing. Māori psychologists have moved beyond mainstream Western knowledge by centring mātauranga Māori and kaupapa Māori theory and practice (Smith, 1999) to achieve excellent outcomes for Māori.

APPENDIX:
Whiti-te-Rā
Interactive Guide
to Wellbeing

Orientation:

1. Introduce concept of Tamanuiterā and innate potential, and the poutama and its relation to the pūrākau of Tāne and his assenting to Toi-ō-ngā-rangi to collect the three baskets of knowledge.
2. Overview each hihi and the range of activities within.
3. Introduce the concepts of Hono and Mahuru.

Exploration:

1. Explore their knowledge of activities within each hihi, including what they have seen, heard of, experienced and/or continue to engage in.
2. Explore their experiences of participating in these activities. What did they sense physically, emotionally, spiritually and socially?
3. Rate Mahuru (level of knowledge and comfort) and then Hono (level of engagement) for each hihi, based on the activities they identified. This is done by drawing a line from the edge of Tamanuiterā (the sun) up the poutama (steps) of each side, rating where they feel they are on their journey (starting on the first step of the poutama and so on). The further along the poutama, the brighter the glow and the stronger the mauri associated with each hihi.
4. Discuss rationale for current ratings (early development – experienced/confident).
5. Discuss the balance and interrelationships of hihi.

Planning:

1. Identify the hihi and, in turn, the activities that are important for their current wellbeing. This may be related to maintaining or enhancing Mahuru or Hono in an activity or identifying a hihi and associated activity that may assist in their mauri ora goals.
2. Identify barriers to engaging in pathways.
3. Identify personal and community resources that may support these pathways.

Review:

1. Re-administer the Whiti-te-Rā interactive guide for the hihi that were incorporated in planning new Hono and/or Mahuru pathways.
2. Explore their experiences of participating in these activities (Hono and/or Mahuru). What they sensed physically, emotionally, spiritually and socially. What were new learnings and/or barriers?
3. Review goals of engaging in each hihi and their sense of Mauri ora. This may include re-administering psychometric measures of symptoms and/or quality of life measures. This may also include consulting with whānau, peers or other significant others identified by the individual.
4. Re-plan (return to step three).

References

ANDERSON, H. (2009). *A confluence of streams: Music and identity in Aotearoa/New Zealand* (Doctoral dissertation). University of Maryland, College Park, MD. Retrieved from https://drum.lib.umd.edu/handle/1903/8478

BAKER, K. (2010). *Whānau taketake Māori*. Research Report No. 2/10. Wellington, New Zealand: Families Commission.

BARLOW, C. (1991). *Tikanga Whakaaro: Key concepts in Māori culture*. Auckland, New Zealand: Oxford University Press.

BECK, A., STEER, R., & BROWN, G. (1996). *Manual for the Beck Depression Inventory–II*. San Antonio, TX: Psychological Corporation.

BOULTON, A., & GIFFORD, H. (2014). Whānau Ora – He whakaaro ā whānau: Māori family views of family wellbeing. *International Indigenous Policy Journal*, 5(1), 1–18.

BOULTON, A., TAMEHANA, J., & BRANNELLY, T. (2013). Whānau-centred health and social service delivery in New Zealand. *MAI Journal*, 2(1), 19–30.

BRAUN, V., & CLARKE, V. (2006). Using thematic analysis in psychology. *Qualitative Research in Psychology*, 3, 77–101.

DURIE, M. (1994). *Whaiora: Māori health development*. Auckland, New Zealand: Oxford University Press.

DURIE, M. H. (1998). *Whaiora: Māori health development* (2nd ed.). Auckland, New Zealand: Oxford University Press.

DURIE, M. H. (1999). Marae and implications for a modern Māori psychology. *Journal of the Polynesian Society*. 108(4), 351–366.

DURIE, M. H. (2001). *Mauri ora: The dynamics of Māori health*. Auckland, New Zealand: Oxford University Press.

DURIE, M. (2003). *Ngā kāhui pou: Launching Māori futures*. Wellington, New Zealand: Huia.

DURIE, M. (2006). *Measuring Māori wellbeing. New Zealand Treasury guest lecture series.* Wellington, New Zealand: Treasury. Retrieved from https://treasury.govt.nz/sites/default/files/2007-09/tgls-durie.pdf

DYALL, L., KEPA, M., TEH, R., MULES, R., MOYES, S. A., WHAM, C., & KEELING, S. (2014). Cultural and social factors and quality of life of Māori in advanced age. Te puawaitanga o ngā tapuwae kia ora tonu – Life and living in advanced age: A cohort study in New Zealand (LiLACS NZ). *New Zealand Medical Journal*, 127(1393), 62–79.

FIARMAN, S. (2016). Unconscious bias: When good intentions aren't enough. *Educational Leadership*. 74(3), 10–15.

GIBSON, K. (1999). *Māori, women and dual ethnicity: Investigating pathways of identity development* (Master's thesis). University of Waikato, Hamilton, New Zealand. Retrieved from https://researchcommons.waikato.ac.nz/handle/10289/876

HARMSWORTH, G., & AWATERE, S. (2013). Indigenous Māori knowledge and perspectives of ecosystems. In J. Dymond (Ed.), *Ecosystem services in New Zealand – Conditions and trends* (pp. 274–286). Lincoln, New Zealand: Manaaki Whenua Press.

HENARE, M. (1988). Standards and foundations of Māori society. In Royal Commission on Social Policy (Ed.), *Ngā Tikanga me Ngā Ritenga o te Ao Marama*, 3 (pp. 7–41). Wellington, New Zealand: Royal Commission on Social Policy.

HENWOOD, W. (2007). Māori knowledge: A key ingredient in nutrition and physical exercise health promotion programmes for Māori. *Social Policy Journal of New Zealand*, 32, 155–164.

HIGGINS, R. (2004). *He tānga ngutu, he Tuhoetanga te mana motuhake o te tā moko wahine* (Doctoral dissertation). University of Otago, Dunedin, New Zealand. Retrieved from https://ourarchive.otago.ac.nz/handle/10523/5193

HOKOWHITU, B. (2004). Tackling Māori masculinity: A colonial genealogy of savagery and sport. *The Contemporary Pacific*, 16(2), 259–284.

HOLLANDS, T., SUTTON, D., WRIGHT-ST CLAIR, V., & HALL, R. (2015). Māori mental health consumers' sensory experience of kapa haka and its utility to occupational therapy practice. *New Zealand Journal of Occupational Therapy*, 62(1), 3–11.

HOUKAMAU, C. A., & SIBLEY, C. G. (2010). The multi-dimensional model of Māori identity and cultural engagement. *New Zealand Journal of Psychology*, 39(1), 8–28.

HURIWAI, T., SELLMAN, D., & POTIKI, T. (1998). A clinical sample of Māori being treated for alcohol and drug problems in New Zealand. *New Zealand Medical Journal*, 111(1064), 145–147.

HYDE, J., LE GRICE, J., MOORE, C., GROOT, S., FIA-ALI'I, J., & MANUELA, S. (2017). *He Kohikohinga Rangahau: A bibliography of Māori and psychology research*. Auckland, New Zealand: School of Psychology, University of Auckland. Retrieved from https://cdn.auckland.ac.nz/assets/psych/about/our-research/documents/He%20Kohikohinga%20Rangahau%202017.pdf

IHIMAERA, L. V. (2004). *He ara ki te ao marama: A pathway to understanding the facilitation of taha wairua in the mental health services* (Master's thesis). Massey University, Palmerston North, New Zealand. Retrieved from https://mro.massey.ac.nz/bitstream/handle/10179/990/02whole.pdf

JAHNKE, H. T. (2002). Towards a secure identity: Māori women and the home-place. *Women's Studies International Forum*, 25(5), 503–513.

KENNEY, C. M., PHIBBS, S. R., PATON, D., REID, J., & JOHNSTON, D. M. (2015). Community-led disaster risk management: A Māori response to Ōtautahi (Christchurch) earthquakes. *Australasian Journal of Disaster and Trauma Studies*, 19(1), 9–20.

KING, P., HODGETTS, D., RUA, M., & WHETU, T. T. (2015). Older men gardening on the marae. *AlterNative: An International Journal of Indigenous Peoples*, 11(1), 14–28.

KINGI, T., RUSSELL, L., ASHBY, W., & THE YOUTH WELLBEING STUDY TEAM. (2017). Mā te mātau, ka ora: The use of traditional Indigenous knowledge to support contemporary rangatahi Māori who self-injure. *New Zealand Journal of Psychology*, 46(3), 137–145.

LOVE, C. (2004). *Extensions on Te Wheke*. Wellington, New Zealand: Open Polytechnic of New Zealand. Retrieved from https://repository.openpolytechnic.ac.nz/handle/11072/182

MARK, G. T., & LYONS, A. C. (2010). Māori healers' views on wellbeing: The importance of mind, body, spirit, family and land. *Social Science & Medicine*, 70(11), 1756–1764.

MARSDEN, M. (2003). *The woven universe: Selected writings of Rev. Māori Marsden*. Otaki, New Zealand: Estate of Rev. Māori Marsden.

MATO, W. T. K. (2011). *Inter-iwi sport can strengthen cultural identity for urban Māori* (Master's thesis). Auckland University of Technology, Auckland, New Zealand. Retrieved from https://openrepository.aut.ac.nz/handle/10292/2494

MIKA, C., & STEWART, G. (2017). Lost in translation: Western representations of Māori knowledge. *Open Review of Educational Research*, 4(1), 134–146.

MILNE, B. A. (2013). *Colouring in the white spaces: Reclaiming cultural identity in whitestream schools* (Doctoral dissertation). University of Waikato, Hamilton, New Zealand. Retrieved from https://hdl.handle.net/10289/7868

MCCORMACK, F. (2014). Being Māori in the city: Indigenous everyday life in Auckland. *Pacific Affairs*, 87(3), 649–652.

MCGIBBON, I. (2010). *New Zealand's Vietnam War: A history of combat, commitment and controversy*. Auckland, New Zealand: Exisle.

MCLACHLAN, A., WAITOKI, W., HARRIS, P. W., & JONES, H. (2020, IN PRESS). Whiti-te-Rā: A guide to connecting Māori to traditional wellbeing pathways. *Journal of Indigenous Wellbeing: Te Mauri – Pimatisiwin*, 5(2).

MCLACHLAN, A., WIRIHANA, R., & HURIWAI, T. (2017). Whai tikanga: The application of a culturally relevant value centred approach. *New Zealand Journal of Psychology*, 46(3), 46–54.

MINISTRY FOR CULTURE AND HERITAGE. (2014). *Ngā hua ā Tāne Rore: The benefits of Kapa Haka*. Wellington, New Zealand: Ministry for Culture and Heritage. Retrieved from https://mch.govt.nz/files/Nga%20Hua%20A%20Tane%20Rore%20%20The%20benefits%20of%20kapa%20haka%20(D-0570327).PDF

MOEKE-MAXWELL, T., NIKORA, L. W., & AWEKOTUKU, T. (2014). End-of-life care and Māori whānau resilience. *MAI Journal*, 3(2), 141–152.

MOEKE-PICKERING, T., HEITIA, M., HEITIA, S., KARAPU, R., & COTE-MEEK, S. (2015). Understanding Māori food security and food sovereignty issues in Whakatāne. *Mai Journal*, 4(1), 29–42.

MURIWAI, E., HOUKAMAU, C. A., & SIBLEY, C. G. (2015). Culture as cure: The protective function of Māori cultural efficacy on psychological distress. *New Zealand Journal of Psychology*, 44(2), 14–24.

NIKORA, L. W., RUA, M., & TE AWEKOTUKU, N. (2007). Renewal and resistance: Moko in contemporary New Zealand. *Journal of Community and Applied Social Psychology*, 17(6), 477–489.

O'HAGAN, M., REYNOLDS, P., & SMITH, C. (2012). Recovery in New Zealand: An evolving concept? *International Review of Psychiatry*, 24(1), 56–63.

PAENGA, M. (2008). *Te Māoritanga – Wellbeing and identity: Kapa haka as a vehicle for Māori health promotion* (Master's thesis). Auckland University of Technology, Auckland, New Zealand. Retrieved from https://openrepository.aut.ac.nz/handle/10292/530

PANELLI, R., & TIPA, G. (2007). Placing wellbeing: A Māori case study of cultural and environmental specificity. *EcoHealth*, *4*(4), 445–460.

PALMER, S. (2004). Homai te waiora ki ahau: A tool for the measurement of wellbeing. *New Zealand Journal of Psychology*, *33*(2), 50–58.

PENETITO, W. (2011). Kaupapa Māori education: Research as the exposed edge. In J. Hutchings, H. Potter & K. Taupo (Eds.), *Kei Tua o te Pae Hui proceedings: The challenges of Kaupapa Māori research in the 21st century* (pp. 38–43). Wellington, New Zealand: New Zealand Council for Educational Research.

PERE, R. (1984). Te Oranga o te Whānau: The health of the family. In K. Whakahaere (Ed.), *Hui Whakaoranga: Māori Health Planning Workshop proceedings, Hoani Waititi marae, Auckland, 19–22 March 1984*. Wellington, New Zealand: Department of Health. Retrieved from https://www.moh.govt.nz/notebook/nbbooks.nsf/0/199037C1AB3E7B724C2565D700185DBD/$file/Hui%20Whakaoranga%20Maori%20Health.pdf

PIHAMA, L. (2001). *Tihei Mauri Ora: Honouring our voices. Mana Wahine as a Kaupapa Māori theoretical framework* (Doctoral dissertation). University of Auckland, Auckland, New Zealand.

PITAMA, S., BENNETT, S., WAITOKI, W., ... & MCLACHLAN, A. (2017). A proposed hauora Māori clinical guide for psychologists: Using the hui process and the Meihana model in clinical assessment and formulation. *New Zealand Journal of Psychology*, *46*(3), 7–19.

PITAMA, S., HURIA, T., & LACEY, C. (2014). Improving Māori health through clinical assessment: Waikare o te Waka o Meihana. *New Zealand Medical Journal*, *127*(1393), 107–119.

PITAMA, S., ROBERTSON, P., CRAM, F., GILLIES, M., HURIA, T., & DALLAS-KATOA, W. (2007). Meihana model: A clinical assessment framework. *New Zealand Journal of Psychology*, *36*(3), 118–125.

PUKETAPU-HETET, E. (1989). *Māori weaving*. Auckland, New Zealand: Pitman.

RAMEKA, L. (2016). Kia whakatōmuri te haere whakamua: 'I walk backwards into the future with my eyes fixed on my past'. *Contemporary Issues in Early Childhood*, *17*(4), 387–398.

RAWSON, E. (2016). Te Waioratanga: Health promotion practice – The importance of Māori cultural values to wellbeing in a disaster context and beyond. *Australasian Journal of Disaster and Trauma Studies*, *20*(2), 81–87.

REID, J., VARONA, G., FISHER, M., & SMITH, C. (2016). Understanding Māori 'lived' culture to determine cultural connectedness and wellbeing. *Journal of Population Research*, *33*(1), 31–49.

RUBIE-DAVIES, C., HATTIE, J., & HAMILTON, R. (2006). Expecting the best for students: Teacher expectations and academic outcomes. *British Journal of Educational Psychology*, *76*(3), 429–444.

SALMOND, A. (2014). Tears of Rangi: Water, power, and people in New Zealand. *Hau: Journal of Ethnographic Theory*, *4*(3), 285–309.

SIMMONDS, H., HARRE, N., & CRENGLE, S. (2014). Te kete whanaketanga – rangatahi. A model of positive development for rangatahi Māori. *Mai Journal*, *3*(3), 211–226.

SMALLBONE, C. (2019). *SpLD – Silent Learning Difficulties? Factors influencing literacy learning of Māori students, as identified by teachers, SENCo, and parents* (Master's thesis). Victoria University of Wellington, Wellington, New Zealand. Retrieved from https://researcharchive.vuw.ac.nz/xmlui/handle/10063/8173

SMITH, L. T. (1999). *Decolonising methodologies: Research and Indigenous Peoples*. Dunedin, New Zealand: University of Otago Press.

SOUTAR, M. (2008). *Ngā Tama Toa: The price of citizenship: C Company 28 (Māori) Battalion 1939–1945*. Auckland, New Zealand: David Bateman.

STAATS, C. (2016). Understanding implicit bias: What educators should know. *American Educator*, 39(4), 29–43.

TE HUIA, A. (2015). Perspectives towards Māori identity by Māori heritage language learners. *New Zealand Journal of Psychology*, 44(3), 18–28.

WAITANGI TRIBUNAL (2018). WAI 2500. *Wai 2500 Military veterans' kaupapa inquiry*. Wellington, New Zealand: Waitangi Tribunal.

WAITOKI, W. (2016). Ngā kete mātauranga: The baskets of knowledge, a curriculum for an indigenous psychology. In W. Waitoki & M. Levy (Eds.), *Te manu kai i te mātauranga: Indigenous psychology in Aotearoa/New Zealand* (pp. 288–299). Wellington, New Zealand: New Zealand Psychological Society. Retrieved from https://pdfs.semanticscholar.org/6a39/cf16490313b5acb58270485c07b81d18bb18.pdf

WAITOKI, W., NIKORA, L., & HARRIS, P. (2014). *Māori experiences of bipolar disorder: Pathways to recovery*. Auckland, New Zealand: Te Pou o te Whakaaro nui.

WIRIHANA, R., & SMITH, C. (2014). Historical trauma: Healing and wellbeing in Māori communities. *MAI Journal*, 3(3), 198–209.

WORLD HEALTH ORGANIZATION. (1996). *WHOQOL-BREF Introduction, Administration and Scoring, Field Trial version*. Geneva, Switzerland: World Health Organization. Retrieved from https://apps.who.int/iris/handle/10665/63529

Glossary

Glossary

ā kanohi, kanohi kitea	face to face, in person
āhua	form/type
ako	practice of teaching and learning
aro	reflection, reflexive practice, to understand, consider, pay attention to
aroha	love, compassion
atua	deities, gods
awa	river
awhi rito	leaves that embrace the centre shoot of the harakeke
hapū	kinship group, sub-tribe, sub-nation, to be pregnant
harakeke	*Phormium tenax*/New Zealand flax
hauora	healthy, well
He Piki Raukura	Te Kura Mai i Tawhiti study title (toroa plume/raukura – emblem of Parihaka)
hihi	sun's ray
Hineahuone	name of a deity
hinengaro	mental and emotional aspects
hoa	friend/s
hoa haere	considered or constant companion
hongi	pressing noses in greeting, to sniff hono join, connection
hui	cultural gathering
hui whānau	meetings of the whānau-collective Huna name of a deity
ingoa	name
ira	life principle
iwi	extended kinship group, tribe, nation, people, bone
kai	food, meal

kaitiaki	teachers
kaitiakitanga	guardianship (usually of the natural environment) stewardship, guardianship and protection
kapa haka	Māori performing arts
karakia	incantation, Māori form of 'prayer'
karanga	ceremonial call of welcome
kareao	supplejack frond
kaumātua	grandparents
kaupapa	floor, platform, topic, policy, matter for discussion
Kaupapa Kōpae	Te Kōpae Piripono approach/philosophy
Kaupapa Māori	Māori agenda, Māori principles, Māori ideology – a philosophical doctrine, incorporating the knowledge, skills, attitudes and values of Māori society; Māori paradigm; based within a Māori worldview
kawa	protocols, customs
kāwanatanga	authority, governorship
kī-o-rahi	traditional Māori ball sport
koha	valued contribution, gift
kōhanga reo	Māori language immersion nests
kōrari	flower stem of the harakeke
kōrero	speak, speech, address, talk
korero whakapapa	oral traditions
koro	grandfather, elder male
koroua	elder male
kotahitanga	unity; united for a cause
kuia	female elders
kupu	word, saying, utterance
kupu Māori	glossary of Māori words
Kura Kaupapa Māori	Māori language immersion schooling
kurawaka	pubic region of Papatūānuku
mahi	work
mahi ā-toi	Māori arts
mahuru	comfort

mamae	pain
mana	spiritually sanctioned or endorsed influence, power, authority, prestige
mana motuhake	authority and capacity to be autonomous
manaaki	hospitality, uplifting mana
manaakitanga	hospitality, kindness, generosity, support; showing and receiving care, respect, kindness and hospitality
manawanui	patience, indulgence
manawaroa	courage in adversity, persisting despite difficulty, and having a positive outlook
Māori	Indigenous Peoples of Aotearoa/New Zealand
marae	traditional Māori meeting ground
Matariki	Pleiades cluster of stars, indicates beginning of the Māori new year
matatau	expert, skilled, competent
mātauranga	knowledge, wisdom
mātauranga Māori	Māori knowledge
Matike Mai	visionary and communicator with the divine realms
mātua	parents
maunga	mountain
mauri	life principle, life force, vital essence
moana	ocean
mokemoke	sadness, loneliness
mokopuna	grandchild, grandchildren, descendant
mōteatea	lament, traditional chant, to grieve
mōtika	right, rights
muru raupatu	state-sanctioned confiscation of Māori land
Ngā Takohanga e Whā	TKP's Four Responsibilities of Leadership
ngā ture	law, lore, rules
ngahere	bush
Ngāti Maniapoto	tribal group located within the King Country region of Aotearoa
noa	unrestricted
Nu Tīreni	New Zealand

oranga	health, wellbeing, vitality
oriori	lullaby, song composed for a baby in utero
ōritetanga	equality, equal opportunity
pā	fortified village
paepae	orators' bench
Pākehā	English, foreign, New Zealander of European descent
pakeke	adult
pakiaka	roots
pakiwaitara	story
Pākoti	name of a deity
Papatūānuku	Earth Mother
Parihaka	a settlement established by Te Whiti o Rongomai and Tohu Kākahi on the slopes of Taranaki
patu ngākau	emotional injury, trauma
pepeha	traditional recital of relational connections
pēpi	baby, infant
pikopiko	small fern frond
piripono	integrity, commitment and responsibility for a shared kaupapa/purpose
pono	to be absolutely true, unfeigned, genuine
poutama	steps
poutama whakawhanakē	staircase of learning and development
pōwhiri	formal ceremony of welcome
Puanga	festival in Taranaki (the star Rigel signals Māori new year)
puāwai	flower, blossom, bloom
pūrākau	ancient/historical narrative, story
rākau	tree
rangatahi	younger generation
rangatira	leader, chieftainess/chief, one who can gather people together
Ranginui	Sky Father
rau	leaf, frond

rito	centre shoot, young centre leaf of the harakeke
rongoā	medicine
tā moko	traditional tattooing
taiao	physical environments
Tainui	waka, collection of tribes around Waikato region
Tamanuiterā	the sun, sun god
tamariki	children
tāne	male
Tāne/Tānemahuta	a deity
Tangaroa	god of ocean elements
tāngata	people
tangata Māori	Māori person/people
tangata whenua	people born of the land – of the placenta and of the land where the people's ancestors have lived and where their placentas are buried
tangi te kawekaweā	the call of the kawekaweā (long-tailed cuckoo) heralds the arrival of spring and the opportunity for new growth (study title)
tangihanga	Māori funeral ceremony
taonga	treasure, anything prized
taonga Pūoro	traditional Māori instruments
tapu	sacred
Taranaki	a tribal nation and region of Aotearoa/New Zealand
Taranakitanga	of Taranaki, or having a tribal affiliation to Taranaki
tātai whakapapa	incantation recounting descent from primal ancestors and connections within te ao Māori
tau	calm, settled
tauheke	elder/s
taurite	balance and harmony
tautoko	to support
tauutuutu	reciprocity
te ao Māori	the Māori world
Te Ara Poutama	the TKP principle and process of open, honest, and solution-focused communication

Te Kōpae Piripono	sanctuary for those committed to the same ideals (Taranaki-based Kaupapa Māori Early Years education provision)
Te Kura mai i Tawhiti	The Sacred Legacy of an Ancient era (title of research programme)
Te Pāhua	annual commemorations of the state-sanctioned ransacking of Parihaka in 1881
Te Pou Tiringa	governing body of Te Kōpae Piripono (the central pillar of our purpose and connection)
Te Pūmaomao	Takawai and Chris Murphy's cultural awareness and nation-building workshop
te reo Māori	Māori language
te reo me ngā tikanga Māori	Māori language and culture
te tiaki a tētehi i tētehi	caring for each other
teina	junior/recent entrants
tiaki	care
tikanga	correct procedure, practice, culture, principles, protocols grounded in traditional values
tinana	physical body
tino rangatiratanga	sovereignty, self-determination, autonomy
tīpuna/Tūpuna	ancestors
tirohanga	vision
tuakana	older sibling/mentor
tuakiri	a secure local Māori identity
tuakiri Taranaki	Taranaki Māori identity
tukanga	agreed processes
tukutuku	Māori weaving
tūmanako	optimism
uiui whānau	scheduled discussions with parents and whānau
ūkaipō	origin, source of sustenance
utu	balance, reciprocity
wā	time, a period of time
wā huihui	tamariki meeting/mat time in the TKP daily programme
wāhi	location, place

wahine	women, female, feminine
waiata	song
wainuku	feeling low and being dragged down
wairua	spirit, spiritual
wairuatanga	spirituality
waka ama	traditional canoe racing
wānanga	gathering for the purpose of learning; to meet, discuss, deliberate, consider
wānanga reo	language workshop
whaene/pāpā	mother/father figures
whai Ora	seeking wellness, consumer, service user
whaikōrero	traditional speechmaking
whakairo	Māori carving
whakamā	shame
whakanoa	ceremony of cleansing
whakapapa	ancestry, familial relationships, genealogical connection/s; to layer one on top of another
whakapono	knowledge of what is true, truth
whakareareanoatia	forgiveness
whakataukī	ancestral saying, proverb
whakawhanaungatanga	to build relationships
whānau	to be born, extended family, family group
whanaunga	relative
whanaungatanga	relationships
whānauranga	Te Kōpae Piripono term for feeling and acting as member of a whānau/community
whare wānanga	place of higher learning
wharekura	Māori language immersion high school
wharenui	ancestral meeting house
whenua	placenta, ground, land
whenua tūpuna	customary lands

Index

Index

Page numbers in bold indicate images.

A

abuse. *See* physical punishment, violence
after-birth rituals. *See* childbirth
Agavaceae, harakeke as 164
Ahipara (Ōhaki marae) 164
āhua (Meihana model) 216
Ahuahu-ki-te-rangi, oriori for 89, 91
Ahuriri, Heretaunga (Te Tahutū-o-te-Rangi) 96
ako Māori 43, 66–67
    ako ā-whānau 24–26
    and mātauranga-ā-whānau framework **119**, 120
    oriori and 86, 88–89
Anderson, Waimarama 105
antenatal weaving clinics 183–84
antenatal workshops (Hapū Wānanga) 180
Aparahi, descent line 96
Archibald, Jo-ann (Q'um Q'um Xiiem) 102
aro and mātauranga-ā-whānau framework **119**, 120
aroha (Whiti-te-Rā model) 227
āta phrases and Kaupapa Māori 117
aunties (whaea), role of 9, 23, 47, 49, 90, 138, 148
    see also whānau, roles of
awhi rau (mātua) **7**
    see also rau
awhi rito/ mātua 165, 170, 194
    Oranga Mokopuna model **195**, 200
    see also rito

B

'baby-wearing' (carrying of infants) 20, 179
back-sleeping 180
bedsharing 178, 180–81
behavioural constructs (children's) 127

behavioural correction, support 66, 134
    whakataukī for 80-81
Behrendt, Larissa (Eualeyai/Kamillaroi) 106
Bell, Leah 105
Best, Elsdon 92, 147, 165
Bock Depression Inventory 221
Braun, V 128
breastfeeding (whāngai ū) 145, 178, 179, 180, 182
    Whāngai Ū programme 180

C

Cameron, N 191
Campbell, D 192, 193
Canada (First Nations) 148
carrying of infants ('baby-wearing') 20, 179
Cartwright Inquiry Report 152
case study (Tamarere) 220-24
    and Whiti-te-Rā Framework 224-27
Centre of Innovation, TKP as 127
Child Poverty Action Group 59
childbirth 20, 152, 178-79
    and hospitalisation 148-49
    kaitiaki of 163
    and wairua 93, 149-52, 168
childless women and oriori 90, 94, 95
childrearing 19-20, 178-79, 180
    collective approaches to 79-80
    as whānau responsibility 21, 23-24, 27, 52-53, 66
children, behavioural constructs 127
    see also tamariki
Chinese community 106
Choices/Kahungunu Health Services (Hastings) 177
cigarette smoking and SIDS 180-81
Clarke, V 128
Codyre, Tim 103
collectivism and settler ethic. *See* colonialism
colonial ethnographers, ethnography 147
colonialism, colonisation, coloniality 44-46, 189-190
    and health care 146-48, 179, 215-16
    impacts of 6, 42-43, 62, 104-06, 113-14, 131
    terminology of 198
Committee on the Rights of the Child 201
Convention on the Rights of the Child **195**, 201

cosmogonies, cosmology, Māori 144–45, 160–63, 196–97
    see also whakapapa
Cram, Fiona 152
cultural appropriation 215
cultural identity, values 52
    practice tools 68–70
    and Whiti-te-Rā model 217–20
    see also tikanga Māori
customary law, Māori 197–98

D

De Santolo, Jason (Garrwa, Barungamm) 102
Declaration on the Rights of Indigenous Peoples (UNDRIP) **195**, 201–02
decolonisation 197, 200
    process of 106, 126, 137
Decolonizing Research: Indigenous storywork as methodology 102
Durie, Mason 18, 215, 226

E

Early Childhood Development Programme ('He Taonga, Te Mokopuna') 21
ecosystem, pā harakeke as 165, 194
education systems 113–14
    and TKP 131–33
    see also ako; wānanga
Edwards, Richard 204
Edwards, S 22–24, 26
Elder, Hinemoa 52
energy, pure (hihiri) 160–61
environments, physical. *See* taiao
Eru, Matiu 177
ethnography, colonial 147
Eualeyai/Kamillaroi (Behrendt, Larissa) 106

F

family violence. *See* physical punishment, violence
fathers and grandfathers. *See* Māori men, roles of
First Nations (Canada) 148

G

Gabel, Kirsten A 21, 144
genealogy, oriori and 89
    see also whakapapa
geography, oriori and 89

grandparents and mokopuna 21–22, 23–24, 63–64, 78, 116
Green, J A 46
Greensill, H 192, 193
Grennell, Di 5

H

Hāpai Te Hauora 51, 170–71
Hapū Wānanga (antenatal workshops) 180
harakeke (korari) 163–64, **202**
    as metaphor 31
    tikanga of 32–34
    whakapapa 162
    see also pā harakeke; raranga; wahakura
harakeke, whakapapa of **162–63**
Harehare (Ngāti Manawa) 95
Harris, R 45
Harte, H 85, 87
Hastings (Choices/Kahungunu Health Services) 177
hau ora (kōrari) **195**
Haumēne, Te Ua 138
Haunui-a-nanaia 95
hauora (kōrari) **195**, 202
Hauora Māori Clinical Guide for Psychologists 216, 220
Hautu, oriori by 92
'He Mokopuna He Tupuna' 59, 60
He oriori mō Tuteremoana 87–88
He Piki Raukura 127–28
He pōpō (oriori) 92
'He Taonga, Te Mokopuna' (Early Childhood Development Programme) 21
He Waka Eke Noa 44
He Whakaputanga o te Rangatiratanga o Nu Tireni 200, 203
    as awhi rito/ mātua **195**, 200–01
health and wellbeing 52, 177, 198–99
    inequities in 44–46, 189–91
    and mātauranga Māori 177
Health Research Council Ngā Kanohi Kitea 127
Hemara, W 25
Henare, James 75
here (umbilical tie) 183
Heretaunga, oriori about 95
hihi (sunbeams) and Whiti te-Ra 217–19
hihiri (pure energy) 160–61
Hinaura. *See* Hine-te-iwaiwa (Hinaura)

Hineahuone 145, 196–97
Hineiterepo **162**
Hinekitawhiti (Ngāti Porou) 89, 91
Hinemukaraiore 162
Hineraumoa 163, **163**
Hinerupe house 93, 94
Hine-te-iwaiwa (Hinaura) 32, 163, **163**
    karakia to 177
Hiroa, Te Rangi 21–22, 24
Hohepa, Margie 18
Hohepa, Patu 79
home births 150–51
Hond-Flavell, Erana 128
hononga, ngā (naming) 64, 180
hospitalisation, childbirth and 148–49
houhi (lacebark) 179
Houkamau, C A 218
hui, wānanga, and mātauranga-ā-whānau 115–16, **119**, 121
hui, whānau 115–16, 137
human rights, international and tangata whenua 191, 202, 203, 204
    decolonisation of 196
Huna (kaitiaki) **162**
hūpē 160
Hutchings, J 192, 200

I

iho (umbilical cord) 164, 179
Ihumātao 105
Indigenous Peoples, colonisation of 189–190, 198
'Indigenous storywork' 102
infant care, traditional practices 178–80
    Kaupapa Māori services for 180
intergenerational learning. *See* ako Māori
Io as grandmaster weaver 161
ipu pito 183
Irawaru 163

J

Jackson, Moana 198, 199, 204
Jacob, H 85, 89
Jenkins, K 85, 87
Jenkins, Kuini 102
Jones, Alison 102

Jones, C 193
Jones, Pei te Hurinui 85
Jones, S 78–79

K

Kahutia (Rongowhakaata) 94–95
Kaikohe Native School 104–05
kaitiaki matatau (expert teachers) 132–33
kaitiaki o te pā harakeke 162–63, **162–63**
Kaiwa (Muaūpoko) 92
Kākahi, Tohu 75, 135, 138
kapa haka (Whiti-te-Rā and) 219
karakia 143, 150–51, 180
    'Tu mai te whare pora o Hine-te-iwaiwa' 177
    see also wairua
karanga and mātauranga-ā-whānau 117–18
kaumātua as educators. See grandparents
kaupapa 44
Kaupapa Māori theory 6, 42, 43–44, 102, 106, 113–14
    āta phrases and 117
    Oranga Mokopuna and 192–95
    see also Hapū Wānanga; Te Kōpae Piripono (TKP);
        Tu Tama Wahine o Taranaki (TTW)
Kawiti, Huia Maihi 160
kia piki ake i ngā raruraru o te kainga 43
'Kids Missing Out' (UNICEF) 59
King, Paula 204
Kingi, Te Kani 46
ki-o-rahi (Whiti-te-Rā model) 219
knowledge forms 75–76, 89–90, 96–97, 102
    see also Kaupapa Māori; mātauranga Māori
koha, tā koha 33, 116–17
Kōhere, Rēweti 75
Kōpua, M 193–94
kōrahi (flint) 179
kōrari (hauora) **195**, 202
korari. See harakeke
'Kōrero Analysis Framework' 193
'kōrero ingoa' (naming stories) 192–93
Kōrero Whakatepe (TTW project) 61
    kupu whakatepe, ngā 67–70
kōrero whakatūpato 80

Kotahi te Aroha **168**
Kōuka **162**
Kuaha, Ihaka 93
kūmara, oriori about 92
Kupe, oriori for 96

L

lacebark (houhi) 179
Lawless, Matekino 33
Lawson-Te Aho, K 196–97
leadership 136–37
Lee, Jenny 80, 88, 114
Lee-Morgan, Jenny 101–02, 192, 200
Lee-Morgan, Kerera 104, 192
Lee-Morgan, Waioro 103, 107
lily, harakeke as 164

M

Maeha, Hemi (Te Aitanga-a-Māhaki) 95
mahi-a-toi 217, **218**, 219
Mahuika, M 203
māhuri (sapling) as metaphor 79
Maikara (Ngāti Manawa) 95
mākahakaha 179
Makaurau marae 105, 106
Makerewhatu, oriori for 94–95
Maldonado-Torres, N 191, 196
Māmā Aroha 180
mana 198
    of tamariki 20, 62, 87
    of words 67
mana wāhine 147
    stories 193
manaakitanga (manaaki tāngata) 65, 68
    whakataukī for 79
    and Whiti-te-Rā model 227
manawaroa 127
Manukau Harbour (Te Manukanuka o Hoturoa) 105
Māori culture (Māoritanga) 35, 75, 193, 201
    desecration of 104–05
    and Whiti-te-Rā model 217–18, 227
Māori customary law, traditions 198, 199
Māori ethnicity as deficit 45–46

Māori health models 189–91, 200–01, 215–20
Māori men, roles of 22–23, 87, 146, 179
    military service and 227
Māori midwives' collective (Ngā Maia o Aotearoa) 180
Māori psychologists 217, 226
    see also psychologists, psychology
Māori Weaving (Erenora Puketapu-Hetet) 31–32
Māori women, colonial ethnography and 147
Māori worldview 35, 160–61
marae, whānau and 63, 160
    see also by name
marginalisation 45, 123, 126, 146, 148, 204
    Meihana model and 216, 227
Marsden, Māori 32, 35, 160–61
masculinity. *See* Māori men, roles of
mātauranga Māori 76–77, 111–12, 121
    and healthcare systems 41–42, 177, 180–81, 183–84, 217
    raranga and 31, 34, 36
    see also mātauranga-ā-whānau
mātauranga-ā-whānau 114, 116
    framework **119**, 119–21
maternal body (whare tangata) 143, 144–46
    and personal dignity 152
Materoa, Heni, Lady Carrol 95
Matiki mai Aotearoa 200
mātua (awhi rito) 9, 33, 36, 65, 165, 194, 200–01
    'matua rautia' 52, 80
    see also Te Aho Mātua
Māui-mua 163
Māui-tikitiki 163
mauri 20, 217
    harakeke and 163, 166, 168, 171–72, 202
mauri ora 217
McCreanor, T 22–24, 26
McRae, J 85, 89
Mead, Hirini Moko 112
Meihana model, the 216–17, 226
mental health, wellbeing 41–42, 46, 193–94, 215–17
    returned servicemen and 226–27
    see also Whiti-te-Rā
Mental Health Foundation 51
Meola Reef (Te Ara Whakapekapeka a Ruarangi) 102–03
Metge, J 78–79

Midwifery Council, the 180
Midwives Registration Act 1904 147–48
Mikaere, Ani 35, 48, 143, 145–46, 148, 153, 200
military service. *See* returned servicemen
Miria marae 160
Mitchell, Aroha 34–35
Moewaka-Barnes, H 22–24, 26, 146
mokopuna (rito/pēpi) 191–92, 194
 grandparents and 22, 63–64, 116
 as rito 7, 164, 170–72, **171**, **195**, 200
 as taonga 5, 53, 201
 and whakapapa 48, 60, 71
 see also Oranga Mokopuna
Mokopuna Ora 180
Monture-Angus, P 190
Morehu, C 19, 23
Morgan, Eruera 102, 103
mothers (whaea) 9, 21, 23, 78
 see also childbirth; whare tangata
Muaūpoko (Kaiwa) 92
muka 164, 168
 as umbilical tie 171, 179
Mumara (Ngāti Ariki) 94
Murphy, Chris 134
Murphy, Ngahuia 145, 192, 193, 196, 200
Murphy, Takawai 134
Muru me te Raupatu (TTW project) 61, 62–63
murunga hara (Whiti-te-Rā model) 227
Musqueam Nation 102

N

naming (ngā hononga) 64, 180
naming stories (kōrero ingoa) 192–93
Nash, R 46
National Centre for Lifecourse Research (University of Otago) 127
Nepe, Tuakana Mate 25–26, 112
New Zealand College of Midwives 180
Ngā Hau e Whā (Meihana model) 216
Ngā Kanohi Kitea (Health Research Council) 127
Ngā Maia o Aotearoa (Māori midwives' collective) 180
Ngā Moteatea 85
 annotated bibliography of 91–96
Ngā Roma Moana (NRM), Meihana model and 216

Ngā Takohanga e Whā 136
Ngākau Māhaki (whare) 101, 169, **169**
Ngake, oriori for 96
Ngāmotu, KM-EYP in 126
Ngapuao, oriori for 96
Ngāpuhi 92, 104
Ngaroto, Meri 164–65
Ngata, Apirana 85
    and oriori 93–94
Ngata, T 190
Ngata, Wayne 85–86
Ngāti Apa (oriori) 92, 95
Ngāti Kahungunu (oriori) 91, 94, 95, 96
    Choices/Kahungunu Heath Services 177
Ngāti Mahuta (Kahukahu Wehi) 105
Ngāti Manawa (oriori) 95
Ngāti Maniapoto 114
Ngāti Pikiao (oriori) 96
Ngāti Porou (oriori) 88, 89–90, 91, 92, 93–94
Ngāti Raukawa (oriori) 91, 93
Ngāti Reko (Kahukahu Wehi) 105
Ngāti Te Ahiwaru (Kahukahu Wehi) 105
Ngāti Te Wehe (Kahukahu Wehi) 105
Ngāti Tūwharetoa (oriori) 87
Ngāti Whakatere (oriori) 91
Ngāti Whātua (oriori) 87, 92
Ngāti Whātua Ōrakei 101, 168, **169**
Niniwa-i-te-rangi, oriori for 95
Nohomaiterangi (Ngāti Kahungunu) 91
nurturing children, whakataukī for 78–79
NZ Council for Educational Research (Teaching and Learning Initiative) 128

O

Ōhaki marae (Ahipara) 164
Oranga Mokopuna 192–94, 203–04
    harakeke as metaphor 194–96
    key concepts 191–92
    Ngā Mōtika Tangata Whenua **195**
O'Regan, H 113
oriori 85–86, 87–89, 90–91, 179
    for child fashioned from wood 95
    childless women and 90, 94, 95

for dead tamariki 89–90
   as pedagogy 88–89
Otago University (University of Otago) 216
   National Centre for Lifecourse Research 127
Ōtorohanga College 105
Ōtuataua Stonefields 105

P

pā harakeke 35–36, **159**, **167**
   as ecosystem 165
   as holistic 35–36
   as metaphor 6–7, **7**, 9, 78, 164–65, 194–96, **195**, **202**, 202–03
   ngā kaitiaki o te 162–63, **162–63**, 167
   tikanga of 159, 164–65
   see also harakeke
Paeko 94
Pāhua, Te (Parihaka commemorations) 130, 137–38
Paiatehau, Ripeka (Ngāti Porou) 89–90, 92
Paiheretia health model 215, 226
pakiaka (roots) 78, 198
pakokori 179
Pakoti **162**
Pani-toangakore, oriori for 91
Papakura, Makareti 21
Papatūānuku 144–45, 146
Parihaka 59
   Te Pāhua 130, 137–38
   Tu Tama Wahine o Taranaki (TTW) and 61
patupaiarehe 103
penupenu 179
Peou (Ngāti Raukawa) 93
pēpeha 77
pēpi (rito) 33
pēpi moenga 166
   see also wahakura
Pēpi-Pod 181–82
Pere, Rangimarie Rose 18, 34, 118, 197
   on tamariki/mokopuna 20, 22, 47, 191–92, 202
   Te Wheke/wellbeing 86
Phormium tenax/ New Zealand flax. *See* harakeke
physical punishment, violence 5, 19–20, 59, 67, 80

Pihama, Leonie 41, 43, 44, 102
    family definitions 47–48
    pūrākau 192, 193
    whakapapa 88, 149, 150
Pinepine te kura (oriori) 94
Pitama, Suzanne 19, 216
pito 164, 179
    burial container (ipu pito) 183
placenta (whenua) **7**, 20, 152, 179, 180
Pohatu, Taina 52, 112–13, 114, 117, 121
Poi (kaitiaki) **162**
porokaraka 165–66
Post Traumatic Stress Disorder (PTSD) 227
poutama whakawhanake 133
Poutūterangi, oriori for 93
pregnancy. *See* childbirth
psychologists, psychology, Māori 215–16, 217, 226
puāwai (rangatira) **195**, 202–03
pūharakeke (harakeke cluster) 165
Puketapu-Hetet, Erenora (*Māori Weaving*) 31–32
pūrākau 67, 76, 192–94
    Hine-te-iwaiwa (Hinaura) 163
    Māori cosmogonies and 196–97
    and Mātauranga-a-Whānau framework 114–19, **119**, 120
    for Te Pā Harakeke 107
    Te Tokaroa 102–04
purposeful activity 66–67
Putukenga, Te Whare Wānanga o Wairaka 166

R

racism 104, 105, 189–190, 216, 226–27
    institutional, systemic 46
Rairoa, oriori for 92
Rakaihikuroa (Heretanga) 95
rākau (tree) as metaphor 78, 79
rangatira (puāwai) **195**, 202–03
Rangiamohia, oriori for 91
Rangihuna, D 193–94
Rangimārie pā harakeke **159**, **167**, 168
Ranginui and birth story 145
Rangitumua, oriori for 91
raranga. *See* weavers, weaving
raranga whatu 32

Raranga-ihu-matua 162
ratonga hauora (and Meihana model) 216
rau (leaves) 9, 201
Rau, Matiu 36
Rau-Kupa, Mararena 59
Raupō (kaitiaki) **162**
reciprocity 19, 34, 51
Reedy, Amster 86
Reid, Melanie 105
Reihana, Poroumati Riki 160
'research' as concept 42
returned servicemen 160–61, 226–27
rito, te 33, 164–65
    as tamaiti/mokopuna **7**, **9**, 170–72, 194, **195**, 200
Rona (pūrākau) 81
Rongawhakaata (Kahutia) 94
rongoā 61, 65
    harakeke as 164
Royal, Charles 36, 196
Royal-Tangaere, Arapera 21
Rūamoko 145
Ruka, Pat 161

S

safe sleep devices (SSD) 181–82
Safe Sleep Programme 181–82
Safe Sleeping 165
Schuster, Cathy 33
Seed-Pihama, J 192–93
self-determination (tino rangatiratanga) 153
self-determination. *See* tino rangatiratanga
sewage, pollution from 105
Sibley, C G 218
Simmonds, N 88
Simmonds, Naomi 149
Simpson, Leanne 148
smacking. *See* physical punishment, violence
Smith, C 227
Smith, Graham 43, 106, 113
Smith, Hinekura 34, 36
Smith, L 44, 46
Smith, Linda Tuhiwai 52, 152
    and indigenous knowledge 146

social programming 190
Southey, K 41
sovereign tangata whenua rights 197
sovereignty, Māori. *See* tino rangatiratanga
spirituality. *See* wairua
storytelling processes 76
storywork 102
    see also pūrākau
Sudden Infant Death Syndrome (SIDS) 180–81
Sudden Unexplained Death in Infancy (SUDI) 165, 177–78, 180–82
    Te Whare Pora as strategy 182–84
'sun traps' 106

T

tā koha 33
taha wairua, spirituality 35
    see also wairua
taiao (physical environments) 50–51, 216, 217
    Whiti-te-Rā model **218**, 219
Tainui district (tongikura) 79
take pū whānau 217
    and Whiti-te-Rā model **218**, 220, 227
Taku Kuru Pounamu 76
Tamanuiterā 20, 217, **218**, 226
    and Whiti-te-Rā model **218**, 226
Tamarere (Whiti-te-Rā case study) 220–26
tamariki 19–21, 60, 87–88, 202
    and leadership 136
    and traditional learning systems 76
    see also mokopuna
tamariki (nurturing), whakataukī for 78–79
Tamati, Aroaro 127
Ta-maunga-o-te-Rangi, oriori for 88, 93–94
Tāne **162**
    and baskets of knowledge 218
Tāne, Wikitōria 33
Tānemahuta 163, **163**, 196–97
tangata whaiora. *See* mental health
tangata whenua rights 191, 197
    see also tino rangatiratanga
Tangi te Kawekaweā 127–28
Taoho (Ngāti Whātua) 87, 92
taonga tuku iho 32, 35, 43

tapu 118–19
    o te tangata 199
        whare tangata and 146–47
Taranaki Māori identity 126–27, 129
    whānau project 59–60
tātai 161
Tātai Whakapapa 125, 128, 138
taurima (whāngai) 64
taurite (balance) 227
Tāwhiao, King 80
'Te Aho Matua' 25–26
te aho tapu 36–37
Te Ahukaramu 93
Te Aitanga-a-Māhaki 92, 95
Te Aokapurangi, oriori for 95
Te Aokaui-rangi 92
Te Aotarewa (Whanganui) 95
Te Ara Poutama **135**, 135–37
Te Ara Whakapekapeka a Ruarangi (Meola Reef) 102–03
Te Arawa (oriori) 96
Te Ataihikoia, Mohi 95
Te Aupōuri 164
Te Awekotuku, Ngahuia 35
Te Hakeke (Ngāti Apa) 92
Te Hauapu, oriori for 91
Te Hīnātore ki te Ao Māori: A glimpse into the Māori world 17
Te Huka-rere (Ngāti Porou) 93
Te Kahu o te Ao 160–61
Te Kanawa, Kahutoi 33, 166
Te Kōhanga Reo (National) Trust 34, 86, 113, 126
Te Kōpae Tamariki – Kia Ū te Reo 126–27
Te Kōpai Piripono (TKP) 125, 126–27
Te Kura Kaupapa Māori o Ngā Maungaronga 171
Te Kura Mai i Tawhiti research programme (TKMT) 127–28
Te Mahi a Atua 193–94
Te Mana Ririki 85
'Te Manaaki o te Marae' 106
Te Manukanuka o Hoturoa (Manukau Harbour) 105
Te Maperetahi (Ngāti Porou) 88, 93–94, 96–97
Te Matapō (Ngāpuhi) 92
Te Matorohanga 96
Te Motu (Ngāti Kahungunu) 91
Te Noho Kotahitanga marae 168–69, **169**, 171

Te Oranga Hinengaro 46
Te Pā Harakeke. *See* pā harakeke
Te Pakaru, Enoka (Te Aitanga-a-Māhaki) 92
Te Parekanga, oriori for 92
Te Pou Tiringa 127
Te Puea Memorial marae 106
Te Pūmaomao 126, 134
Te Rangimatarau 102
Te Rangitakoru (Ngāti Apa) 95
Te Rangi-wahipō, oriori for 92
Te Rapunga 160
Te Rara-o-te-Rangi (Kawana te Hakeke, Kawana Hunia), oriori for 92
te reo Māori 75–77
    and power of words 20, 67
    Taranaki dialect 126
    TKP and 132–33
    Whiti-te-Rā model and **218**, 219
Te Reo Rangatira **68**
Te Rongomau, (Te Kōhanga Reo) 171
Te Rōpiha 91
Te Tahuri, oriori for 93, 95
Te Tahutū-o-te-Rangi (Ahuriri, Heretaunga) 96
Te Takai (Ngāti Kahungunu) 96
'Te Taonga o Taku Ngākau' 9, 41
Te Tihi (oriori for) 92
Te Tiriti o Waitangi 200, 204
    as awhi rito/mātua **195**, 200
Te Tokaroa (pūrākau) 102–04
    carving **104**
'Te Tuhi o Hine-te-iwaiwa' 151
Te Ua-o-te-Rangi, oriori for 89–90, 92
Te Ūkaipō 145
Te Umurangi, oriori for 94
Te Waka Hourua 216
Te Whakataha-ki-te-Rangi, oriori for 94
Te Whanaketanga (TTW project) 61, 63
Te Whānau a Kai (Tupai) 94
Te whare pora o Hine-te-iwaiwa 182–83
Te Whare Tapa Whā 44, 215, 216
Te Whare Wānanga o Wairaka, Unitec 171
Te Whatanui (Tohe, Tohe-a-Pare, Whata) 93
Te Whatapoto (Ngāti Pikiao, Te Arawa) 96
Te Wheke (wellbeing framework) 44, 86

Te Whiti o Rongomai 69, 75, 135, 138
    and Taranaki KM-EYP 138
teachers, expert (kaitiaki matatau) 132–33
Teaching and Learning Initiative (NZ Council for Educational Research) 128
teina/taina (tuakana/teina) relationships 64–65, 120, 129, 196
Tiakiwai, S 41
tikanga Māori 8–9, 25, 43, 65–66, 68, **119**, 120
    disconnection from 6, 45, 62
    as law 193, 198
    Meihana model and 216
    Oranga Mokopuna model **195**, 198–200
    te whanaketanga and 63
    see also mātauranga-ā-whānau
tikanga pā harakeke. *See* pā harakeke
tikanga-tukanga (KMP principles and processes) 134–37
Tikao, Teone Taure 20
Tīkapu **162**
Tinirau 163, **163**
tino rangatiratanga (self-determination, sovereignty) 43, 106, 199, 202
Tipene-Leach, David 165–66, 170, 193–94
tīpuna/tūpuna 191
    Declaration on the Rights of Indigenous Peoples **195**
tirohanga, shared vision (TKP) 137–38
tohi rite (oriori for) 93
Tohunga Suppression Act 1907 147–48
Toi (as kaitiaki) **162**
Tokitoki (Waerenga-a-Hika) 94
Tokorau (Ngāti Raukawa, Ngāti Whakatere) 91
tongikura (sayings) 80
'Tu mai te whare pora o Hine-te-iwaiwa' 177
Tu Tama Wahine o Taranaki (TTW) 59–61
    interviews 61–68
tuakana–teina (teina/taina) relationships 64–65, 120, 129, 196
Tuakiri Taranaki 130–32
Tūhoe (Tupai) 94
Tuhotoariki (Ngāi Tara) 87–88, 93
Tūhuruhuru (as kaitiaki) 163, **163**
tūmanako (Whiti-te-Rā model) 227
Tupai (Te Whānau a Kai, Tūhoe) 94
Tūpuna. *See* whakapapa
tūpuna, naming children after 64, 180
tūpuna rau **7**, 165
Tūranga, oriori about 95

Tūranga Kaupapa 180
Tuteremoana, oriori for 93
Tūwhakairiora 94

U

uiui (whānau hui) 115–16, 137
ūkaipō 77, 226
umbilical cord (iho) 164, 179
umbilical tie (here) 179, 183
unborn children, teaching of 25
UNICEF ('Kids Missing Out') 59
Unitec Institute of Technology (Auckland) 166, 168–69, **169**
United Nations Convention on the Rights of Persons with Disabilities 201
United Nations Convention on the Rights of the Child (UNCROC) 201
University of British Columbia 102
University of Otago (Otago University) 216
    National Centre for Lifecourse Research 127
utu 199

V

vision, shared (TKP) 137–38

W

wā and wāhi **119**, 121
Waerenga-a-Hika (Tokitoki) 94
wahakura **159**, 165–72, **168**, **169**
    SUDI and 180–82
    Te Ware Pora and 183
    and whakapapa 161–62
waiata as teaching tool 76
waiata oriori. *See* oriori
waikawa (woven container) 183
Waikerepuru, Huirangi 59
    Tatai Whakapapa 125
wairua (spirituality), wairuatanga 65, 68, 143–44
    and childbirth 146–51
    research and 152–54
    and Whiti-te-Rā model **218**, 219
Waitoki, W 88
Wakefield, Rura 23
Walker, T W 18, 192

wānanga 32, 118, **119**, 121
    Te Mahi a Atua and 193–94
    weaving wahakura as 166–70
    whānau development 133–34
    whare wānanga view 160–61
waterways, harakeke as kaitiaki of 163
weavers, weaving (raranga) 31–34, 36, **166**
    oriori about 92
    as worldview 160–61
    see also wahakura
Weaving Waiora Wānanga 168–70, **169**
Wehi, Kahukahu (Ngāti Mahuta, Ngāti Te Ahiwaru, Ngāti Te Wehe, Ngāti Reko) 105
wellbeing guide (Whiti-te-Rā) 217
whaea. *See* aunties
Whai Māia (Ngāti Whātua Ōrakei) 168
Whakaawe (Ngāti Tūwharetoa) 87, 91
whakaheke 161, 162
whakapapa 18–20, 149, 161, 197
    Oranga Mokopuna model **195**
    oriori, whakataukī 77, 88, 89, 90–91
    rights and responsibilities 118, 197, 199
    te pā harakeke as **202**
    weaving and 32, 161–62
    as Whānau Ora goal **68**
    and whānau structures 18, 48–49, 51–52
    and Whiti-te-Rā model **218**, 220
whakapapa grid 160
whakapono **68**, 115
Whakarae (Ngāti Porou) 93
whakatauākī, whakataukī 60, 67, 75–76, 77
    childrearing 52
    harakeke 164–65, 195–96
    Oranga Mokopuna and 192
whakatere (navigation), Meihana model 217
    case study 222–24
whakatū weave 166
whānau 5–6, 17–18, 43–44, 49–50, 63, 112–13, 192
    collective networks 44–46
    Convention on the Rights of the Child as **195**, 201
    and KM-EYP programme 127, 128–30
    and Meihana model 216

whānau (*continued*)
  protective role of 23, 46
  and tamariki 21–26
  tools for 67–70
  weaving wahakura as **167**, 167–68
  Western appropriations of 47–48
whānau hui, uiui 115–16, 136
whānau kaikōrero 47–52, 53
Whānau Ora goals 68–70
whanaungatanga 18, 21, 63, 199
  and mātauranga-ā-whānau framework **119**, 120
whānauranga 127, 129–130
whāngai (taurima) 64
Whāngai Ū programme 180
whāngai ū (breastfeeding). *See* breastfeeding
Whanganui River, naming of 95
Wharaurangi, oriori for 95
whare kahu 179
whare kōhanga 179
whare pora, kaitiaki of 163
whare pora o Hine-te-iwaiwa (karakia) 177
whare puhi 179
whare rauhi 179
whare tangata (maternal body) 143, 144–46
wharepaku, inappropriately sited **104**, 104–05
whatu. *See* raranga whatu
whenua (land/placenta) **7**, 20–21, 152, 179, 180
  Meihana model and 217
  Oranga Mokopuna and 197
Whiti-te-Rā interactive guide 217–19, **218**
  case study (Tamarere) 220–25
  as wellbeing tool 226–28
WHOQOL-BREF Quality of Life measure 221
Wihongi, Mata (Ngāpuhi) 104
Wikitera, Joy 34
Winiata, Whatarangi 111–12
Wirihana, R 227
Wi-Romana 91
women. *See* childbirth; mothers; whare tangata

X

Xiiem, Q'um Q'um (Jo-ann Archibald) 102

Y

Yates-Smith, Aroha 151